Narrative of the Village

Centre of the Periphery

Narrative of the Village

Centre of the Periphery

Edited by
JASBIR JAIN

RAWAT PUBLICATIONS
Jaipur • New Delhi • Bangalore • Mumbai • Hyderabad

ISBN 81-316-0008-4

Published by
Prem Rawat for **Rawat Publications**
Satyam Apts., Sector 3, Jawahar Nagar, Jaipur 302 004 (India)
Phone: 0141 265 1748 / 7006 Fax: 0141 265 1748
E-mail: info@rawatbooks.com
Website: www.rawatbooks.com

New Delhi Office
4858/24, Ansari Road, Daryaganj, New Delhi 110 002
Phone: 011-23263290

Also at Bangalore, Mumbai and Hyderabad

Typeset by Rawat Computers, Jaipur
Printed at Chaman Enterprises, New Delhi

to Veena with love

Contents

Preface

It was disturbing to be always working with the polarities of margins and centres. These kind of divisionary approaches are overlaid with power struggles and inequalities. Increasingly one feels the need to dismantle such juxtapositions and oppositional categories and replace them either with multiplicities or with similarities and simultaneities. In order to explore these issues, IRIS organized a seminar, *The Village as Protagonist: Centre of the Periphery*, 2-4 May, 2005. It was concerned with a multiplicity of issues: identity construction, role of communities, conformity vs. non-conformity and the absorption of a global citizenry. It was also concerned with religious affiliation and religious strife as it operated in the sub-continental village. Choosing to limit ourselves to literary and filmic constructs, the discussion ranged over the historicization of the pastoral idyll, Gandhian movement and political activism, writers' perceptions and personal accounts, a juxtaposition of values and the emergence of 'regional' writing.

A majority of the papers in this volume were presented at the seminar in abridged versions. Some have been invited: Anisur Rahman, Avadhesh K. Singh, Usha Bande, Ameena Ansari and Kumool Abbi were gracious enough to contribute to this volume. We express gratitude to them and to all the other contributors. At the same time, it is regretted that some papers could not be accommodated. The arrangement of the papers has three implicit sections. We have the issue-based papers that introduce morphology, folk impact, films, crises focused writing, and transitions in the first section. Then follow the writers of the 30s, with an attempt to maintain chronological progression and last of all come the single novel-based articles.

The editor expresses gratitude to all the contributors to this volume who have joined us in this endeavour. This is a special volume for more than one reason. First it is concerned with the village as an entity, placed not in isolation, but in a diverse context of narratology, landscape, reform and revolution, as mirror and interrogator both, and as memory and nostalgia. Second, because this is meant as a volume that celebrates friendship, and the sixtieth birthday of a colleague, Professor Veena Singh. We wish her every happiness in the years to come.

Introduction

JASBIR JAIN

The idea of a village works in relation to a reference point. No space, not even an enclosure is totally self-defined or self-contained. Village cultures and people have travelled back and forth. The mind's eye, as it travels in imagination, works through half-remembered images, fragmentary pictures and mixed values. How does one describe a village? A layman's idea of a village would be a place with a dominant agrarian economy, open spaces, separate household units with some cattle or goats around them, a shared community life and a unique bonding between the inhabitants. Words like gaon-bhai are likely to strike a chord in the hearts of many. A city would conjure up images of factories, chawls and narrow lanes and a sense of anonymity in the crowded streets. Yet, despite these contrasting images, the two are inhabited by people and at times the same people, who move from one place to another and carry their lifestyles with them.

Literary constructs of the village reflect the changes that have taken place over the years. It is possible to distil some images that distinguish one from the other. Classical literature depicts the city as a seat of royal power while the village is seen as inhabited by peasants, artisans and the food suppliers. Stories from history and mythology reflect a similar dichotomy. The narrative of Krishna-Sudama, the *vrat-kathas*, all of them separate the two on the basis of the quality of life. Between the two are the highways, travel and the risks associated with travel, dacoits and thugs, huge forestlands and literally the unknown and the adventurous. Yet, they are not treated as opposites. The city has always had its attraction for the villager, primarily as a land of opportunity. It is difficult to erase the scenes of city life or the poet's meanderings in the lanes of Delhi.[1]

At the same time, it is not possible to treat the city as an expanded version of a village. Perhaps, at one time, it may have been with cultural practices being carried over to the new environment but city space is different from village space. The nature of employment in offices, factories, ports and docks is also markedly different. Housing patterns, nature of community relationships and bonding also differ. The feeling of belonging that one can sense in the village people is considerably subdued and often missing in city people. A sense of alienation, and a feeling of anonymity, often pervade the urban scene. Lifestyles are governed by the nature of employment, infrastructural facilities, domestic space, community relationships and educational levels. And, when landscapes change, over a period of time, the change in values is inevitable.

Girish Karnad, at a recent seminar (15 December, 2005),[2] made the observation that city culture became distinctively different from the village culture with the coming of the British. The British expectations, cultural entertainments and distinctively foreign presence subjected the Indian lifestyle to modification in order to accommodate the element of foreignness. In matters of dress, socialization, gender roles and a host of other practices, this accommodation became visible.[3] The shifts become perceptible as one moves from writer to writer, from Bankim Chandra through H.N. Apte, Tagore to Sarat Chandra Chatterjee and Premchand. And, from the 30s to the end of the 20th century, Indian villages have further changed. These changes have been initiated, hastened and brought about by a series of factors, foremost among them is migration to city centres and other employment centres outside the country and the money generated by this employment. Other factors are education, economic development (5-year plans and the green revolution), technology, roads and transport.[4] Villages have changed and so have village communities. This time the flow is reversed: no longer is village culture being brought to the cities in matters of values and emotional bonding, in family relationships and neighbourly concern but the flow is from the city to the village in terms of skills and technology and in the competitive spirit. Village lifestyle, folk forms, handicrafts are duly framed and exploited by the market economy. This framing reflects a nostalgia for the myth of a village.

What then is the myth of the Indian village? The romantic ideal conceives it as an organic community, a place of harmony and belonging, an emotional bonding and a sense of protection towards the vulnerable, a place of stability and of innocence with the village banyan tree and the panghat presenting places of congregation along gender lines. But this myth remains a myth. The feudalistic social patterns and the family feuds of village life are legendary. The gender segregation, the caste divisions, the economic exploitation are all reflected even in the myth of an organic community. It is a fractured community, where the individual is coerced into conformity.

Between the romanticized ideal and the harsh economic reality, there is still a very livable world, meaningful and vibrant. The village hearkens its people back, it imparts a strong sense of belonging and represents a rootedness. It responds with an unusual immediacy to its immediate environs. Through the length and breadth of the country, no two villagers are the same. Landscapes, histories and local compulsions vary from place to place. Development projects and the rise of rural leadership are other factors responsible for the change. Hilly areas, national highways, forested land, flowing rivers and construction of dams all contribute to the way village life shapes itself. The village is placed on the periphery and yet it remains the centre of the periphery, effectively destabilizing the very notion of a city centre, and dislocating the centre-periphery equation.

The essays in this volume address a whole range of questions, approaching them through literary constructs, films and folk cultures, activism and narrative strategies. Anisur Rahman's excellent essay on Kajri explores continuities and establishes connections between the folk and the classical; Renuka Pamecha looks at the two aspects of village politics as it moves from passive reception to active participation and the persistence of certain mindsets. The message is not merely the need to acquire a political right but to exercise that right through an empowered agency – *tu khud ko badal, tab hi to zamana badlega* – change yourself, only then will the world change.

Narratology, music, activism all feature in contemporary films with varying emphasis and aesthetic choices. Kumool Abbi in a detailed analysis works through parallelism, critiquing the projection of subaltern histories through colonial-postcolonial constructs in films from the 60s to the present. Having opened the various dimensions of the village narrative, the stage is set for an intensive analysis of village-focused issues. Santosh Gupta takes up the transformation from reform to revolution through fictional illustrations, while Avadhesh K. Singh's concern is with novels that work with crisis situations and the different narrative strategies they demand. Concentrating on the depiction of the peasant, Ameena Ansari takes up Premchand's work and Bandana Chakravorty goes on to offer a structural analysis of a near-contemporary's work – Sarat Chandra Chatterjee's *Palli Samaj* comparing it with "*Abhagi ka Swarag*".

Usha Bande's essay is gender-oriented and locates the woman in the rural context. She takes up texts spread over a period of time and located in different spaces, while Veena Jain takes a leap in time to place the dalit question within a comparative framework as she places Premchand and Limbale side by side. Madhuri Chatterjee works with Bhibhutibhushan Chattopadhaya's novel *Pather Panchali*, The Song of The Road (1928), which evokes memories of a pastoral past, and Neelum Raisinghani essay takes up one of the first 'regional novels', a novel that made literary history, Phaneshwar Nath Renu's *Maila Anchal*. Fairs and festivities, an integral part of life, reflect a celebratory side of village India. Vrinda Mathur takes up this colourful aspect as reflected in films and the purpose these serve in the narration of the story.

The partition and its aftermath in terms of human relationships, conflicts and memories is the subject of four papers. Sarojini and Rama Rani Lall focus on Khushwant Singh's 1956 novel *Train to Pakistan* while both Urmil Talwar and Avinash Jodha work with Rahi Masoom Reza's *Adha Gaon*. Partition has also featured in Avadhesh Kumar Singh's essay where amongst other novels, both *Train to Pakistan* and *Adha Gaon* have also found a place.

The difference in location has a strong impact on both the narrative and its concerns. While Jasbir Jain, by selecting novels from four different locations, had brought out the regional differences effected by landscape, Jessy Mani takes up a fisher folk's village in her analysis of *Chemeen* and Preranna Bishnoi works with O.V. Vijayan's *Legends of Khasak*. Another article, which highlights the kinship patterns and social ambience of the region, is Preeti Bhatt's on David Davidar's *The House of Blue Mangoes*. Village India has also travelled through memory to distant lands. By focusing on Ashis Gupta's *Dying Traditions*, Supriya Agarwal has worked with the diasporic analysis of the past. Gupta, who lives in Calgary, relates to his past through a fictional presentation, and is concerned with the weakening of the hold of traditional values. Sonu Shiva's essay on *Gaon Ka Aadmi* is focused on the urban-rural relationship and the nature of commitment. While the insider despite moving centre stage prefers to return to the roots, the outsider watches it with a sense of cynical disdain.

Together, the essays draw attention to the complex variety of the village narrative and the journey it traverses from region to region, from time to time and from perspective to perspective. It explores the reflections, the counter questionings and resistance and the myriad narratives of the village, its centrality to change, growth and national constructs. In their variety and multiplicity these village-based novels together weave a narrative of the village, a narrative that is complex, multi-layered, elusive and yet eternal.

Notes

1. Though it is possible to distinguish between village and city landscapes, between village gatherings and city mohall as, the friendly village neighbourhoods and the prying eyes in the chawls, it becomes difficult to distinguish between the cluster of people sitting under the shade of a banyan tree, the village chaupal and the portrayal of the poets' gathering in the film *Mirza Ghalib* (1954) as the poets create poetry through repartee. The film based on the life of Mirza Asadullah Ghalib (1797-1869) chronicles Ghalib's rejection and later acceptance by the royal court. Some of the scenes are unforgettable and one such is when Ghalib and his fellow poets are having a mango feast in the open. Ghalib's love for the streets of Delhi constitutes a legend in itself.
2. Karnad made this observation in his 'Keynote Address' in an International Conference on Theory in a Counter Mode (15-17 December, 2005) at Mangalore.
3. Social histories of nineteenth century India have commented on the change in dress code, footwear (specially where women were concerned) and modification of social habits. Reform movements like the Brahmo Samaj also affected changes in dress and behaviour.
4. These brought prosperity to the village and as newer, technology-aided products became accessible to the average household, ways of cooking altered and traditional leisure activities gave way to newer methods of grinding, churning etc. removing some of these acts from collective participation to the lonely kitchen. Fashion and the nature of village fairs also changed. It became difficult to draw a line between the city and the village, especially in Punjab.

1

Narratology and the Narrative of the Village

JASBIR JAIN

A story about a village need not be very different from an urban narrative in its relationship between plot and character, character and action, cause and effect and between theme and form. Yet, one begins to recognize that the shift in location – what may be called the 'law of placement' in Bakhtinian terms (Holquist 21) – also marks a shift in narratology and upsets the conventional processes of interpretation, unfolding a different kind of poetics (the making of the tale) at work, and gives birth to a new aesthetics (the overall relationship between the act of writing and that of reading). Between the two ends of a literary process are a large number of constituent elements: location, language, style, imagery, momentum, development of action, cohesion or disintegration, linearity or interrupted temporality, narratorial positions, time-space relationships and endings. Even this long list is incomplete. Somewhere in the background lurks the presence of the narrative framework and the narratorial tradition adopted.

What is a 'village'? What does it signify and how does one define it? Each one of us imagines it differently, our imagination is partly shaped by some vague memory, some tales our grandmothers and mothers told us, our travels, a casual visit to a village, villages as portrayed in films or in literature. Premchand's villages are marked by poverty. The villages in films either house lonely women waiting for their migrant husbands as in *Rihayee* or *Gaman*, or are a place of fairs and melas, targets of dacoities, zamindari power and tyranny, unequal societies, or a world of nature as in *Pather Panchali* and *Bhuvan Shome*, of exile as in *Ankur*, and of tribal clusters as in *Rudali*. But these imagined constructs tell us very little about the definition of a village. It cannot be conceived as a segment of a city, or a depopulated town. Demographic studies reveal that towns were surrounded by a cluster of villages, which supplied their needs. Villages were defined primarily on the basis of agricultural activity.[1] Narayani Gupta, in her article "Urbanism in South India," writes that writers in south India have for centuries been quite clear that town and country were distinct; the suggestion that the town is merely a large village has begun only with sociologists recently (Gupta 122). But she goes on to trace a common element of planning in both rural and urban settlements with division into the Brahman area (*agraharam*) and the non-Brahman area (*cheri*), (Gupta 123). Development has recently been seen as a new identifier of village versus town versus city. Thus, trade, industry and money-centres would mark a town or a city to a higher extent than a rural society,[2] which would be marked by agriculture, artisan crafts and known as supplier of migrant labour. A village as such is nowhere an idyllic space. Its great strength, however, lies in the formation of a community.

How do these imagined concepts, perceived realities and geographical spaces affect narratology? Krishna Sobti in her novel *Zindagi Nama*, has one of her characters say: "My submission is, a village is not a city. Even the rustling of a leaf is within the knowledge of everyone" (347, translation mine). Such a view throws away the element of suspense or secrecy to the winds, discards the centrality of the individual and brings forth the difference between a village-centred and a city-centred narrative. But, despite this, the difference is not so simple. Any attempt at a morphological analysis would be varied and heterogeneous. Following Vladimir Propp's morphological classification of the fairy tale, I offer a similar broad classification:

(i) Village as raw material: used merely as a memory, nostalgic recovery, or portrayal of oppression. Rohinton Mistry's use of the village in *A Fine Balance*, Shanta Rama Rau's *Remember the House*. These are personal/political novels.

(ii) Village as nation: Premchand's novels where city-educated men find their purpose of life or alternatively Raja Rao's *Kanthapura* where Murthy acts as a negotiator between national politics and the village awakening. These are primarily ideological constructs building up sagas of nationalist struggle.

(iii) Village as refuge/exile: a place of ideal peace. Nirmal Verma's *Antim Arnay* in which the hills become a refuge for the aged protagonist. City dwellers come here in search of peace and fugitives for help. There are embedded village structures as in Attia Hosain's *Sunlight on a Broken Column* where the ancestral village is first seen as a homeland, a discovery of self and recovery of roots and later portrayed as a place of exile and punishment. Reverse exile takes place when villagers move out in search of employment as in Kamala Markandaya's *Nectar in a Sieve.*

(iv) Village as source of revolution: a place where hegemonic power is questioned. Buddhadeva Guha's *Kojagar*, Raja Rao's *Kanthapura,* Mahasweta Devi's several narratives including the historical *Titu Mir* and novels about the Naxalite movement both in Bengal and Punjab (Gurdial Singh's *Parsa*), all fall into this category.

(v) Village as homeland: place of birth as in Rahi Masoom Reza's *Adha Gaon* and Intizar Husain's *Basti.* This kind of a novel is an experiential novel, not one of an imagined reality.

(vi) Village in confrontation with modernity: Markandaya's *Two Virgins* and Meeran's *The Story of a Seaside Village.* It is not necessarily anti-modern or necessarily anti-tradition.

(vii) Village life as formative experience. Dalit writing is an example of this as in Baby Kamble's *Jeevan Hamara* and Limbale's *Hindu* and *Narvanar.*

(viii) The ethnographic novel: Several of the above-mentioned novels would also fall into this category but a classic example is Krishna Sobti's *Zindagi Nama. The Story of a Seaside Village* also falls into this.

The above categories are broad divisions based on the dominant feature of a novel, the narrator's relationship to space, the space-time conjunction and the embedded purpose of storytelling. The act of writing itself would fit into more than one category. Further, as the above classification is based on my own reading, it simply cannot be exhaustive for there is the huge language barrier as one crosses from one language to another, and other barriers of rituals, myths and customs. Several other narratives come to mind – Gurdial Singh's *Marhi da Diva*, M.K. Indira's *Phaniyamma* and Vijaydan Detha's folk tales ("Duvidha" – made into *Paheli*) – narratives, which are village-centred and work with the everyday struggles of the village folk. There are embedded village narratives in several of Shashi Deshpande's novels, specially in *Roots and Shadows* and *The Binding Vine* but these are personal narratives, the village as such is not problematized. Anita Desai's *Where Shall We Go This Summer?* is another such novel where the village is a place of childhood memories.

For the purpose of this paper, I propose to work on four novels: Buddhadeva Guha's Bengali novel *Kojagar* written in the late 80s and translated as *The Bounty of the Goddess*, Rahi Masoom Reza's *Neem ka Ped,* a fictional version of the 52-episode TV serial of the early 90s, Krishna Sobti's *Zindagi Nama* (1979), a novel located in district Gujarat (part of undivided India and a district of undivided Punjab of the pre-1947 period) and Thoppil Mohammed Meeran's *Oru Kadalora Kiramathin Kathai* (1988), translated from the original Tamil as *The Story of a Seaside Village.* These four narratives represent different kinds of locale, regional languages and historical periods. They are representative of different geographical spaces and their histories of struggle and survival also are different as are the ecological environs and religious power structures. Krishna Sobti's *Zindagi Nama* takes up the first two decades of the 20th century and the story of her ancestral village; Meeran similarly takes up the southern-most tip of the country, probably his own native village Tengaipattanam in the erstwhile state of Travancore. Meeran is also concerned with the pre-independence period. Rahi Masoom Reza's novel is located in U.P. in Madrasa Khurd, a village near Lucknow, in post-independent India, with elections in the background and aspirations for a better life in the foreground. The fourth novel *Kojagar* is located in the tribal region of Palamau with the forest as its landscape.

These novels are by no means pastoral poems. It is difficult to place them under any uniform category but some of their main characteristics are: (i) working backwards through memory; (ii) ethnographic documentation; (iii) stylistically they use dialects. (It is not possible to make any statement about translated texts but both *Zindagi Nama* and *Neem ka Ped* use local dialects); (iv) the imagery reflects the local landscape. This is most prominent in *Kojagar*, which is surrounded by forests, birds and animals; (v) rituals, ceremonies, community-gathering events are centrally placed in these narratives where often spectacle assumes greater importance than reflective monologues; (vi) relationships acquire greater importance than the notion of self; (vii) the reality depicted is more earthy than in the urban novel and the materiality of the body is more recognizable; (viii) the negotiations with outer spaces are an ongoing disruptive process; (ix) and, more important than all else, is the space-centredness of the village narrative.

A natural fallout of the space-centredness is the gradual unfolding of the theme. The narrator/writer sets about to describe the community, the family, the place or environment at a slow pace. For more than sixty pages, Sobti describes episodically the various incidents, which do not seem to have any apparent connection. Similarly, Guha indulges in a descriptive narrative about the landscape, Reza about kinship and political rivalries, and Meeran about the mosque, the Mudalali and the Revered One.

The narrative voice in *Kojagar* is neither omniscient nor that of an insider; it is Sayan Mukherjee, the bamboo-babu. An interesting feature is this narrative voice which is in a constant state of movement between the two worlds. He looks at nature as a city-bred sensitive man would do. He indulges in bird-watching, wants to identify them with the help of the 'bird' book (Salim Ali's), whereas the peasants look at them as harbingers of good or evil, as indicators of a snake or a leopard or of seasonal change. Again, while the city-bred officers and government policies are concerned with the preservation of wildlife, protection of the environment and family planning, the tribals find in the animals a constant threat to their life and property. The lurking presence of the leopard imposes a nightly curfew on them. They are exploited and the natural means of livelihood are denied them; their children die while the medical officer imposes family planning upon them. The animals also become a metaphor for this exploitation as well as of the courage of the villagers. Nankua, the village rebel, is often compared to a tiger. The tiger with his bold ways and the leopard with his stealthy ones are contrasted. The two main exploiters are Mahato Babu and the local bania and money-lender, Goda Seth. A third exploiter is the upper caste police officer, who visits the village along with Hiru Oraon and rapes Hiru's sister. In fact, the structure is fascinating. There is no single protagonist, lives are interwoven, exploiters are multi-headed and dissidents are many. Valumar, despite its enclosure in the forest area, is a microcosm of the nation.

Bamboo Babu is the outsider who marries Titli, the tribal girl, gives up his job with the forest contractor, becomes an insider, opens a school, all this while negotiating the difficulty of becoming the 'Other'. Crazy Sahib remains on the fringe, a sympathizer, an adviser, but not a participant. Hiru Oraon becomes Hira Singh, disowns his family, only to come back to kill his sister's rapist and his own pregnant sister and ends up serving a jail sentence. Nankua is the native rebel, the protector, the elusive benefactor, always on the run but one who dares take up cudgels against the local powers. Nankua is in communication with the Naxalites, in love with Tusiya, Hiru's sister, and is willing to own her bastard child. His is the most courageous figure and the one who sacrifices the most. There is also Uncle Karua, the poacher, who dies in his attempt to kill the leopard. There is a constant strife with the powers that be through defiance, rebellion, violation of law and of custom. Bamboo Babu alienates his uncle and aunt, Crazy Sahib and his other upper caste friends through the act of going across to the tribals.

Though the main narrator is Bamboo Babu, who occupies an observer status, there are a few sections that have an omniscient narration and then there are letters that fill up other gaps. Bamboo Babu also slides from his observer status once he becomes a participant. His own emotional conflict is problematized and his dissatisfaction with only a sexual and bodily relationship begins to tell on his relationship with Titli. Through this both the nature of the 'self' and of the 'centre' are dissected. The many leopard deaths, the drowning of Bulki and Pareshnath, their mother's selling her body to Mahato, the broken dreams of Muniya, Tusiya's murder – all these tragedies punctuate the narrative of the place as they repeatedly ask the question – What is the meaning of freedom?

Freedom is an elusive idea, even in *Neem ka Ped*, where the tree is the narrator, the target and the definer. It is an unusual narrative strategy, which equates the tree's life with human existence. Planted in 1946, it shares its birth with Sukhiram,

Buddhai's son. Buddhai has planted it in the hope that his son will not be exploited in a free country, he will not be Sukhiya but Sukhiram. But Sukhiram, the son of a bonded labourer, grows up to become a manipulative politician and exploiter. In a brief prologue to the novel, the all-controlling voice of the writer states that the characters play out the larger political reality. The two cousins, Zamin and Muslim, *khala-jad bhai*, and brothers-in-law, play out the game of all nations where honour is bartered and territories are claimed, gained and lost – "*yeh to mujhe mulkon ki adawat ki tarah dikhayi deti hain*" (vi). Truth is another category which contends with reality. Does the tree know enough and does it tell the truth? If not, then, the falsehood is the tree's falsehood. Using this framework, the narrative proceeds to build on the allegorical significance of the tree. It is planted on the master, Zamin Miyan's land. This piece of land is then gifted to Buddhai by the new master, Muslim Miyan, when the property changes hands. But, the ownership is in name. With the change of masters, loyalties are required to be transferred. Buddhai, an important witness in a murder case, can save or destroy Zamin Miyan through his testimony. When he is transferred to a new master, he is required to change his testimony, despite the fact that the earlier evidence was also faked.

The tree symbolizes various things, but the dominant image is that of the dream of freedom. The shade of the tree is equated with a son's love and care and a father's protection (66). It represents a living history – "*Zinda itihas hun main*" (50). It is conscious that when its shadow lengthens, the sun is about to set, and is afraid that the sun in Sukhiram's life is also going to set as his shadow has lengthened. Under Sukhiram's regime, the coolness of the tree's shade has 'disappeared' (50). Rooted in the earth, the tree has observed generations of politicians as the game is played from father to son or to daughter-in-law, tearing families apart and resorting to murder with ease. In its role as narrator, the tree is free to turn to itself as a reference point and to reach out to the reader/listener for purposes of commentary and analysis. Its loneliness is conveyed when even Buddhiram abandons its shade and not even a stray dog turns up to bark under its branches. This alienation spells ill for the dreams of the nation and its future (56). There are references to the partition and its aftermath, the time when blood flowed freely and there were no swings on the trees even during the rains, people were uprooted and carried away by the flood of violence and political events took an unexpected turn (19). Court cases, false witnesses, police corruption, family rivalries, and the widening schism between friends become a part of daily life putting an end to dreams of freedom. It is a sad story with the tree willing itself to forget its memories and Buddhiram left to mourn the death of his dreams. He had loved the tree more than his son, Muslim Miyan deprived him of its shade and Sukhiram sold the tree – towards what end? When a brother can murder a brother under its shade and children are aborted even before they are born, the tree is flooded by a mother's tears, the tree is up for sale – "*ped bachayo, neem ka ped bachayo, khoon deke bache to bachayo*" (192). At this point, the tree turns into the image of a nation, as in Manzoor Ehtesham's *Sookha Bargad*. A nation is made by its people and their ability to materialize the dream of freedom.

The village narrative interacts with the political reality because the strands of national life go back to the village for life and sustenance. The spatio-temporal context is also never out of sight. There is a constant interaction with past histories, past revolutions, an interaction which prods the reader's memory every now and then (97) and thus reinforces its presence (50, 55-56). The tree's constant interaction, the use of the local dialect and the tone of storytelling are all elements of an oral tradition. An inland place, it is *land* that is foregrounded here – land, territory, belonging and nationhood.

In contrast, the scene changes to a coastal region in Thoppil Mohammed Meeran's *The Story of a Seaside Village*. The role of the sea is first foregrounded when the Revered One arrives in the village from Maldives (3), again when Farid goes away, perhaps to Colombo (142), and then when the daughter of the house commits suicide (171). For the rest it is an enclosed village, absorbed in the religious hold of the mosque and the Mudalali. Located in the pre-independence period, the village welcomes the Revered One who has arrived in pursuit of an 'escaped' evil spirit but is hostile to Mehboob, the school master. This is the central conflict of power – religious versus secular power. The Mudalali moves towards his own ruin – economically he is eaten out of his inheritance by the Revered One, morally he stoops to committing murder, emotionally he marries off his young daughter to a mad man, repeating the story of his sister who, at thirteen, had been married to a man of sixty and widowed a year later. Mudalali finally loses his sanity and his madness becomes a symbol of a total loss of control. His daughter commits suicide and his nephew goes away. The village dissident is Mehmood who cannot understand why prayers cannot be said without Mudalali, and why people have to get off the road to let the Mudalali pass. Later, he wants a school to be established in the village. Despite being a poor man he offers his own land, a stretch intended as dowry for his daughter, for the school. Further, he marries off his daughter without a dowry and without a priest, thus violating the conventions of this society. At one level it is the conflict between superstitious belief and a modern mindset, at another between life-denying power and the desire for freedom, and at yet another between appearance and reality. Farid who is said to be not 'fully' there is wiser than his uncle. The women of the household, Mudalali sister Noohu Pattuma and daughter Ayesha, are wiser than the men. As the story proceeds, the most loyal of Mudalali's people who had so far unquestioningly carried out his wishes, begin to question his orders. When he asks Karuppan to burn down the school, he refuses:

> I killed when Mudalali told me to. I stabbed when I was told to. Not once did I disobey. But I refuse to do this.
> ...

> I am an ignorant brute and a cruel man..... But I shall not destroy this Saraswati temple which is going to show light to our children. (138)

The final blow is struck when the noon prayers take place "without him, without his knowledge" (146). Dress, marriage, education, loyalties, sex all are controlled to such a degree that the society has become moribund and static, leading to isolation, confinement, separation and madness. In Ayesha's view it is like serving "a life term in a dungeon" and she finds it intolerable to continue living in "a society that was numb and blind to the plight of a young woman and denied youth its due" (168). The novel ends with Ayesha's suicide, but before that the horse has died, her father has turned mad, and the noon prayers have taken place without him. One is compelled to ask – is it a negative ending? or does it display the impossibility of suppressing the human urge to freedom, of living in closed societies, and demonstrate the irrelevance of practices which deny the human? There is hope in the death of the Revered One, in the refusal of Karuppan to obey Mudalali, in Mehboob's struggle to continue with his school, in Mehmood's continuing questioning. All these lead to a decentring of the power of Mudalali and of the mosque.[3]

In contrast to the above three narratives Sobti's *Zindagi Nama* is totally decentred. It does not choose to work through a central symbol or a single narrator. While it shares with others the resort to dialect, the stress on graphic details, the dependence on rituals and ceremonies, the community-centred narrative interwoven with politics, it goes beyond them in its expansion of time and space, and its extensive documentation of cultural attitudes and mindsets. *Zindagi Nama* depends heavily on orality and the oral tradition. This is stressed throughout by the articulated requests for storytelling as for instance: "*Lalaji kahani! Lalaji bujhartein. Lalaji koi kissa*" and then references such as "*Shahji ne mannka piro diya*" as beads are threaded in the narrative (147). Later, when the story is interrupted, Dodiya explains his silence as the breaking of a string with the beads all scattered *mala tut geyi, manke bhiker gaye,* (181). There is an equal stress on listening, the importance of response of '*hunkara*' is pointed out by direct reference – that the response is given (*hunkara dena*) and acknowledged and becomes a dialogue. There is the men's *majlis* where they get together to exchange gossip, pass on rumours and indulge in expositions. They provide a debating ground as well as a channel for transmission of knowledge. Discussion is important as it facilitates circulation of ideas and becomes a way of learning for the simple village folk.

The dependence on oral tradition is first of all framed by the long poetic poem which stresses the importance of oral histories, what one way refers to as people's or folk histories, which are instrumental in building the spirit of patriotism, of national belonging and the sense of pride that one has in one's own land. This is reinforced over and over again throughout *Zindagi Nama*.

Another important dimension is the role of the 'mirasis', the professional singers and family hagiographers, who participate in the act of narration. They do not merely sing songs, but recite histories, continuing to reinforce memory and facilitate the presence of the past in the present. History is passed on as a story – *Mashoor kissa ho guzra hai* – and invasions are described (122), and contemporary reality is also presented in a story form (151-152). History is used to offer a comparative framework, to discuss power, to invoke patriotism, to relate to the problem.

Rabiyan, Lali Shah's nursemaid, is also a singer. She sings couplets from Bulle Shah and Waris Shah, thus rendering them contemporary. Everyone requests her to sing and even the men feel that "Heer and Ranjha are alive amidst us" when she sings of them (163). The characters of the romances are role models for lovers as their sacrifices project the highest ideals of love. In Rabiyan's case, it becomes the blueprint of her behaviour when she sings Bulle Shah's kaafi:

Nan main bihahi, nan kanwari
Per beta goad khilaonyungi
Ek duna achraj gayongi
Main pyara yar manaungi. (110)

But before we come to that there is about eighty pages of preparing the setting for the saga. The story doesn't move forward in terms of happenings; instead, nursery rhymes, children's verses, riddles and games are introduced and the change of seasons mark the passage of time.

Rituals can be religious or social. *Zindagi Nama* uses social rituals rather than religious ones, primarily because social rituals are participatory and work across caste and religion. These collective celebrations are occasions like childbirth, marriage ceremonies and other conventional practices of inculcating social behaviour like Lali Shah's school entrance ceremony. They occur at regular intervals in the narrative and provide a space for the surfacing of cultural practices: *suhaags* and *ghoris* are sung, lullabies find a place and the child Lali Shah gets the blessings of old and young as he sprightly prepares for his first day at school. Before that a *trinjan* – a spinning and embroidery get-together when young girls compete with each other and work throughout the night – a shared activity and space which may be lost to them once they are married. Festivals like Lohri are celebrated when children go from door to door singing songs and collecting funds for their celebration (37). The concept of privacy or individualized space is totally rejected. In direct opposition is the male discourse of honour and masculinity, of passion and revenge, incidents of which are interspersed at regular intervals – a soldier proceeding on leave with the government issued gun to avenge dishonour, a son coming home to kill his uncle he suspects of having a liason with his mother and party to his father's death (in the true Hamletian manner (339-342). Both the discourses reflect regional compulsions: the merry-making which is part of a transient life and the passion which is easily excited. People who live in uncertainties do not think of long-term immortalities but of the present. They give themselves to it as they are constantly being tested for their courage and bodily strength and are engaged in battle and yield to the passion of the moment when honour is balanced with life. The materiality of this discourse is balanced by the underlying anguish which tugs at the heart of many – the unfulfilled love of Rabiyan, the loss of childhood innocence and the war always at their doorstep.

In terms of time, perhaps, it is a narrative spread over a period of fifteen years or a little more. We have many markers – the 1905 partition of Bengal, the 1911 bomb blast in Chandni Chowk, the 1913 formation of the Gadar Party in Washington, the 1914 Komagatamaru incidence when 27 Sikh immigrants were killed, the recruitment during World War I (345-351), Gandhi's resistance to the South Africa regime – comfortably located it in the first two decades of the 20th century. But time is not segmented, nor is it linear. All histories are rooted in the past and all progress has a history. Other wars have been fought and either won or lost. And, the great Kohinoor won by Maharaja Ranjit Singh in 1813 was lost due to the defeat in the battle of Chillianwala in 1849 (181). These are narrated and enacted by the mirasis in *swanga* masquerade. Throughout the 19th century the borders of the Sikh Empire were constantly shifting, either expanding or contracting. Other invasions and battles are recounted by the villagers going as far back as Alexander's and Ghazni's invasions (358-359). These references explode the myth of the ignorant villager and reinforce the strength of oral history which is recapitulated through sifting, repetition and myth-making and projects role models to be emulated. These histories also stress the openness of the frontier, the constant need to be vigilant and to adapt to change. And more than that to invest their values in survival strategies and human memory.

Writing is a fixed entity (transcription), it is distant and does not have community participation. And, the whole effort in *Zindagi Nama* is directed towards making the act of writing and of storytelling come alive, to make it rise out of the page. An indication of this is given by the rapid succession of songs and rhymes, and by the long episodes of discussion and conversation. The descriptive passages, passages which do the 'telling', are limited. To the same-culture reader the reality comes alive while for the other-culture reader it is transformed into secondary orality. Orality, whether primary or secondary, evokes a cultural context. This challenges the belief expressed by Colby in *Narrative*, "words within inverted commas give a false sense of freedom and are controlled and manipulated by the words outside it, character is subordinated to the narration" (101-102). This does not happen in a community-centred narrative because the centrality of the character is never at stake;[4] its relationship with narrative is more intimate, less obtrusive than in the individual-centred novel.

When the British policies for land development are placed side by side with the policies and farsightedness of earlier rulers, it is a direct critiquing of the British economic interest. Other targets of criticism are religious conversion, missionaries, urban lifestyles, corruption and the offering of *nazaranas* (264-266). The villagers argue that the canals are also god given. If Punjab had not been a land of rivers, could the British have drawn water from a desert? Earlier rulers had likewise looked after the people, the British are not the only ones. Even during Shah Jahan's rule canals had been dug and rain water harvested (268-269). Progress is seen in indigenous terms. But, in all discourses of war, the people's power is stressed, logically building up the narrative towards the freedom struggle of 1919 and Gandhi's launching of the Non-Co-operation Movement. Not only are there umpteen number of references to the Bengal revolutionaries but examples are also unearthed from past histories. Even as territories change hands, from the Hindu to the Turk, to the Moghul, people remain where they were – "*Apne mulk ki dyodhi to rahe Kabul Kandhar*" (99):

> The threshold of our country has always been Kabul and Kandhar. The truth is this that thousands of invaders have come and gone but Lahore belongs to the people of Lahore and Kabul to its people. What I wish to point out is that kings and rulers, Sultans and Shahenshahs come and go, political regimes change but no one can displace the populations of these countries. (99)

There is a restlessness amongst the young, they even resent the hierarchy and the economic inequality, they also resent the racial discrimination abroad:

> The truth is that the country is ours but political power is in foreign hands.

And, as the spirit of revolution is aroused, inspiration is drawn from the Guru's words:

> When all other paths have come to a dead end, then it is legitimate to pick up the sword.

As these narratives move into history and record the flux of time, they are simultaneously engaged in projecting an idea of the nation. Freedom is very central to all of them – political and personal freedom, justice and equality. Buddhai's whole life is geared towards working for this freedom, the tree laments the strangling of freedom by the manipulative politicians, *Zindagi Nama* calls for a revolution to free the country of the foreign ruler, and Mehmood questions the hegemony of the Mudalali's control. The natural constituent of freedom is power – the power to be – and lack of freedom is also a lack of power with the village rebels like Nankua, Mehmood, the naxalites and revolutionaries, the freedom fighters rising up against the strongholds of power, the course of power is diverted and the Foucauldian circulatoriness emphasized. Even Buddhai, the bonded labourer, rebels in the end. Again, all four novels stress the role of education as a channel of change, as a medium of entering the temporal flow. Mehboob's school, aided and helped by Mehmood, is the counterpoint to the power of the mosque, it is the temple of Saraswati. Sayan Mukherjee in *Kojagar* himself starts a school for the tribal people; Lali Shah enters the school ceremoniously and with the community's blessings in *Zindagi Nama*. Buddhai is all praise for Zamin Miyan because he was the one to establish the school which helped Sukhi to become Sukhiram. That this very school is used as a pawn in the game of politics and it is this political game which corrupts the ends of education is an altogether different matter.

What happens to narratology in these community-centred, space-specific narratives? If, on the one hand, they connect with the nation's political life and social goals, on the other, they stress the rootedness of value structures and the refusal to be marginalized. The choice of the narrative voice becomes important. All four writers have adopted different strategies. Guha's use of an outsider, who wishes to identify himself with the people, is a narrative voice on the border – the border between belonging and not-belonging. Sayan Mukherjee's observations are those of a city-bred outsider. His critiquing likewise has to travel inwards into their lives to understand them. His is a disruptive voice, yet he is a link between the two worlds as he identifies himself with the dissidents and also because, through marriage, he owns them. *Zindagi Nama* has a decentred narrative, an ethnographic purpose where a collage of memories is built up out of Sobti own's background. But, by using two different time frames – one from 1905 to 1919 and the other which goes back into the early 19th century and even to earlier times – and also by travelling in space to other regions like Calcutta, to countries like Afghanistan, it refuses to be enclosed in a small village. Meeran's omniscient narrative voice works with an enclosed space. But it too travels outside it through marriages, through journeys and through aspirations. Yet it is a claustrophobic, concentrated narrative – the interior of Mudalali's house and the lives of the two women inside it, the decadence and bankruptcy which gradually creep into it – all these demonstrate the larger truth and play a significant role in the matter of shaping our attitudes and the way we think. The village narrative to my mind is a limited term: it uses the village merely as a setting, the 'narrative of the village' goes further than the 'village narrative' because it looks at the formative patterns, the community interaction and villagers as cultural carriers rather than as individual lives located in a particular space. When it uses individual characters, they are either archetypal figures or acquire a mythic role (like Nankua) rendering the end of a life irrelevant to the narrative. The advantages of each narratorial approach are different but the constant shifting of perspectives as in *Kojagar* and *Zindagi Nama* introduces a multi-subjectivity. This is absent in *Neem ka Ped*[5] where the journey is towards the representation of a nation and in the *Seaside Village*, which centralizes the oppressive nature of mindless power.[6] The narrative of the village is about many things – the faithfulness of memory, the construction and perception of reality, the self-image of a community.[7] It is situational rather than personal and uses autobiographical material as ethnography.[8] It goes on to link memory and desire.

Notes

1. Refer R.S. Sharma's "Urbanism in Early Historic India" and Narayani Gupta's "Urbanism in South India", both included in *The City in Indian History*. Ed. Indu Banga. A third article which discusses the residual village culture as continued in urban communities is Nita Kumar's "Urban Culture in Modern India: Words of the Lower Classes" in the same volume.
2. Shahid Amin in his *Event, Metaphor, Memory: Chauri-Chaura* throws light on the interesting way rail junctions affect a village. In 1872 Chaura had only 132 inhabitants (19). It was the railways that 'made it a bazaar'. Between 1872 and 1881 the population increased considerably.
3. Khushwant Singh's *Train to Pakistan* is also located in a village, Mano Majra, where the mosque and the gurudwara are the two spaces which

despite being religious spaces are secular and humanistic, while the third space of the Rest House where the magistrate hands out his orders is manipulative.

4. Refer Bhalchandra Nemade's essay "The Semantics of Orality". Nemade stresses the collective enjoyment of the oral narrative and this in itself is a censoring on the purely intimate. He also draws attention towards the poetic nature of the oral narrative, which is more 'proletarian and rural' than the written (201).
5. *Neem ka Ped* was begun by Rahi Masoom Reza but given its fictional form by Prabhat Ranjan. There may have been other collaborators. In any case a TV serial is a collaborative effort. This kind of participatory writing can go a long way in recreating a community narrative.
6. Thoppil Mohammed Meeran's novel has been used as a text book both in Tamil Nadu and Kerala. This is important because if it is to be read as a critique of religious power, it would be seen as explosive material. Instead, the focus is on superstition and on social, class and gender oppression. Tradition, when it ceases to evolve, becomes a crippling burden.
7. Also refer Colby 32.
8. Rahi Masoom Reza writes about his own village, as do Krishna Sobti and Thoppil Mohammed Meeran.

References

Amin, Shahid. *Event, Metaphor and Memory: Chauri Chaura.* New Delhi: Oxford India Paperbacks (1995), 1996.

Banga, Indu. ed. *The City in Indian History.* New Delhi: Manohar Publications and Urban History Association of India, 1991.

Cobley, Paul. *Narrative.* London: Routledge, 2001.

Foucault, Michel. *Power/Knowledge. Selected Interviews & Other Writings 1972-1977.* Ed. Colin Gordon. New York: Pantheon Books, 1980.

Guha, Buddhadev. *The Bounty of the Goddess.* Translation of *Kojagar* from the original Bengali by John W. Hood. New Delhi: Rupa and Co., 2004.

Gupta, Narayani. "Urbanism in South India: Eighteenth and Nineteenth Centuries". *The City in Indian History.* Ed. Indu Banga, 1991.

Holquist, Michael. *Dialogism: Bakhtin and His World* (1990). London: Routledge, 2002.

Kumar, Nita. "Urban Culture in Modern India: World of the Lower Classes". *The City in Indian History*. Ed. Indu Banga, 1991.

Meeran, Thoppil Mohammed. *The Story of a Seaside Village.* Translated from the Tamil original by M. Vijayalakshmi. Hyderabad: Disha Books, Orient Longman Pvt. Ltd. (1998), 2003.

Nemade, Bhalchandra. "The Semantics of Orality," *Creating Theory: Writers on Writing.* Ed. Jasbir Jain. Delhi: Pencraft International, 2000.

Ong, Walter J. *Orality and Literature: The Technology of the Word.* London: Methuen, 1982.

Reza, Rahi Masoom. *Neem ka Ped.* Translated by Prabhat Ranjan (2003). New Delhi: Rajkamal Paperbacks, 2004.

Sharma, R.S. "Urbanism in Early Historic India", *The City in Indian History*. Ed. Indu Banga, 1991.

Sobti, Krishna. *Zindagi Nama*: Pahla Bhag *Zinda Rukh* (Hindi) (1979). New Delhi: Rajkamal Prakashan, 1994.

Visweswaran, Kamala. *Fictions of Feminist Ethnography.* Delhi: Oxford University Press, 1996.

2

Rethinking Kajri When Black Clouds Hang

ANISUR RAHMAN

Aap ko achha lagey ya nahin...hum to kajri bajayengey.
I will play kajri...whether you like it or not.

—Ustad Bismillah Khan

A Folklorist Interlude

An unassuming person, a charismatic musician, Bharat Ratna Ustad Bismillah Khan made this frank and justifiably fair statement in a musical soiree in Jammu quite recently.[1] He was enamoured by the beauty of the valley and wanted to play the various tunes of nature. He chose kajri as one of his offerings to the charmed audience, completely undeterred by the fact that the acoustics of the hall were poor.

Kajri is played, staged, or sung when black clouds, announcing the rains, literally hang in the sky. When the Ustad chose to play, there were no such clouds. He probably wished to make a metaphoric statement to suggest that we all live in times of great anguish and need soothing. Today, even though black clouds hang all over and we exist in various states of uneasiness, we have little hope that we shall have the redeeming rains. The Ustad's offering may thus be taken as a folklorist interlude of hope, faith and redemption that his music might bring to listeners.

Music has a healing touch. The same is true of literature. The two may sometimes join together to reinforce the modes of human expression, both through words and performance, and become a source of deliverance. The folk forms of tales, fables, legends, myths, sagas, songs, or even proverbs and riddles have long been known to have the capacity to rejuvenate the human beings. We relate to folk arts rather naturally as they represent our history, memory and myth, both in direct and imaginative/creative terms. While they do so, they also allow us to connect with our environs and ourselves. In this process, they help us live, imagine and dream, and seek roots in our race and culture. They re-affirm our identity and provide opportunities to extend our selves beyond time and space. Folk arts and forms also call the past to bear upon the present and make the two points of time mutually relevant. They offer us with a principle of sustenance that proves vital in how they operate upon us and impart meaning to our existence.

The way inimitable players and singers like Ustad Bismillah Khan and Begum Akhtar have rendered kajri, it has acquired the potential of being a major point of reference in culture studies. When Begum Akhtar sang *Chha rahi kari ghata...* (The black clouds are gathering...) in the 1930s, she did so in a manner that was more spontaneous and less embellished. However, when she sang the same kajri in the mid 60s for All India Radio, it was quite artfully conceived and proficiently delivered. The two renditions of the same kajri represent two modes of artistic apprehension: one marked by immediacy and the other by deliberation. While the tonal and musical impact of the two renditions differed greatly, they remained united in one way: they represented the essential pathos associated with the plight of the sufferer in a particular season of the year.

Many classical, semi-classical, and popular musicians and singers have found their appropriate medium in kajri. This has been happening over a long period of time. In its classical rendition, it may be set, for example, to a play of keharva (eight beats) and other styles. It may also be sung in Misra Piloo, which is a light raga. *Kehana va Madho* by Mala Ramadurai is an example of this. Even though a large number of kajris have been lost forever (because they were not recorded and lived only in the memories of the singers), the institution has not been dead altogether. They have existed in a variety of languages and dialects, have been composed on a variety of themes, and sung in innumerable styles. In all these manifestations, kajri has provided an emotionally fulfilling and aesthetically sound interlude in the humdrum existence of human beings. Other folk songs like chaitri (chaita, chaiti), sohar and malhar, the eulogies of the bhands and the fine satirical comedies of the bhands also provide similar interludes and supplementary source of emotional sustenance.

Kajri: Origin, Form, Value

There are various views about the origins of kajri. According to a popular belief, kajri had its origin in the black clouds of sawan, which has a stock symbolic significance with respect to love and longing. The days of scorching heat that gave birth to chaitri look forward to the arrival of black clouds and rains. These clouds and rains raise the songs of love and longing in what we know as kajri. Traditionally, it is a folk song composed and sung in the regions of eastern Uttar Pradesh, Bihar and in parts of Rajasthan on the eve of Teej of Shrawan Shukl Paksh.

As a folktale of Mirzapur, the home of this song would have it; kajri had its origin in the story of a woman called Kajli whose husband had gone to a far off land. Even when the monsoon arrived and her love did not return, her suffering grew unbearable. She wept at the feet of goddess Kajmal and her imploring turned into pathetic songs known as kajri. The story sounds familiar. There are many such in the literatures of the east and the west but this one goes so well with the story of kajri.

Bhartendu Harishchandra has enumerated three sources of kajri.[2] First, he has related it to the death of king Dadu Rai of central India and the sati of his widow queen, Nagmati. These two tragedies brought immeasurable pain to the people of the kingdom. They, thereafter, evolved a new form of expressing their woes in a song that came to be known as kajri. Second, he has related kajri to the beautiful wild forests in the kingdom of Dadu Rai. The forests were called kajli and the songs named after them, later came to be known as kajri. Third, he has proposed that the songs sung on the eve of Teej in the months of sawan and bhadon were known as kajli or kajri. The explanations given above often bring the two expressions kajli and kajri together. It could be proposed that many of the expressions in the regions of eastern Uttar Pradesh and Bihar replace 'l' with 'r' as they fit well with the spoken dialect of the people in these regions. As such, *kali badli* (black cloud) is often spoken or sung as *kari badariya, kajal* as *kajar* etc. It is only natural, therefore, that kajli was called kajri.

The origin and development of kajri as a folk art form is almost impossible to ascertain, as it has mostly been a manifestation of impassioned speech, an oral art *par excellence*. The composers were neither self-proclaimed poets nor were they otherwise acknowledged as such to form a possible part of any literary history. Hardly aware of the remarkable literary feat these composers (better called poets) were achieving, they did not make any conscious effort to write or preserve their creations. They did not also consciously follow the norms of poetic composition yet their kajris emerged as fine creations of remarkable literary worth. As it kept emerging and consolidating as an independent folk genre, it posed several important questions, hitherto unattended, regarding spontaneity in verbal expression, vigour and vitality of the spoken lexicon, cultural roots, musicality, drama, and community entertainment.

Kajris may be read as eminent examples of secular poetry rooted in history, culture, region, spirituality, and patriotism. Apart from other constituents, nature and woman remain at the centre of this composition. Kajri is an emotional and dramatic representation of life in village. It spells out the longings and despairs of a community of people enjoying close emotional bondage. Kajri represents an individual history as forcefully as it does the history and geography of a people, its sociology and its philosophy of existence. Kajris may also be read as the dream indices of the village men and women living their lives so very passionately and in an environment of their own. They spell out the beat of life, its internal rhythm, and association with the lives around. Kajri has had various forms ever since its origin at some point of time in the past and has passed through several variations in techniques of composition and styles of rendition. They may best be read in two of their inseparable manifestations: as written or recorded songs for their broad rhetorical and prosodic, cultural and historical, philosophical and religious significance, and also as a text in performance with adequate emphasis on the principles of presentation like *tek udan*, off-and-on stage presentation, and community participation. There are regional variations in the styles of singing that may clearly be noticed in the way kajris are sung in Ramnagar (Kashi) and Mirzapur. In this respect, kajris may also be read as manifestations of the tones and tunes characteristic of a community of people living in two areas of the same region.

While Ramnagar (Kashi) has been the home of Ramlila, Mirzapur has been the home of Kajri: *Leela Ramnagar ki bhari/ Kajri Mirzapur sarnam/sardar* (Ramnagar excels in Ramlila, Mirzapur in kajri). Sometimes, it holds close to jhoola, another form of folk devotion to Radha and Krishna: *Jhoola lagal kadam ki dari/Jhoolein Krishna Murari na/Radha jhoolein Kanha jhulawein/Kanha jhoolein Radha jhulawein, Pari-pari na.* (There is a swing on the kadam branches/Krishna enjoys swinging/ Both Krishna and Radha swing each other/one by one). As men and women sit in swing in the month of sawan and sing kajri, so are the gods made to sit in a swing and listen to kajri sung in great devotion and delight. Kajri and jhoola, therefore, appear to be holding close to each other as both represent facets of romantic love and also complement the acts of singing and listening.

As a typical example of a folk song sung in sawan, a kajri by prominent Hindi poet Chaudhary Badri Narayan Premghan[3] as quoted by Abdul Bismillah in *Lok Kavya Vidha: Kajri*[4] is produced here as follows:

Rimjhim rimjhim barsaiy re badariya
More chadariya bhiji jai.
Kahan Jai ab hai bachaun mein
Daiyya jiya ghabrai.
Lai chhata tar chhati se lagi
Preeti reet barsai.
Priya Premghan Paiyan lagaun
Begi bachawa aiye. (13)

(The clouds send drizzles; my sheet is drenched
Where shall I hide myself; I'm wet, I'm scared
He drew me close under the umbrella
He embraced; he showered his love
Dear Premghan! I must touch his feet
How soon he appeared to save me from distress)[5]

At Home in Mirzapur

Ever since Kajli sang her song of separation at the feet of goddess Kajmal in the folk tale mentioned above, Mirzapur, a small town in eastern Uttar Pradesh, has been the real home of kajri. It has become synonymous with the place and it is more than a folk song for its people; it is Mirzapur's culture icon. Many of the landmarks here, including a pond, have been named after kajri. On the occasion of Nagpanchami, women bathe in this pond every year and come back home singing kajri. Kajri is also sung on other religious occasions and has become a kind of ritual for the people who have been practicing it for a long time now.

Following the forlorn Kajli, women in Mirzapur sing kajri while working in the fields or swinging on jhoolas. They also do so behind a curtain by the roadside. On the eve of Anant Chaturdashi these performances from behind the curtains increase in number as more women join in. A popular couplet says that the women of this place would not go to their husband's homes in the month of sawan for that is when the sons of the soil would return and kajri would be sung. It is a very special occasion when one could participate in festivity and enjoy oneself in a community of kindred souls.

Men join in singing kajri in a different manner. They form groups and sing their chosen songs in a number of *akhadas* spread all over the town and even in the peripheries. The two *akhadas* of Jehangir and Siddhnath are better known than others as these groups pose questions, seek answers and try to establish their supremacy over each other. Singers also change their parties or groups with the exchange of cardamom. The kajri composers or poets pass on their creations to the singers, who earn praise and pride for themselves as also the poets.

Kajri in Mirzapur is sung and performed in three different ways. Men sing it in a classical, semi-classical or popular manner with nostalgic fervour and enjoy its emotional flavour. Women sing in folk tunes in the fields, on the *jhoolas*, or behind the curtains. Then there are actors who perform them enthusiastically in local *dangals*. Turning their gestures into language and language into gestures, they add to the given text and perform in *dangals* with a keen sense of competition. This sense of competition is heightened when kajris are presented as questions and answers. As the imagination of the poets is required to soar high to seek gems of questions and jewels of answers, the actors too have to keep pace and sound overpowering. Parties lose and win, receiving public applause and criticism for the quality of their performance. An example may be seen here:

Question song

Chaat rahi chakchhu se chakori kora katora chandi ka
Bhara hua lau hai amrit se weera katora chandi ka (tek)
Lagaiga kya koi use jo bada anal se laga hua
Dhalengey kis sanchey mein jo chheer Sindhu mein dhala hua
Tab se suraj tapayega kya tar karai usey jo tala hua
Churayega kya chor usey wah khud choron ka bala hua
Meley ke mehfil mein ghoomein chunh ora katora chandi ka (udan)
(16-17)

(The *chakori* is licking with eyes the empty bowl of silver
It's filled with *amrit* to the very brim, that bowl of silver
Who can fill it better; it's already filled with fire
In which cast shall it be moulded; it's already moulded in Sindhu
With what heat would the sun burn; it's already soaked in frying
How can the thieves steal it; it's already a bane for them
I wish to stroll in the fair all around with an empty bowl of silver)

Answer song

Latka hua adhar mein hai ek lal katora soney ka
Lalit prathat paaya Shankar khushhal katora soney ka (tek)
Nahi baid na puran mein na kuran mein iska barnan
Na ye katora zameen mein na na yeh rahta yaar gagan
Naqsha jiska duniya ke karigar na paye mitran
Nashey mein ek din Shiv Shnakar thhe Parvati se lagey kahan
Liya pratham sakti se terey yeh lal katora soney ka (udan) (17)
(There hangs in the space a red bowl of gold
A bright, a beautiful, a happy bowl of gold
Neither the Vedas, nor the Purana, nor the Quran mention it
This bowl is neither here upon this earth, nor there in the skies
No craftsman can ever draw its figure, my friend!
Drunk to the brim, one day Shiv Shankar spoke to Parvati:
Only from your prime powers, I got this red bowl of gold)

The questions and answers are presented in complex ways and as riddles to the rival party. The intention is to make it too difficult to answer and bring defeat to the rival party. More than mere exercises in kajri singing, these competitive items create a keen sense of participation by training and sharpening the sensibility of the listeners.

These exercises not only underline the creative vitality of the poets, they also bear witness to their sharp logic, deep knowledge, and command over the art of rhetoric. The lexicon used in the kajris of Mirzapur is a rich admixture of the Hindi-Sanskrit, Urdu-Persian expressions in addition to those drawn from Bhojpuri and Avadhi. Kajris are not written in any particular style or form; they are composed in any metre, line or text length, and in any manner that might appeal to the poet. These are the free expressions of untutored imagination but deserve to be read as serious literary texts.

The Kajri Protagonist

Considering how kajri had its supposed origin and what seminal references it grew with, it would not be improper to assert that village is the essential protagonist in a typical kajri handed down to us through generations of poets and singers. This village does not exist in isolation; it is lively as it enjoys and suffers, and has a whole lot of references associated with it. It represents various facets of romantic love, socio-political concerns, historical situations, cultural manifestations, linguistic registers, mystical apprehensions, and patriotic expressions.

The female persona in the romantic kajri is composed of delicate material that makes the lover pine for her. She often wears a bright costume and nature envies her youth and beauty. This is the stock character of a romantic folklore. Both in image-making and phrase-formation, some kajris exhibits strong Persian influence. Written in the couplet form, they represent a gesture on the part of the narrator. It is on this account that the couplets acquire a certain dramatic/melodramatic tone and tenor and that is how they become suitable enough to be sung on the stage. Given below are examples of Mirzapuri kajris characterized by overt Urdu-Persian influence as most of the poets and performers in that region belonged to the Muslim community, spoke Urdu and represented that culture in its localized form. Two examples are quoted below to confirm these readings. In the third example, a different image may be seen where the beloved pines for the lover who is away; her tattered thatched roof leaks, the night is dark and, she is too scared to step out of the house. All these examples, taken together, represent romance, gesture, pathos, and the courage to live life.

Wo nazneen jab libas badley
sitaron ke dil jigar phatengey
Jo chashm-e khooni lagaley surma
Hazaron ke sar yahan phatenge. (19)
(When that dainty love shall change her dress
The heart and soul of the stars shall tear
When those killing eyes shall put in *surma*
Many injuries the heads shall bear.)
Aaj terey majnoo ki tasweer sarasar roti hati hai
Bigad gayi taqdeer meri tadbeer sarasar roti hai. (20)
(Your lover's portrait cries unstopped today
I have a bad fate; all my methods fail today.)

Mori tutahi madaiyya chuwai bun mori sajni
Mohi chhad balamua de gailein dukh dun mori sajni.
Chadhat Asadh gagan ghan chhaye boond birah ki bares ho
Sawan jhoole sakhi hindola birhan baithhi tarsey ho
Bhadon andhyari dar se ho, kadam na nikle ghar se ho
Pi pi papeeha boley uthai junoon mori sajni. (20)
(My thatched roof leaks; repair it my friend
My love has left me alone; I am in pain my friend
Asadh is there, the sky is full of clouds, drops of separation fall
My friends swing in sawan; I pine for love alone
I am scared of the dark Bhadon; I can't step out of home
I hear papeeha's pi pi; I grow wild.)

Several examples may be quoted to show the variety of moods in romantic love that pertain to hope, then despair, and ultimately a sudden recuperation to face the odds. The female protagonists in all these conditions of being hail from different points of times. The poets also recall the images of Gaura, Shaivya, and Ahalya; Draupadi, Urvashi, and Uttara, apart from those of Sita and Radha, who are the stock characters of the ideal woman and ideal beloved respectively. While thinking of Radha, the poet is naturally drawn towards Krishna and their playfulness. Both become one as if in a moment of magic realism. As opposed to them are the women who belong to modern times and wish to be treated differently. These divergent images may be seen in the following lines:

Urvashi sun re Dhananjaya kaha bigad ke batiya ho
Sawatia such ke dahey jiyara.
Aayi saja ke saj sab nakhra dikhaney ko yahan
Lagi na aiko chal tohri maan ja m era kaha. (22)
(Listen Urvashi, said Dhananjaya in anger
Your heart burns in jealousy against the other woman;
You have come here so embellished to have your way
Nothing would work; you should better understand what I say.)

Sajjano aaj Ahalya nari ki lachari suniye
Indra ki atyachari suniye (23)
(Gentlemen! Hear today how helpless was Ahalya
Listen! how cruel Indra was to her)

Aadhe Radhika aadhe Nand ke lal ba re balmu
Ek roop mein dono roop bisal ba re balmu (tek)
Aadhe sir per mukut biraje aadhe mein beni chamkey
Aadhe math mein chandan sohe aadhe mein bendi damkey
Ek aankh mein dor gulabi ek aankh mein mohini damkey
Ek kan mein kundal ek mein bari aur jhumka jhamkey
Ek sanwaro ek hain gore gaal ba re balmu (udan). (25)
(Half Radhika half Nand, shine bright in one image
In one image are two united, the image looks splendid

On half the head sits a crown, on half is a plait of hairs
On half the crown dazzles *chandan*, on half the *bindiya*
In one eye a line of pink, in another a rare enchantment
In one earlobe hangs a *kundal*, in another dangles a *jhumka*
One is brown, another a fair-cheek, my love.)

Hamein cycle pe chadhhna sikhai da piya
Mirjapur ghumai da piya na. (24)

(Love! Teach me how to ride a bicycle
Take me around and show me Mirjapur.)

Maheen kapda badan ke ooper pehnai khatir karai jatan
Darjan darjan sabun mangwai lagwai ghas ghas ke badan
Powder, alta, othh ka lali, ingur kajar karai rachan
Latka ke choti peeth ke ooper khol ke sar ghumai banthhan. (24)
(She makes efforts to put on a thin material on her body
She gets dozens of soaps; she rubs them on her body
She applies powder, nail polish, lipstick, kohl
She dangles a *choti* at her back, walks bare-head as a painted doll.)

Along with references to Hindu mythology and religious personages, kajri has enough space for Islamic thought and mysticism. The poets have referred to man's spiritual yearning and desire to know the eternal truth. As stated earlier, kajri is a purely secular form of folk tradition and both the Hindu and Muslim poets have executed their own mythical and religious references to construct their individual apprehension of the impending reality. References to *burraq*, *karbala*, *advait*, *shariat*, *tariqat*, *marifat*, *haqeeqat*, *lahoot*, *fana*, *baqa* recur in the poets with Islamic backgrounds. These references, however, do not limit the appeal of their creations as all of them can be most appropriately sung with tonal variations or performed on the stage with gestures and lively action. Some examples would bear this out:

Baba duwariya dhum machal hoor-o ghilman karti mujra
Panhuchi barat meraj ki raat dayi jhimjhimat gherey badra. (28)

(Baba! there is festivity in the yards as the sylphs dance,
The *barat* has arrived on the night of Meraj,
The clouds have gathered all around.)

Din juma mubarak masjid mein azaan pukari jaati hai
Karbala mein Bibi Zohra ki looti phulwari jati hai (28)
(It's a holy Friday; the call to prayer comes from the mosque
Ah!, In Kerbala, Bibi Zohra's garden is being ravaged.)

Tod chuke zunnar Brahman taj baithhe butkhanon ko
Bana liya zahid ne masjid ab merey maikhane ko. (29)
(The Brahmin has broken his thread; he has deserted the temple
The *zahid* too has turned the tavern into a mosque.)

Mai pee kar Mansur anal-haq kehta thha bazaron mein
Sarmad ne sarkatwaya mashhoor thha jo maikhwaron mein. (29)
(Mansoor drank his cup and said in the marketplace: I am God
Sarmad got himself beheaded; his name spread
Among those who drank from this cup.)

Hai paish-e nazar tasweer-e sanam guftar hai apne aape se
Ajpa jap hota hai apna apne aap ke japey se. (29)
(I have my beloved's face before me; I speak to my own self
The best worship is the worship when you worship your own self.)

Saaf nazar aati hai amaan ab khuda ki qudrat shishey mein
Chashm-e haqeeqat se dekha hai yaar ki surat sheeshey mein. (30)
(I can clearly see God's magic in the glass
I have the eyes that see reality
And I have seen my beloved's face in the glass.)

Baqa fana se kaam nahin kucch gharz na marne jeeney se
Mit gaya khud bekhudi mein ek jam wasl ka peeney se. (31)
(I have nothing to do with eternity or with annihilation
There is nothing for me in life or in death
My self got merged with selflessness
After I drank a cup of union.)

Maraz ishq ki dawa dair aftar se nikley Allahu
Lahoot ki mnazil tai ho dil-e afkar se nikley Allahu
Noor se nikle allahu aur nar se nikle Allahu. (30)
(Love's patient needs to wait; he would himself utter Allahu
When the stage of *lahoot* is crossed the heart will cry Allahu
Heavens would utter Allahu; hell would echo Allahu.

These verses deny the impression that the kajri poets depended on sheer inspiration and on merely developing the art of spontaneous utterance. In fact, these poets were quite informed and chose their references with considerable critical sense and discrimination. Their renditions remind the common readers and listeners of Tulsi, Sur, Jaisi and Kabir. They may, in this respect, be considered to be the descendants of these poets. The thesis proposed earlier that the kajri poets were no less intellectually aware gains further ground here. These poets did not assume an intellectual stance as they were much too rooted in the folk tradition of composing and sharing rather than the elitist literary tradition of constructing a self-conscious text and getting it canonized. There are various other manifestations of deep religious and philosophical apprehensions on the part of the poets hailing from both the traditions of Hinduism and Islam, including their mutual acceptance and secular understanding for each other.

Many of the kajri poets have been truly concerned with constructing their nation, a concern that has occupied the postcolonial writers in the recent past. These poets have been concerned with events in history and their impact on the making of the new India. They are aware of the contemporary relevance of new developments and the sacrifices of Gandhi for creating a political democracy. They also reflect upon the partition of the country, the suffering of the people in the wake of this event, and importance of vote banks for narrow personal ends. Some examples are quoted here:

Jhula pada ahimsa ka, Bharat ke lalanwa jhool gaye
Liye hatheli paranwa jhool gaye, kata kata gardanwa jhool gaye (37)

(The swing of *ahimsa* is swinging
The sons of soil have swung in them—
They all have sacrificed their lives.)

Naye chhe paise mein purana ek aana ba
Badla bhai jamana ba na. (38)
(There is an old *anna* in the new six *paise*
See how the times have changed, my dear.)

Hey Bhagwan kawan gati hoiheinyenhan ghuskhoran ke
Chalbaj au chorwan ke na. (39)
(O God! What will happen to these bribe seekers;
These deceitful ones, these thieves)

Garib janta se vote lekey ban ge aflatoon suna
Kahen pahunchtai assembly banwaub kanoon suna. (39)
(I hear he would thrive on the poor man's vote
He says he would reach the assembly and have the laws made).

It would not be improper to assert that kajri as a folk form has transcended the limits of time and space; it has moved beyond the confines of the village and brought in the outside world to bear upon it and *vice versa*. It has drawn upon a world of broad references, images, symbols, and archetypes. It has created its own lexicon and absorbed the contemporary diction of the village and the town. Kajri has long been a cultural icon of the village and the two have kept the people together in a common bondage. They have helped them tell a tale, and taught them to be keen and sensitive listeners. Kajri and the village together provide a mode of acculturation, and a way of holding hands.

A Case for Kajri

Folk literatures deserve serious critical attention. There is a postcolonial need to remember one's history and identify one's cultural heritage. These literatures help us do that precisely. The sprawling industrial city has pushed the village out of sight. The city stands next door as a dark, impending reality claiming all that the village stood for once. The village is now re-writing itself, it is revisiting its myths, and acquiring new references. Its ethnicity and iconography have all undergone drastic changes. With all these happening and with such speed, the folk tradition is in a state of neglect and would, subsequently, stay only as a point of reference while talking of our rich cultural heritage.

Kajri is a far cry from the complicated, artful, urban text. That artful text would sound hollow and remain isolated if severed from the roots. Far from being a song of the sawan, kajri may be read as a culture text, a performance text, an artistic text, a text of history, society and politics. In brief, it may be approached as a meta-text that reflects our primeval associations. It may broadly strengthen other texts that fail to seek their sustenance from the soil and have been looking for readers who elude them again and again. While other texts, including the elitist ones, may elude the reader for a number of reasons, kajri can only help connect and justifiably seek its space in our collective psyche.

In spite of all its virility, kajri has lived in hand-written manuscripts and human memory. Both are subject to decay and may be effaced in due course of time. Even those texts that have been recorded and preserved suffer the indifference of general readers, and certainly of those who have remained isolated from the essential sources of human sustenance.

It would be wholly erroneous to say that an art form like kajri is a weak literary form, devoid of literary merit, or that it refers to a certain community of less educated beings. In fact, there are a number of compositions that call for informed interventions. It may be easily marked that those written in classical and semi-classical styles, as also those composed for the popular taste have their individual merits and affirm the poets' ability to command the form. Their artistic vitality may only be verified by referring to the tools that the kajri poets employ to make their compositions meaningful, both for the popular and the informed literary reader. A critical reading of 'kakahra', which in Hindi poetry is known as 'Akhrawati' and had been employed by poets like Kabir, would show how keenly conscious the kajri poets were of their tools and techniques. It would also establish how sensitive they have been to sound, as much of their appeal depends on the modulation of music and tones of voices. Similarly, many of their alliterations are not conceived on the repetition of certain sounds alone but on the arrangements of alphabets in order of their appearance, and with emphasis on a certain sound at the beginning of each line. Some poets have also composed kajris of mixed lexicons and created a unique linguistic and auditory impact upon the listener.

We may relate to kajri rather naturally. We may approach it as a literary text, a song, as also as a potential reference to our heritage, our fauna and flora. The variety of themes as reflected in the titles[6] of some of the kajris and the rhythm that they create could be the two simple reasons for us to approach them. Once we do that, it would open up a world of strange mysteries and rare delights, a condition many literary texts aspire to achieve. There are a thousand merits but lesser number of seekers. The following couplet tells it in no uncertain terms:

> *Kabiyon ke kavita sey kahoon hoteen hain kalaein ek hazar*
> *Khabar karo hain kalp vriksha ki sakhaaein ek hazar (tek). (88)*
> (Let me tell the poets' creations
> There are a thousand arts in them
> As there are thousand branches
> In the *Kalp* tree.)

The strange world of kajri awaits exploration. That is surely why Ustad Bismillah Khan said, "I will play kajri whether you like it or not".

Notes

1. The event was organized by Jammu and Kashmir Academy of Arts, Culture and Languages in collaboration with University of Jammu and Spic MACAY, Jammu Chapter at Abhinav Theatre, Jammu on September 8, 2005.
2. See http://www.abhiwyakti_hindi.org/parva/alekh/kajri.htm
3. Chaudhari Badri Narayan Premghan had considerable space for kajris in his poetry. He also published an anthology called *Kajli Kadambini.* The Kajri by Premghan, quoted in the text, is included in *Lok Kavya Vidha: Kajri* ed. Abdul Bismillah, Delhi: Anang Prakashan, 2000. Extracts of other kajris quoted in the text with page numbers are all taken from this anthology.
4. The anthology of kajris edited by Abdul Bismillah contains sixty-two compositions on a variety of themes and experiences. They were mostly written for dramatic presentations in *dangals* where people gathered to enjoy themselves and encourage the performers. The scenario presented a great sense of excitement and festivity. Some of them draw heavily upon Persian-Urdu vocabulary and relate to religious and philosophical themes. This reader-friendly volume also contains an introduction and annotations to words and concepts that many of the readers may need to know. Extracts of kajris quoted in the text have been taken from this book.
5. All translations of the extracts quoted are by the author of this paper.
6. Some of the kajris included in *Lok Kavya Vidha: Kajri* has titles like: 'It Ut Nain Niharey Pant,' 'Ichhuk Prasang Pee Mai Anang,' 'Kalpat Birah Biyogin,' 'Adhey Radhika Adhey Nand Ke Laal,' 'Aainey Mein Hai Aaina Saaz,' 'Pauwwan Pauwwan Hari ke Gauwwan,' 'Brahm Roop Brahmand Alakh,' 'Neek Nipun Nutan Nartat,' 'Hud Hud Har Har Shor Machawey,' 'Bhaiwa Milal Faisani Humkey Ek Mehraroo Ba'. The first line of each kajri has been used as its title for the convenience of identification as kajris do not have titles like other poetic compositions.

3

Village as Protagonist in the Socio-Political System

RENUKA PAMECHA

Hey apna Hindustan kahan?
Woh basa hamare gaon mein.

* * *

Tu khud ko badal, tab hi to zamana badlega.

The centrality of the village cannot be disputed. It is the protagonist both of our successes and of our failures as a nation. It is space inhabited by contradictions. Today, we look towards it in hope as the source of change, a place which can help the nation recover its vitality, from where a new India will come into being. And, at the same time, it is a place which holds us back, calling a halt to development. Over the last eight decades or more, the Indian village has travelled a long distance. It has changed, and yet in a mysterious way, it still remains the same.

Mahatma Gandhi had a dream for villages and he imagined a totally self-reliant village with a people-dependent system, minimal intervention of the government, social audit and participation of the common masses in every activity. Based on these core issues many facts have been incorporated in the

Indian Constitution. Panchayati Raj came into effect and community development schemes have been launched. To further strengthen these the 73rd Constitutional Amendment was made. It would not be an exaggeration to say that even today 75 per cent of the population resides in villages. Villages cannot be thrown into oblivion. And to keep them in focus and to talk of them is essential for politicians and political parties. Voters living in villages stay there and yet they affect politics right from the villages up to the centre. The slogan *Garibi Hatao* (eradicate poverty) has affected the entire political system. The excesses of the family planning campaign during the emergency affected rural voters so much that the political balance in the entire country turned topsy-turvy.

Globalization and liberalization have demolished the boundaries between the city and the village. Now, even in the village markets, consumerism and materialism have become important. On the basis of the census categorizations, villages would have to be called villages, but on the surface level at least they are fast becoming the reflections of cities. The search for employment has pushed the villagers towards the cities, which are getting overcrowded. They do not necessarily accommodate the villager. Instead, they reflect on an entirely different set of values. Even today, the socio-cultural landscape of villages is different. They have a composite culture that has been spoilt by the spread of the blight of casteism. Communal harmony has changed into communalism. At one time every Hindu considered it auspicious to go across under the *Tazia* during the Moharram procession. But, today, it has become the nucleus of hatred.

In villages casteism and caste panchayats have now gained more strength. The desire to get the advantages of reservation and to reap political benefits on caste basis has further strengthened casteism. Vote bank politics has split the village. When politicians talk in terms of Hindu vote and Muslim vote, the village population also gets divided along religious lines. This hatred comes to the fore during elections, especially, those of the panchayats. The profession of politicians does not prevent them from spreading hatred whole-heartedly if doing so can fetch them votes. Today, in the villages of Rajasthan, communalism has sunk roots to such depths that it is difficult to get rid of it. Bhilwara in Rajasthan like Gujarat has also become a laboratory of communal hatred.

The Constitution of India is a modern one in spirit. It negates caste and communalism. But the socio-political reality reflects an all together different picture. Caste, which was downplayed at the time of independence, with secular values and the spirit of freedom gaining an upper hand has resurfaced as a source of vote banks with a vengeance. Today's caste struggle is different in its nature from the position Ambedkar adopted. It has transferred itself into a political strategy that governs vote politics and sidesteps other important issues. Casteism has become more strongly entrenched in the national consciousness than ever before.

Today, whatever happens in villages has an affect on national level politics. Three important things that become clear are:

1. The changing political system has changed casteism and caste system in India.
2. Due to this, political dynamism and political activity and understanding have been affected.
3. Caste system is, on the one hand, taking the modern political system forward, and on the other pushing it backwards. It sometimes appears like a boon and at other times, a curse.

On analysis of these three factors it becomes clear that the political system has affected the structure of casteism in villages. It has increased political dynamism and activity and castes have become organized. On the other hand, in order to attain power, bonding within castes has become weak. To gain votes a Brahmin would readily ally with the Dalits. This change in the villages is often for political benefits, it is more of a show and the discrimination within castes still remains the same. In politics there is a lot of difference between practice and precept. Secondly, caste plays an important role. In villages caste panchayats are very powerful. All groupism centres in and around caste. This percolates down from the state to the village level. In Rajasthan, the conflict between the Jats and the Rajputs affects politics in more ways than one can imagine. In the villages of Rajasthan there is a conflict even amongst the upper castes. As is evident during elections, particularly on the issue of reservation, it is a means to gain political power. With their ability to influence social issues, caste panchayats have gained influence. In Shahadpur village in Rajasthan, Neelam Gujar, who was in love with a Dalit youth, was murdered by her family in the name of family honour. Top-level leaders and caste leaders gathered in a grand meeting of the Gujar Mahasabha to get the case of murder dismissed. Likewise, Bhanwari, who was gang-raped, was ex-communicated by the Kumawat caste when she demanded justice. And, the Gujars took out a huge procession in support of the rapists. This Mahapanchayat had the support of several MPs and MLAs. Similarly, in 1987, when Roop Kanwar was burnt alive, the Rajputs formed a "Dharam Raksha Samiti", took out a large procession and hurled invectives at progressive forces demanding a stringent Sati Law enforcement. They even attempted to prevent the criminals from being punished.

Thirdly, in functioning as a pressure group, caste has increased political awareness and has also organized people. From this point of view it is a blessing. While, on the one hand, the participation of people in Panchayati Raj has increased, on the other hand, there is also an increase of groupism in the villages. Increasingly, one can see, that the villagers are losing their initiative. The sense of a community is on the decline. With caste divisions having become so sharp, solidarity is now a thing of the past. The strong Hindu-Muslim unity of villages has been replaced by hatred. During elections all the major parties lobby candidates of the same caste so as to divide votes.

They raise slogans like "Jat's vote for a Jat, Jat's daughter for a Jat".

Jats wield such awe and power that they organized and got reservations in 1999. The structure of caste appears different in every village and every election. In every election caste panchayats actually hold meetings to decide who to vote for. It has even greater affect on Panchayati Raj elections. These decisions can even change overnight. The village head, who connects the village folks to top-level politics and senior leaders, is an important link for both. The leaders of tribal societies are also very important as they have an overwhelming influence on what their people do.

In villages the decision whether or not to support someone is a group activity. In these caste panchayats women do not have any participation but when pressure has to be created on women-related issues they may even be sent for demonstrations. In villages, individual identity still centres around caste. That is why, when Bhanwari was ex-communicated, she had to make lots of effort to be included again. It is not good for a democracy that politics should promote casteism. But, the scene is not so dismal, village communities cut across these barriers and organize themselves around social issues.

In Rajasthan, water, forest and land revolutions have brought tribal people together. People's movements can still draw the village people right into the centre. The Right to Information movement of the Mazdur Kisan Shakti Sangthan, public hearings and minimum wages are revolutions that have greatly affected rural politics. There is a new ray of hope in democracy. Village people have now begun to understand the meaning of democracy, transparency and accountability. People have started asking for information, "Our money, our account(ing)", (*Hamara paisa, hamara hisab*) is their slogan. Panchayats now have to show their entire account to the masses. The Kuchalpura Panchayat in Rajsamand has given an account of each and every paisa spent over five years. The inclination towards social audit is increasing. It ensures public accountability.

Rural youth is taking out peace processions against communalism. “We want work, not *trishuls* (tridents)”, “work and full value for it” – is the slogan being raised by the rural society to get the employment guarantee law enacted. Most of the schemes of the centre and the state are pro-rural. Although it is a different matter that the villagers are not getting all the benefits of these schemes. There is a lot of corruption and non-accountability of money. That is why, everywhere, a need is being felt to strengthen the right to information.

But, one wonders whether this awakening is really widespread. There are a whole lot of problems which rural communities face, and through them surface in the larger social world. Educational and employment levels still remain low; large-scale migration to urban areas does not necessarily relieve the situation. This is so because the feudalistic mindset still persists, specially where gender is concerned. Again, looking up to the government as *mai-baap* is also a hangover of the colonial past. This makes them sit and wait passively for the government schemes rather than rely on self-effort.

The rural poor, divided on caste basis, fall easy prey to the designs of political parties which use them for their benefits by giving them petty allowances. Due to this, democracy has not been able to thrive at the base. Whenever there is threat to the top leadership, power becomes even more centralized. A leadership-dominated democratic system, thus, caters more to its own power and benefit than to the welfare of the community. As a fallout of this, the power of villages has been divided and the villages of olden days no longer exist.

To sum up, the reality of the village as it exists today is as follows:

1. Cooperative movement and the feeling of cooperation has become weak.
2. The initiative of the society has also declined.
3. Traditional caste panchayat has acquired a new role.

4. Groupism in villages has become politicized.
5. State and Zilla level politics has reached villages.
6. The status of castes having more population has increased.
7. Relations between opposing groups and castes are formed for short-term power-centred political goals.
8. Political leaders have become ruralized.
9. Materialism has increased.
10. Right to information has created an awareness of the increasing power of the masses, thus generating a counter-force.

There is no disputing the fact that the centrality of the village, both as a source for political change as well as a yardstick of social progress, is of importance to society as a whole. Marginalization of the rural populations would be a shortsighted, myopic way of addressing the issues of socio-political progress. Even today, the country is known by its villages. But, the concentration of wealth and power on caste basis is something that needs to be guarded against, and alternative means of decentralized power worked for.

Translated by Preranna Bishnoi

4

Interplay of Rural Social Change, Urban Middle Class and Filmic Depiction

Recovery of the Village in Popular Hindi Cinema

KUMOOL ABBI

This paper attempts to understand an emerging trend in the filmic construction of rurality represented by such films as *Raja Hindustani* (1996), *Virasat* (1997), *Lagaan* (2001), *Gadar* (2001), *Veer Zaara* (2004) and *Swades* (2004), where either a young man staying put in the village, or an urbanized villager returning to the village after a prolonged urban residence, finds the village a congenial setting to wage a struggle to achieve certain personal or social or community-centric values. The appeal of such films for the producers or investors to risk their capital, for the stars to stake their reputation or popularity and the public to spend their time and money to see the film again and again, specially when such appeal occurs after a long interval of neglect of the rural is an interesting issue which this paper seeks to explore. While doing so, the paper looks at the changing contemporary significance of the village and the city as part of the liberalized globalized world. Here one comes across a paradoxical situation. While the failure of the village to provide for the family subsistence needs of most of the small cultivators and to generate an adequate employment, pushes the village towards the city, there is a corresponding rise in the symbolic significance of the village for certain sections of the middle class, particularly who are long term, or second generation migrants to the city or to foreign lands and have experienced upward social economic or professional mobility. How the village is imaginatively created in filmic or artistic production and what purpose it serves for whom is part of the exploratory understanding this paper seeks to achieve.

The paper is divided into four parts. The first part deals with the changing conceptualizations of the village by the administrators, historians, social science scholars and others till the 1950s, the second looks at the village as informing Indian common sense and looks at films and other aesthetic creations, the third examines the sociological and other empirical studies of the village from 1960s onwards to the present and the fourth provides an analysis of *Lagaan* as an important film representing the recovery of the village in popular Hindi cinema in the late nineties.

The Village: Changing Historical and Sociological Viewpoints

India being a predominantly village society, the village has always had a special place in it. The village "was not merely a place where people lived; it had a design in which were reflected the basic values of Indian civilisation" (c.f. Beteille 1998: 108). It was essentially during the "British rule that concrete steps were taken to describe and classify the village community. This was necessitated by the administrative and revenue needs, as also the desire to understand the socio-economic conditions of the people who were being governed. Census reports as early as 1880s along with gazetteers, district handbooks and village surveys brought together varied information on the village community" (Madan 4). Sir Charles Metcalf's famous statement of 1810, which described India as a land of mini-republics of immutable villages became a broadly shared colonial view. The two-level conceptualization of India as a land of changing ruling outsiders and unchanging village republic carried an implied justification of the British rule as no more alien as than that of traditional Indian rulers. However, for most Indian nationalists despite their different "ideological orientations" and political agendas, the village remained an "important given of Indian reality" and the core category to conceptualize India (Jodhka 3343). Moreover, for them, unlike the colonial administrators, the 'village' represented the 'real' India, the nation that needed to be recovered, liberated and transformed.

In Indian scholarly studies, particularly those of sociologists and social anthropologists, the above overly static view of the Indian village came to be increasingly questioned. They began to find more sociologically plausible the views of American anthropologists A.L. Kroeber and Robert Redfield, characterizing peasants as part cultures and part societies, the other part being made up by trade and social cultural exchanges with the towns. "Mckim Marriot, writing on the aspects of village life in the 1950s spoke of how the ties that related the village to the outside world also brought wider society to the villages. He called these "the processes of universalisation when elements of the village culture are being incorporated into a wider regional or even larger society and parochialisation [when cultural elements of a pan-Indian nature filtering down to the village level through various modes of communication such as storytelling and folk drama" (Marriot 1955), (qtd by Madan 9).

Many village studies were carried out from 1950 to 1970 or there about which greatly contributed to the in-depth understanding of the internal structure and functioning of the village, the manner in which it relates to the neighbouring villages, the region and the world beyond. The studies, while exposing the limitations of the village studies as a framework for the understanding of society and polity in India, they did help contest many dominant stereotypes of both local and foreign provenance. In addition to generating great deal of authentic information and concepts relating to Indian socio-cultural dynamics such as sanskritization, dominant caste substantialization of caste, etc.

These studies clearly show that the dynamic relationship of the village and the city, their mutual interlinkages, conflict as well as co-operation and the manner in which they have shaped each other's constitution and development. Although the major emphasis of the studies was on the functional integration and interdependence, they also brought about areas of disruption, fissures and flashpoints in these relationships. These studies and those of historians, economists and others left little doubt that earlier emphasis on the unchanging nature of Indian village, or for that matter Indian caste, culture or tradition was more of an ideological construction than a historical fact.

Village in the Indian Common Sense, Films and Other Artistic Creations Leading to *Lagaan*

Notwithstanding the above scholarly evidence the myth of the lack of change, together with the view that real India lived in the villages came to be an accepted part of common sense understanding about India – both Indian and foreign, to which not only Gandhian and nationalist politicians but also British administrators and Indian intelligentsia, journalists writers and others shaping public opinion broadly subscribed. The fact that India has continued to remain preponderantly rural even till now, has lent this construction certain plausibility. The most important ways in which this common sense construction informs Indian writings, literary fiction, filming and other aesthetic creations is in terms of a posited contrast between the village and the city by which the village characters are shown to be close to nature, simple, tradition centred and lacking in sophistication as compared to clever corrupt, sophisticated and exploitative townsmen. The contrast, according to Dwyer and Patel (63-64) "depicted in the films, is not between 'the real India' of villages as Gandhi called it and the problems of increasingly overburdened Indian cities, but it is more to do with a contrast between the pre-modern or timeless village and the city as an icon of modernity". However, the aspects of the contrast selected for emphasis varied with the theme of the story and the nuances focused upon.

Raj Kapoor, for instance, presented village women "as representative of pure unsullied India and highlighted their innocence and purity. On the other hand he showed the city as a place of corruption, glamour and sophistication and lacking in warmth" (Dwyer and Patel 62-63). Mehboob Khan's film *Mother India*, however makes little mention of the city "The film presents a romantic version of the village in the early days with farm workers singing and romancing in the fields in Soviet type images before showing the problems that beset the villages such as money lending, humans labouring as beasts of burden illiteracy and natural disaster. Nehruvian modernity is promoted as the solution to the village problem, symbolized by the opening and closing images of the configuration of the dam...". There were also some more realist attempts in the 50s such as B.R. Chopra's *Naya Daur* in which the villain brings modern technology to the village already beset by modern problems of caste and religion (Dwyer and Patel 64), and *Do Bigha Zameen* which presented "a double vision showing the village through the perspective of city people and the city through the eyes of village protagonists" (Chakravarty 95).

The theme of simplicity, honesty and relatively incorruptibility of the villagers continues to be depicted but the village and the city are seen more in regular interaction and the virtuous qualities of the villagers are more often shown to emerge in that context, further, the village is now deemed to need reform or development and freedom from exploitation, and so, a number of films articulate the nature of the need and the manner in which it is taken care of, the cooperative effort conflict or struggle it leads to and the kind of heroes, villains and other supporting characters the struggles throw up.

A few films like *Upkar* (1967), which by working on the slogan 'Jai Jawan, Jai Kisan,' popularized during the 1965 war linked the imagery of the village, town and nation and

Aashirwad (1968) articulate this theme, though a gradual drift takes place from the visible markers of Nehruvian models of development leading to a sense of cynicism and disillusionment with the nascent Indian state. At times the hero, a village product himself, or a doctor or engineer seeking redemption in the village, takes upon himself the task to reiterate a commitment to the goals set out after Independence and attempts to retrieve idealist values, *Anuradha* (1960), *Satyakam* (1968) and *Tere Mere Sapne* (1970) articulate this existential crisis and its ultimate resolution. The question of freedom from exploitation being more complex and being closely related to some other themes will be discussed presently in that context.

The landscape and the village people of Kashmir or some other scenic hills are often co-opted to represent the contrast between the urban world of the Indian hero and the purity of the innocent Kashmiris, particularly women, as shown in such films as *Junglee* (1961), *Kashmir ki Kali* (1963) and *Jab Jab Phool Khile* (1965), though here an innocent Kashmiri boy falls in love with the city bred girl.

The exploitation of innocent villagers by unscrupulous zamindars, greedy moneylenders, and dishonest officials conniving with the exploiters is a significant theme articulated in many films of the 60s, 70s and 80s with numerous variations, e.g., *Jis Desh Mein Ganga Behti Hai* (1960) and *Mujhe Jeene Do* (1963) take up this theme. Here the dacoits including the hero are mostly innocent villagers who had become outlaws to protest and avenge the indignities and injustices meted out to them. The films portray them sympathetically as Robin Hood – like characters and suggest, as a solution to the dacoit problem, the surrender of the dacoits to the state, which would ensure social rehabilitation. Later films dealing with lawlessness and violence get linked up with the so called 'angry young man' trend connected with the emergence of Amitabh Bachan as an avenging lower class hero fighting urban smugglers, black marketeers, corrupt police and other similar government officials. The hero in these films is basically pro-poor and fair minded but does not hesitate to take the law into his own hands to defeat the corrupt, cruel and lawless elements. Films of this kind have been very popular, like *Sholay* (1975), *Adalat* (1976), *Don* (1978) and *Namak Halal* (1983).

A significant aspect of the village-city relationship as depicted very often in films is the villager's need to make a journey to the city for employment, or for a friend or relative to provide shelter or patronage or other connecting link to the city. Here the filmic depiction of male or female journeys to the city shows more contrasts than similarities. The male protagonist after initial setbacks or comic or amusing interlude establishes his dominance in the city through resilience, superior intelligence, honesty, decency, and steadfastness. He is often shown to charm a rich sophisticated, wilful or spoilt girl and transform her into a devoted beloved wife. Sometimes he succumbs to the corrupt ways of the city but generally in the end his basic rural decency surfaces to redeem him. On the other hand, the female journey to the city is shown to be more degrading, she often falls prey to pimps, cheats and other immoral elements and ends up as a prostitute or kept woman and is forced to indulge in illegal or shady activities. Her initial experiences are always degrading even if she, with superhuman perseverance emerges triumphant in the end, the films, *Haryali aur Rasta* (1962), *Bandini* (1963), *Teesri Kasam* (1966), *Mausam* (1975) and *Ram Teri Ganga Maili* (1986) exemplify this.

The Changing Village: Sixties to the Present

During the British period itself, many steps were taken to further integrate the village with the provincial and federal politics and structures of government, the establishment of revenue and police administration, setting up of provincial and federal legislatures, elected municipalities, the village block and district level panchayats – all these and associated development of industrialization and urbanization brought the village economy and society in closer integration with the governmental structures as well as the British established system of local, regional and international trade.

After the country gained independence, the government intervention in various levels as well as sectors of the country's social and economic life including the village increased greatly. New institutional links with both towns and villages multiplied. Space will not permit even a brief discussion of these links and associated interventions. I shall therefore refer briefly to a few of the most relevant steps and events. According to Appadurai, three of the most important diacritics of modern subjectivity are electronic media (cinema, television, computers, telephones, internet, etc), migration and the everyday quotidian mental framework of ordinary people as against that in the expressive face of art, myth etc. (Appadurai 2-27).

These diacritics have now come to characterize not only Indian towns and cities but also Indian villages in varying ways. Further, with the establishment of the World Trade Organization and the related liberalized framework of cross-national movement of commodities, capital communications and, to a limited extent, people also forms the broader context affecting India and its villages. Thus, Indian village agriculture with its characteristic small scale farming and limited mechanization has now to compete with highly subsidized products of advanced European, American Canadian and other similar economies.

Indian agriculture is already feeling the pinch though the full effect of the WTO regime is yet to be felt. The spread of capital intensive agriculture with hybrid seeds, chemical fertilizers, pesticides, etc together with tractors, trolleys, threshers and other mechanized equipment, despite its limited productive potential already created a diminishing trend between employment generation and per hectare yield of output severely restricting the employment potential of agriculture. Further about 80 per cent of small and marginal holdings hardly leave any room for greater employment generation. Thus, village India suffers from unemployment and underemployment pushing able bodied villagers to seek employment elsewhere (Gupta 1-2). The capacity of the peasant farmers to extend patronage to the Scheduled Caste labourer and artisan castes is also similarly diminished. Virtually, all transaction are carried out in cash or in terms of cash calculation of work done and wages paid even if a particular wage may be paid in kind.

Farming as a valued and honourable occupation has lost its sheen (Gupta 15-17). Neither farmers (because of uncertain and inadequate income), nor labour (because of long hours of hard work and poor wages) want it. Every village now has a number of educated unemployed, mostly sons of farmers, who may loaf around the village doing nothing but would not lend a hand at farming even on their own farm. The village as a living space lacking in hygiene, properly paved streets, drainage, medical, educational and shopping facilities, has also come to be devalued. However in most villages there are a small minority who have ample non-farm income to be able to afford a middle class or upper middle class urban life style while enjoying some of the advantages of living in the countryside. They have well furnished *pucca* houses, fitted with air conditioners, televisions, and other modern household gadgets, expensive cars, scooters, motorcycles etc. to take them away to town and cities for business and pleasure (Abbi and Singh 1997; Gupta 2005). Presence of these people while indicating the levels of class and caste differentiation in the village, also gives the village an appearance of being more modernized than it really is.

It is not only the rich who move regularly or frequently between towns and cities and countryside and vice-versa but ordinary people with a variety of socio-economic statuses too do likewise. Presence of the proliferation of small and medium towns and semi-urban qasbas, link arterial and main roads and the availability of public transport and such cheaper private means of transport as bicycles, scooters, motorcycles have made to and fro movement of people between towns and country an ubiquitous fact of life. The village people not only go for occasional work, shopping, socializing and pleasure trips to cinema etc., but more important many of the villagers regularly commute for work as clerks, labourers, shop assistants, rickshaw pullers, drivers, etc., making the village not much different from a suburban location in town.

This has many implications in the social and community life in the village. The internal cohesion of different segments of the village, the overall village solidarity, the cooperation and conflict between caste, religious communities and other social divisions maybe affected by the internal linkages. In particular the lower castes who are not dependent on the village for their livelihood are apt too be more strident in their protest against unequal or discriminatory treatment meted out to them. Many of the tensions between the dominant peasant castes and dalits and other lower castes are traceable to this situation.

This is specially evident in Punjab where in many village dalits are in numerical majority and economically diversified and not much dependent on agricultural labour. The extension of protective discrimination in education, scholarships, jobs, election to legislature have also ameliorated the situation of the dalits and other backward sections of village society, though most of them still suffer from various disabilities and iniquitous treatment meted out to them. The above marginal improvement itself has become a source of social tensions in the village society. With the 73rd Constitutional Amendment Act of 1992, the Government of India established a modified three-tier system of Panchayati Raj Institutions markedly extending power and authority of Panchayati Raj bodies. Some notable features of this extended system are: (a) the reservation of seats in favour of SCs in proportion to their population, (b) reservation of one-third seats for women at all levels, (c) reservation of one office of a panch for backward classes in a Gram Panchayat where their population in the panchayat areas is over 20 per cent of the total population of the area.

These compulsory reservations of Panchayati Raj seats and offices have made dalits, women and backward castes a force in the village society and pose a serious challenge to the dominance exercised by the peasant and other upper caste males. How much power is to be extended to these Panchayati Raj bodies and resources placed at their command are a matter of serious contestation between the village and higher state level bodies. Whatever the final outcome constitutionally and formally, at least the village has undergone a major change with a very considerable potential for democratic reform and related conflicts. The above is only a sketchy account of some of the changes the village has undergone. It clearly shows the gap between the changing reality of the village and these conceptual or commonsense understandings of the village which still see it as a repository of pristine purity of changing Indian values. No less pronounced is the gap between the conceptions of those who themselves or their parents have migrated out of the village and acquired a prosperous upper middle class status while living in the city in India or abroad. The romanticized recreated village of the urban middle classes of rural provenance is evidently both a product of a distorted memory and present search for community and identity in the competitive world of urban existence. In any filmic or other artistic creations an element of inter-textual, i.e., other films, novels, fictive creations is inevitably always there, along with calculations of profit and other practical considerations and a film represents a compromise or balance arrived at among them. I have however attempted to intellectually supplement these considerations by trying to understand the construction of rurality in *Lagaan* and other films in the context of lived realities of middle classes in cities and of their co-related work of imagination.

Construction of 'Rurality' in *Lagaan* and the Urban Middle Class

The impact of the film *Lagaan* has been tremendous in the academic circles having generated a great deal of response and debate. Majumdar in the his article: (a) makes a commemoration of the film as a commentary on the evolution of cricket in colonial India, (b) views the mastery of the game by the natives as a tool for subverting colonial rule, (c) sees the images of Champaran as an invocation of a Gandhian critique particularly in the context of the role of the farmer: "The aspirations of the village of Champaran to enjoy their own agricultural produce, the history of rural goodness over imperial craftiness can be seen as an evocation of a Gandhian Critique", (d) limits *Lagaan* as a film representing the politics of leisure in colonial India. He finally appropriates *Lagaan* as an invocation of a lost history (2001:3399).

For Mannathukkaren, *Lagaan* is a film, which "ostensibly has the subaltern the protagonist, ultimately ending up reaffirming the hegemonic nationalist project in which the subaltern has no place". He discusses the "strategy which still re-inscribes the nation is by positing the 'other' as an outsider...in this case, the other becomes defined as belonging to outside the 'nation' – the white colonizer. This happens through the effacement of other 'others' within the film". In this manner, "the film's portrayal of subaltern action grossly misinterprets history", since "the subaltern's history is tied to the destiny of the 'nation', the question of caste, class and gender oppression has to wait till such time that the 'nation' is strong and able to stand on it's feet" (4581).

Chakravorty, while critiquing Majumdar and Mannathukkaren, attempts to show how *Lagaan* extends the "subaltern studies project in the visual medium in a country which produces the largest number of films in the world...." Using *Lagaan* as a case in point. She argues that "popular Bollywood films with their appeal to the mass audience of uprooted peasants, factory workers, unemployed, uneducated and poor can decolonize the imagination of the Indian masses." She further asserts that "the film reiterates the subaltern studies projects call for "an opening up and restructuring of the received disciplinary boundaries for the study of peasant movements' by writing the dispossessed of the colonial margins into the history of a popular sport". This is accomplished as "*Lagaan* recuperates the subaltern as a conscious agent of history, similar to the attempts of the subaltern studies contributors" (2003:1879-1881). She further highlights that "Bollywood films like *Lagaan*, can go beyond the parameters of the 'educators' to include and engage the masses, 'the people' to actively and critically engage with mass culture in order to re-think forms of received knowledge, discourses and of course, history" (2003:1883).

Anand (1-7) focuses on the 'repressiveness' of *Lagaan* and links it to cricket in India "being a casteist game", he critiques the inclusion of the Dalit Kachra in the team and sees "such a rationalising of a dalit's ability coming as it does in the post-Mandal, post-liberalization phase where the brahmanical/statist mood is pronouncedly anti-affirmative action, is an ontological and epistemological assault on Dalits and disabled people. It makes a mockery of Dalit 'merit'"(6), thus making *Lagaan* a ruse which "claiming to recreate a piece of imagined history, ends up being yet another clever brahmanical tale..." (7). Deshpande sees *Lagaan* as a film, "which actually manages to run counter to the dominant trends of the market...." The hero of the film and all his associates are peasants and other rural folk. They are poor, smelly, sweaty, and they work with their hands...." He discusses the criticism of the Dalit in the film on two points: (a) he is included in the film not for his ability but his disability (b) he is never asked if he wants to be in the team, so his subjectivity is erased. He offers an answer in terms of seeing *Lagaan* as a "tale that constructs a Gandhian utopia" and while accepting the 'erasures', of the film he highlights the unique feature of the film, "in imagining a peasant-dalit-Muslim combine leading India to victory" (243-245).

Doraiswamy focuses on the construction of the "benign community that bridges differences of caste, class and religion and is seen in the Hindi film after a long time as a positive, creative and constructive force. This resurrection of the benign community is all the more significant in the context of the fact that, since the 80s villainy in films has come to be represented, through characters belonging to minority religious, regional or caste grouping". She discusses two important songs 'ghanana ghanana' and 'chalo chalo' to show the community, 'captured as tableaux' reflecting a feeling of 'oneness and bonding' with a deliberate focus on the 'community of bodies' (2003: 218-219).

These studies on *Lagaan* elicited a biting if perhaps a bit harsh comment from Guha (354) about the way scholars of "post-colonial studies.... have been swarming around it like hyenas around a carcass, surfing its shots and dialogues for traces of misogyny and collaboration". Indeed there has been a bit of both theoretical overloading and skewing to extract the maximum ideological mileage. In the process the autonomy of the text has also been disregarded along with a near total neglect of the viewpoints of spectators who made such a large contribution to the success of the film. The director of the film Ashutosh Gowariker has commented that he believes in "combining realism with larger than life situations. The ambience in *Lagaan* is real. But the situation is large than life. That has clicked with the audience" (*Filmfare*, August 2001: 73).

My study was conducted outside the Piccadilly Theatre in Chandigarh in June-July 2001. Approximately 150 respondents were interviewed. The informants were usually gathered through the snowballing technique. Initially it were the usherers, the security people as well as the peddlers who helped me earmark the audience coming out of the theatre. But soon it became easy to organize impromptu sessions. One or two spectators would stop by, arousing the curiosity of some others to join in an impromptu discussion. While discussing, I was able to mark out those who had seen the film more than once. Out of those 60 were identified, to be interviewed in detail at time and place of their convensience.[2]

The people who came out of the lower stalls had little to say, except '*achi hai*', '*pasand aayi*' which contrasted with the enthusiasm witnessed when I conducted a similar preliminary survey of *Gadar* released at approximately the same time. It was largely the middle class: students, teachers, white collar workers, doctors, professional bureaucrats etc. who responded to the film, felt fascinated by it and were interested enough to discuss it at length. This was also pointed out by Harjinder Singh the manager of Jagat Theatre in Chandigarh, "*Lagaan* was the film of the educated, *Gadar* the film for the masses". A point confirmed in the film trade journals which have emphasized that *Lagaan* worked better in the A grade centres (West and South Metros urban centres), while *Gadar* fared better in B/C class cites. Similarly the distributors have seen *Lagaan* as a "*Lambi race ka ghoda* (Long distance runner) with a potential in the overseas market" (*Outlook*, July 9, 2001. 60-62, Anand 2001:4).

An initial trade figure of the two films show/this comparison:

Table 1

First Week Collection of Gadar and Lagaan

Territory	*Gadar*	*Lagaan*
	28 shows	*21 shows*
Bombay-Circuit	Rs. 2.00 cr.	Rs. 1.75 cr.
Delhi UP	Rs. 2.25 cr.	Rs. 1.50 cr.
East Punjabs	Super Hit	Hit
CP Berar (parts of MP and Maharashtra)	Rs. 1.00 cr.	Rs. 30 lakh
CI	Rs. 20 lakh	Rs. 25 lakh
Rajasthan	Rs. 50 lakh	Rs. 30 lakh
Nizam	Rs. 40 lakh	Rs. 50 lakh
US	Rs. 90 lakh	Rs. 1.50 cr.
UK	Rs. 50 lakh	Rs. 1.00 cr.

Source: Outlook, July 9 2001.

This is further confirmed by the following table of members of the audience I interviewed:

Table 2

Occupations of Respondents having Watched the Film more than once

Occupations	*Number of Persons*
Engineers	4
Doctors	7
Teachers	5
Lawyers	6
Computer Professionals	9
Clerks	5
Students	11
Bank Managers	6
Entrepreneurs	7
Total	60

While the above sample may be too small to make any large-scale generalizations, it clearly shows a distinct preference of the middle class for the film.

The film like most other films, addresses different interests and levels of knowledge and comprehension. At one level it combines comedy and suspense and makes a populist appeal ensuring the defeat of the powerful, the strong-willed and sophisticated by the poor, ignorant weak and inept, at another it celebrates community consciousness within which Dalit consciousness, if any, is subsumed, at another it has an anti-colonial national appeal not as sharp-edged and cut-throat one as that associated with the days of freedom struggle but a muted one of the post-colonial globalized world. It has a nostalgic appeal and feeling of lost consciousness of a rural world, which can only be recreated, imaginatively in personal memory or fictively in literary or filmic construction like *Lagaan*.

The audience, as most of the comments highlighted, was impressed by the 'ethnic touch of the film' as Mahesh Kumar, a cardboard manufacturer, elaborated, "*badi ethnic feeling aati hai*", (one gets an ethnic feel by going to see the film), while Rajender Khosla, a computer engineer, felt, "as if the Rajasthan emporium had been raided for the film". Ginni a student of LL.B talked about the 'Gurjari touch'. Maninder, the wife of a mechanical engineer was very impressed by its 'fancy dress'. Similarly Balraj Metha a retired bank manager and his wife remembered that, "the costumes were done by the same woman who had worked for the film *Gandhi*". A majority of the audience was clear that the setting of the film was 'perfect'. They felt that the film tried to show a 'real village'. For Rajeev Arora who deals with the furniture business, "Champaran, was like the village he had visited in Rajasthan (the name he forgot) perhaps Chokhi Dhani near Jaipur, where one could go and enjoy the ambience, with people dressed in village outfits serving food in thalis, offering bajra rotis and white butter. The water was served in kullars, and the evening ended with a camel ride". Raj Purohit, a graduate student felt that going to see *Lagaan* was like "visiting food festivals where cuisine of different regions was served and one enjoyed the ethnic flavour." Urmila, a student of NIIT, was attracted by "Aamir Khan wearing a designer dhoti, perhaps it was a slip around, like a new kind of Bermudas".

Similarly Gurleen, a medical student, noticed "the pencilled eyebrows of Gauri, perhaps they forgot, that *ye to gaon hai* (that this is village)." Similarly for Rishi Kumar, an executive, "I like *Lagaan* because it is ethnic and it is 'in' to be ethnic." Similarly the girls among the audience pointed to the film as 'cho sweet', 'so quaint', '*kuch alag*' (something different), and so typically village type, and "Aamir Khan managing to look sexy despite his dhoti". Or as Rani, another LL.B student commented, "after all how could we forget that Bhuvan was no ordinary villager but Aamir Khan, we had to see the film'. In this context, it may be pertinent to cite Vishwanathan describing Aamir Khan as "a disembodied farmer let loose in a rural imagination. The farmer returns not as a real character but as a fantasy, a historical figure" (*Outlook,*

January 18, 2001: 56-57). Typically another clear and common response was that '*hai kitne simple the woh log*' (how simple were those people).

The above remarks clearly show what has come to be recognized as 'an international tendency among elite groups who live in urban, industrialized environments, to idealize nature and the village" (Tarlo 1996: 34). Tarlo whose work centres on the revival of Haus Khas also sees the "Indian version of 'village dressing' very much a part of the international trend of villigising the city." But at the same time it builds on a more specifically Indian precedent: "It combines the colonial image of the village as timeless and unchanging, with the nationalist idea of the village as a means of re-asserting Indian identity... All these elements together, and combined with the tendency of a global elite to idealize the village-within-the city, have contributed to what Indian journalists call the 'ethnic revival' in food, fashion and décor" (Tarlo 35).

Nandy too sees this trend in terms of how, "the village of the imagination has become a serene, pastoral paradise. It has become the depositary of traditional wisdom and spirituality, and of the harmony of nature, intact community life and environmental sagacity perhaps even a statement of Gandhian austerity, limits to want, and anti-consumerism. The village, too, is no longer a village in itself, it is a counterpoint to the city.... The village symbolizes control over self; the city reeks of self-indulgence and the absence of self-restraint. Beyond the temptations and glitter of the city lies the utopia of an idyllic, integrated, defragmented self, not tyrannized by the demands of atomized individualism. It is the utopia of village as a self, controlling the self-that-is-the-city" (Nandy 13).

This middle class appropriation of *Lagaan,* also in a stroke seemed to individualize colonialism, racial prejudice and cruelty, reflecting more the attitudes of liberalism and contemporary relationship between India and the English. This liberal attitude reflected in terms of the new wave of globalization and the presence of a huge Indian Diaspora. The entire audience was clear that "*Saare angrez marre nahi hote*" (all the British are not bad). They emphasized "it is the individuals who are bad". They would clearly state, the 'umpires' and 'Elizabeth' '*ache the*' (were good). This cooptive aspect was elucidated clearly by Manoj Prakash, an accountant, "*agar un dono ne madad nahi ki hoti to, Bhuvan kaise jeet sakta tha*" (without the help of those two how could Bhuvan win) or as Bahadur Thapa, a manager in a restaurant commented, "Captain Russel was the Amrish Puri of *Lagaan*". Similarly Saurab, a gazetted officer stated, "I just hated captain Russel. So cruel but just look at his sister". This was also elaborated by Phool Chand who has a shop in Sector 22, "Elizabeth must have been an Indian in her previous birth. She was so self-sacrificing". Thus, unlike what has been pointed out in various critiques of *Lagaan* it is not Indian vs. others. It is the individualization of colonialism, which becomes significant. Reiterating Maithali Rao's point that "our response to *Lagaan* holds the key to what films mean to us. Entertainment plus an uplifting moral, making us feel good, about ourselves, our lives and the inevitability of ultimate success if we work hard enough and the gods decide to be kind" (Rao, *Outlook*, August 20, 2001).

The other most important aspect of watching the film was the interesting juxtaposition of the past and the present through the mirroring of Bhuvan's cricket team. Almost all the members of the audience interviewed had drawn parallels with contemporary cricketing heroes. This tendency was also reflected while observing the audience during my five screenings of the film. This tendency they were willing to discuss at length. They would generally comment: "that shot was pacca Sachin yaar", or "that character was Waseem Bhai", or "*Cha gaya* Kapil", "*Oui* Harbhajan, *Oui*, *hamara* Chandrashekar", or even "*aaja aaja* Andy Roberts." They would laugh and contest each other comparing the *Lagaan* XI with their contemporary heroes and trying to find attributes common to them. Even Lakha, the saboteur, was compared to

Azharuddin, "*apne Azhar bhai to kamal ke the*" (Azhar bhai was just too good).

The other important issue of *Lagaan* relates to the politics of leisure in contemporary India. To a large extent the success of *Lagaan* would not have been possible without the knowledge of cricket and its nuances, which is largely due to cricket being a very important part of leisure during these periods. This is related largely to the development and transmission of cricket particularly the direct telecast of both one day and test matches, first on Doordarshan and later lucrative deals through private television channels. Thus making cricket as much a part of the "privatization of leisure activities of middle class India as watching soap appears" (Appadurai 101).

This process of "indigenisation and decolonialisation" (Appadurai 90) has put "Television at the cutting edge of the privatisation of leisure in contemporary India... as public spaces grow more violent, disorderly and uncomfortable, those who can afford television consume their spectacles in the company of their friends and family" (Appadurai 101). Guha too feels that, "with the spread of television and growing of integration of India into the world market, cricket has successfully consummated its marriage with consumer capitalism" (331).

Here I would like to assert that the enjoyment of the film *Lagaan* would be unimaginable without an understanding of the subtleties of the game. Here the audience show not only knowledge but a certain sense of 'superiority' in relation to the characters of the game. They make a clear distinction between cricket played 'then' and cricket played 'now'. They also patronize the 'naiveté' of and 'innocence of the villagers' as they struggle with the game. The intricacies of the game, run outs, appeals, bowling and batting action particularly Goli's appeals, lbw decisions, handling the ball, tampering of the ball, nuances of using the new ball, the tendency of the old ball to spin, retired hurt etc. can only be relished if they are seen with a certain familiarity.

Connected with this is the issue of humour in the film, which the entire audience points out as its most interesting feature. Largely it is essentially through the exaggerated comic, improbable farcical situations that the film depicts and brings into focus certain political and social issues: dependence of Indian farmers on the vagaries of rain, realities of British colonial government, the local Raja's subordinate status in relation to the government's representatives, weakening of community structure due to colonial rule, compulsions of revenue collection etc. However, the audience was very clear, it was the humour of the film which tickled them the most, specially that related to the game of cricket, which they tremendously enjoyed for they knew what 'real' cricket was all about. Compared to that the cricket played by Bhuvan and his friends, "made them laugh their heart out" or as Ram Kanwar a clerk who has watched the film twice, pointed out: "*yaad kar ke bhi hum khoob haste hain*" (we laugh at the very thought of it). For a majority of the audience narrating these sequences from *Lagaan* is like re-enacting the fables that they have absorbed. The enjoyment of the humour in the film as well as the suspense, which the film creates, depends on the audience familiarity with the basics of cricket. The suspense is maintained till the last ball, which is caught feet across the boundary, making all the difference between success and failure.

Our point about the middle class audiences and their leisure activities becoming a significant force influencing commercial cinema's calculation of film production, finds support from Dwyer who writes: "a major component of this new audience for films and film music was formed by the new middle classes who emerged with economic liberalization in the early nineties. They enjoyed different patterns of leisure, consumption and spending power, and were soon targeted by astute film producers, usually quick to seize on indicators of social change. They were among the audiences who returned to the cinema when the VHS rental market was killed in the 1990s by the cable and satellite Asian TV channels and the practice of video holdback. There was also a return to cinema in the west at this time, so other considerations, such as technical advances, modernized cinemas and so on may also have been instrumental in the revitalization of cinema going" (Dwyer 190). Our figures on the box office collections of films like *Swades* and *Veer Zaara* exemplify her contention (see sharukhhkhan.org and Indian-express.com).

The other significant issue raised by most critics relates to the issue of nationalism. Interestingly the responses of the audiences rarely alluded to the nationalist ideology or related struggle in history. The audience reacted strongly to and responded to *Lagaan* in terms of a new kind of patriotism. As a majority of the audience commented, seeing the film was like participating in a 'one day match'. They were all impressed by the 'spirit of *Lagaan*'. As Ranbir a (10+2 science stream) student, like so many others commented, "Bhuvan does not give up till the end and makes India win". Many in the audience felt that the *angrez* was incidental, "the excitement built up was just like watching an Indo-Pak match." They felt glad that this film showed that India too had developed a "killer instinct" and "a never-say-die attitude". Or as Balraj, an entrepreneur commented, "at least they don't live up to their image as good losers. They growl, snarl and abuse". Tarsem K., a BBA student, too endorsed this view by emphasizing that "with nothing the *Lagaan* team won, if our boys work a little hard they would do India proud and win the world cup". Similarly Gurdev Bhalla, a lawyer, too commented that "in *Lagaan* they do not give up, the Indian team should learn something from this, become strong, win the world cup and make us proud". Lastly the majority of the audience was clear, "*Lagaan* should teach a lesson to the Indian team." Rakesh Chib, a BA student commented, "It should be compulsory watching for the Indian team. How they make 'us' suffer when, they go and lose to others."

At this stage, it would be apt to state that "cricket has been at the cutting edge of modernization in the region, and it is in the subcontinent that the one day game – an attempt to squeeze cricket's amorphous pre-industrial sprawl into its designated niche in the modern market place has been most ruthlessly exploited by both the commercial and the nationalist forces" (Marquese 1996:158). The commercial and nationalistic exploitation of the modern form of cricket, 'the one day game' its impact on the culture of the game as well as on the Indian social cultural life generally is commented upon by Ashis Nandy and Ramchandra Guha, two of the most astute academic analysts. While admitting that cricket has been changing globally, Nandy observes, "as it has become a billion dollar enterprise, it has softened as a cultural form. Spectator demands have begun to push it further away from its original cultural role as a typically 19th century game enshrining pre-industrial values in an industrial society and serving as a part of the cost of being mediagenic and business friendly, the game is showing a growing tolerance for its atomized uprooted urban spectators... The dominant model of heroics in cricket today depends more and more on the values of global market and the nation-state-system and is designed to alleviate the routine and tedium of life through a nationalist project dreamed by up paradoxically by transnational capital" (xii-xiii). Further he takes note of "the passions – the free-floating violence and the sectarian venom seeking targets that constitute the under belly of India's public life today" (xviii).

While acknowledging that, "after independence the new nation has come to identify cricketing prowess with patriotic virtue" (341), Guha discusses the plight of the genuine cricket lover who has been "displaced by the overworked overpaid, half-drunk and hyper-nationalist yuppie... He is quick to praise and quicker to blame – a temperament to match the sport, for the limited over game punishes players heavily; no second innings for the batsman, no second spell for the bowler. One honest mistake can swing the game leading to abuse, innuendo and violence" (405). In a graphic description, Guha quotes, "the cell-phone-toting yuppie, the sunscreen-lotion-smeared Raybanned girls, the pan masala chewing rotund businessman as typical examples of the audience in cricket" (413-414).

Lagaan thus constructs for the Indian middle class an Arcadian village of their imagination where they are able to give expression to their passion for and expertise of cricket in an important three-day match (modelled on the present one day match), against their former colonial masters. And unlike what more often happens in real life games they are able to show the grit to fulfil their wish to win the contest. Moreover, the game of cricket in *Lagaan* satisfies the need of the middle class for an ideal hero in the person of Bhuvan, the captain of the village team who riding the crest of success "... seems more super-human than most of the other sportsmen. He takes on and defeats fate itself" (Nandy xiii).

Notes

1. The periodization through this paper is only approximate, for rather difficult problems of reconciling time periods in different areas of national and social life are involved. For instance, the rural community is continued to be represented with little significant change in diminishing number of films till the early 1990s.
2. I would like to thank the manager and usherers of Piccadilly Cinema, Chandigarh for their numerous kind gestures during my periodic visits.

References

Abbi, B.L. and Kesar Singh. *Post-Green Revolution Rural Punjab.* Chandigarh: CRRID, 1997.

Anand, Siriyavan. "Eating with our Fingers, Watching Hindi Cinema and Consuming Cricket", in Himal South Asia. Kathmandu (download), 2002.

Appadurai, Arjun. *Modernity at Large: Cultural Dimensions of Globalisation.* Delhi: Oxford University Press, 1997.

Beteille, Andre. "The Indian Village: Past and Present", in E.J. Hobsbawn et al., *Peasants in History: Essay in Honour of Daniel Thorner*. Delhi: Oxford University Press, 1980.

Breman, J. "The Village in Focus", in J. Berman et al., *The Village in Asia Revisited*. Delhi: Oxford University Press, 1997.

Chakravarty, Sumita, S. *National Identity in Indian Popular Cinema 1947-1987*. Delhi: Oxford University Press, 1987.

Chakravorty, Chandrima. "Subaltern Studies, Bollywood and *Lagaan*". *EPW*. May 10, 2003.

Dehpande, Sudhanava. "What's so great about *Lagaan*?", in *India International Centre Quarterly*. Winter-Spring 2003, Vol. 29, Nos. 3 & 4, pp. 236-245.

Dirks, Nicholas, B. *Castes of Mind: Colonialism and the Making of Modern India*. Princeton: Princeton University Press, 2001.

Doraiswamy, Rashmi. "Image and Imagination: Reconstructing the Nation in Cinema", in *India International Centre Quarterly*. Winter 2002-Spring 2003, Nos. 3 & 4, pp. 211-223.

Dube, S.C. *Indian Village*. London: Routledge and Kegan Paul, 1955.

Dwyer, Rachel. *Yash Chopra: Fifty Years in Indian Cinema*. Roli Books: New Delhi, 2002.

Dwyer, Rachel and Patel, Divya. *Cinema India: The Visual Culture of Hindi Film*. Delhi: Oxford University Press, 2002.

Guha, Ramchandra. *A Corner of a Foreign Field: The Indian History of a British Sport*. Delhi: Oxford University Press, 2002.

Gupta, Dipankar. "Whither the Indian Village: Culture and Agriculture in 'Rural' India". *EPW*. February 19, 2005, www.epw.org (download).

Hardgrave, R. *The Nadars of Tamil Nadu: The Political Culture of a Community in Change*. Berkeley: University of California Press, 1969.

Hardiman, David. *The Coming of the Devi: Adivasi Assertion in Western India*. Delhi: Oxford University Press, 1987.

Inden, Nicholas. *Imagining India*. Oxford: Basil Blackwell, 1990.

Jodhka, Surinder Singh. "From 'Bookview' to 'Field View' Social Anthropological Constructions of the Indian Village", in *Oxford Development Studies*, Vol. 26(3), pp. 311-331, 1988.

—. "Nation and the Village: Images of Rural India in Gandhi, Nehru and Ambedkar", *EPW*. August 10, 2002.

Kessinger, Tom P. *Vilayatpur (1848-1968): Social and Economic Change in a North Indian Village.* Berkeley: University of California Press, 1971.

Majumdar, D.N. *Caste and Class in an Indian Village.* London: Asia, 1956.

Majumdar, Boria. "Politics of Leisure in Colonial India '*Lagaan*': Invocation of a Lost History", *EPW.* September 1, 2001, pp. 3399-3404.

Mannathkkaren, Nissim. "Subalterns, Cricket and the 'Nation': The Silences of *Lagaan", EPW.* December 8, 2001, pp. 4580-4588.

Marquese, Mike. "Nothing Official About It? The World Cup", in *India International Centre Quarterly.* Summer 1996, Vol. 23, No. 2, New Delhi, pp.154-169, 1966.

Nandy Ashis. *The Tao of Cricket: On Games of Destiny and the Destiny of Games.* Delhi: Oxford University Press, 2000.

—. *An Ambigious Journey to the City.* Delhi: Oxford University Press, 2001.

Niranjana, Seemanthini. "Conceptualising the Indian Village: An Overview of the Village Studies Tradition", *Indian Journal of Social Science.* Vol. 4, No. 3, Sage: New Delhi, 1991.

Pandey, Vikash, N. "Re-presenting Rural: From Definition to Discourse", *Sociological Bulletin.* 52(1), March, 2003.

Prasad, Madhava, *Ideology of the Hindi Film: A Historical Construction.* Delhi: Oxford University Press. 1998.

Sharma, Satya Prakash. "Indian Village as a Unit of Study 1 & 2", *EPW.* August 23, 1969, pp. 1347-1387.

Tarlo, Emma. "Ethnic Chic: The Transformation of Hauz Khas Village", in *India International Centre Quarterly.* Summer 1996, Vol. 23, No. 2, New Delhi, pp. 30-60, 1996.

5

Revolt and Reform in Rural India

SANTOSH GUPTA

The village in India is not a singular entity and not necessarily always at the receiving end. One can trace histories of peasant revolt and resistance movements against colonial oppression even in the first half of the nineteenth century. In *India's Struggle for Independence* (1987) Bipin Chandra *et al.*, give details of the widespread revolts in rural India, which represent the village communities' reaction to injustice and oppression at the local and regional levels. These historical evidences belie the myth that the Indian peasant was cut off from the world outside his small village which had remained unchanged "from time immemorial".[1] Researches by social anthropologists and subaltern historians in recent times find that the Indian village has maintained a constant dialectic of resistance, autonomy and a consciousness of its own during the colonial period.[2] Some of these rebellions were supported by the intelligentsia, as was the case during the Indigo planter's rebellion during 1859-60 (Chandra 53). Harish Chandra Mukherji, editor of the *Hindoo Patriot* "published regular reports from his correspondents in the rural areas on planters' oppression", Din Bandhu Mitra dramatized this uprising in a play titled *Neel Darpan* which was widely read at that time (Chandra 54).

Texts like *Neel Darpan* that focused on the villagers' struggles were few during the nineteenth century; the intelligentsia, located in the cities, was mostly caught up with other colonial issues and debates. True, the quantum of village based literature across languages may not be very large or not accessible to us at present, though there is evidence enough in folk tales and fables, now being collected and rewritten by writers like Lakshmi Kumari Chundawat and Vijay Dan Detha. When one examines the role of the villagers in political movements is the question of agency must also be considered. Village narratives are formulated on several principles but the two most evident are: (i) one, where the villagers are themselves the agents of consciousness, they constitute the 'subject' and it is the extremes of oppression that leads them to their revolt or resistance; and (ii) the second is where the village community is shaken out of its passive suffering by an outside agency, whether it is education, political leadership or reform for economic motives. It is a matter of travelling knowledges, of threat to the status quo where hierarchy of religion or power is concerned. Given India's sprawling countryside, the agrarian nature of its economy, the rootedness of village communities in cultural and artisan traditions, no political movement could ignore the village at the turn of the century. The oppositional relationship between the city and the village could no longer be sustained. Of these the Gandhian movement was a major force in focusing or the recognition of the importance of village communities. The Communist Party's activists also penetrated some of the rural locations where they found the people unorganized against their oppressor. They helped the local villager to rise against their oppressors. This shift of focus on the village influenced the urban youth who were politically active, and the gap between the village and the city began to be bridged.

Jawahar Lal Nehru records in *The Discovery of India* (1947) how Gandhi sent his followers to go to the villages so as to know the villager "in the intimacy of his mud-hut and with the stark shadows of hunger always pursuing him" (Nehru 365). The close encounter with the villagers changed both the visitor and the village. In the villages a new kind of political awareness made entry, as these workers spoke to the villagers about the nationalist movement based on some political point of view. Nehru recounts this impact in these words: "The countryside hummed with the activity of innumerable messengers of the new gospel of action. The peasant was shaken and he began to emerge from his quiescent shell" (Nehru 365). The villagers were involved in the nationalist movement organized on a pan-Indian level, integrating the different sub-cultural groups. The villagers, who had their own distinct sense of culture and traditional roots, were drawn into the movement. The early twentieth century saw a new phase of villagers' participation in the broad-based movement. As more interaction between the city and village took place, a larger number of literary works depicted the village. The village became an important protagonist in Indian literature where political and social intermingling took place. In the writings of Rabindra Nath Tagore and Sarat Chandra in Bengali, Premchand in Hindi, Thakhazhi Shankar Pillai in Malayalam, Gopinath Mohanty in Oriya, and R.K. Narayan, Raja Rao and M.R. Anand in English the marginalized village community is brought to the centre, as these writers depicted the multidimensional emotional experiences and lives of the villagers. These writers saw the villagers and the other down-trodden poor sections of their society from a close and sympathetic viewpoint, and showed their sufferings, hardships as well as the strength, beauty and joys of their lives in their writings. The works of these writers glow with the deep authenticity of their observation and sympathy.

Premchand's portrayal of the diverse aspects of the village community has been among the most realistic, moving and enduring in Indian writing. His greatest work, *Godan* (1936) presents the complex colonial Indian society, divided as it was in the city and the village. Premchand focuses on the peasant community in Belari, a small village in U.P. The middle and upper classes are also presented in their self-centred and narrow materialistic pursuit. They visit Belari, at the invitation of the Zamindar, but their involvement with the village community remains very distant.

The villagers are caught in their own struggle for survival. Hori, the central character, is a poor peasant, forever on the brink of total deprivation, even of the basic necessities. His wife, Dhania, and the rest of the family struggle along with him, as do most of the villagers, in order to survive. The long struggle against the odds that they face is hard and back-breaking, but Premchand depicts the blossoming of romance, love, marriages taking place, brothers who fight, separate, and reunite, festivals are celebrated, and several other activities that are part of the lives of these people in the village. They live their lives with gusto and courage; sometimes they break down and are unhappy, yet life goes on and they continue to struggle.

Premchand's peasants have a hardiness that is the result of long suffering, low expectation from the world, and a realization of one's existential loneliness. Hori struggles hard to fend for his family, he tries to maintain his dignity and decency in every kind of struggle and lives by some simple moral values. Often his wife and son disagree with his moral scrupulousness, but Hori's own faith never wavers. His deep wish to own a cow is the desire of any peasant to have some livestock – to feed his children milk, so that they grow up well; the cow is also a symbol of material prosperity. He manages to own a cow for a few days. But his economic degradation continues and he dies a poor, struggling man. Dhania, his wife, gives him her full support, working equally hard with him. She readily agrees to give shelter to the Jhunia, the woman her son has chosen to marry, but is afraid to tell to the parents. So on in several incidents, the bond of love, sharing and understanding between Hori and Dhania is remarkably strong, giving them both moral strength.

The integrity and honesty in human relationships that is seen in the dealings of Hori and Dhania in their relations with different characters stands contrasted with the obvious lack of such qualities in the dealings of the urban, upper class characters in the novel. Premchand shows that amongst the more educated, middle class people of the society, there is a marked tendency to be opportunistic and self-centred. His portrayal of Mr. Khanna's relationship with his wife Govindi, and Miss Malati, a young doctor satirises the shallowness of the his infatuation and desire. This is shown as a materialistic concern, nurtured by the wave of 'modernity' of the educated class. Premchand depicts the increasing trend towards self-centred commercial concerns of the educated and well-to-do, upper class men and women. The business dealings between Pandit Omkar Nath, editor of a newspaper, Mr. Khanna, and Rai Sahib are based on selfish, unscrupulous dealings, where one partner does not hesitate in exploiting the helplessness of the other.

The city based characters remain, for the most part, involved in their own activities. But Mr. Mehta, who is a lecturer of Philosophy, and Malti, a doctor, learn to respect the qualities of hard work, sincerity, in the villagers during their visits to the village. When Gobar takes up work in Malti's house as a gardener, Malti becomes attached to Gobar's child, and looks after it selflessly during an attack of chickenpox. These changes in her also bring about a change in Mr. Mehta's attitude towards her, who then declares his adoration and love for her.

Life does not remain dull and drab all the time in the village. At the time of Holi, Gobar organizes a programme in which there is a skit. The village elders are mocked for their hypocrisy and exploitation of the poor. Dancing and singing are also held, giving expression to the irrepressible spirit of joy of life. The younger generation is critical of the exploitative practices around them but do not know any way to get out of the trap. Gobar moves out of the village. But after spending a few years in the city, he gains a mellowness, which helps him in understanding the dignity and goodness of Hori and Dhania. He respects Hori and promises to help him financially.

The village in *Godan* is perhaps in its most degraded economic stage. There is an element of rebelliousness and restlessness in the younger generation, who do not know how to remove the stronghold of the colonial system and exploitation. The peasant is the worst sufferer in the chain of the colonized citizens but right from the Zamindar down to Hori, they are all caught in the colonial machinery, where no light seems to be coming from outside. As already pointed out Gandhian and communist ideologies were instrumental in providing a base for resistance motivating the villagers to support to the non-cooperation and civil disobedience movement in the following years. By referring to only two novels, I wish to depict this stage in the villages' history where awakening and their participation in the nationalist struggle is seen, namely, Raja Rao's *Kanthapura* (1938) and Niranjan's *Chirsmarniye* (1955).

Kanthapura like *Godan*, has gained the stature of a classic. It dramatizes the revolutionary message transforming a small, sleepy village in the distant regions of South India. How completely it changes the orthodox unchanging mindset of the villagers into reconsidering the boundaries of gender and caste are reflected in the final uprising (in the novel) where all the villagers stand up to offer a non-violent resistance to the brutal encroachment upon the villages by police. Women participate equally in the struggle. Moorthy, a follower of Gandhi, brings to the entire village the ideas of pursuit of Truth through Ahimsa and Satyagraha. He preaches against untouchability, enters the houses of the village pariah and has to face the wrath of his own mother. However, the impact on the villagers is made; he is able to persuade them to give up some of these old practices. The village participates in the nationwide movement, recasting itself in the process.

This transformation is achieved through a careful coating of the political message by religious colours. The contemporary conflict against the British rule for the country's freedom is presented to the villagers in a religious terminology, thus entering into the hearts of the deeply religious village very easily. Using the space and rituals of the temple and the narration of religious tales, the 'Harikatha', Moorthy, the Gandhian, who comes to the village, tells the villagers about the new incarnation of God in Gandhi, who will fight the mighty Empire with the humble means of Ahimsa and non-cooperation.

Raja Rao presents the translation of the political actions into religious parables, dramatizing through the scenes in, Kanthapura, the wider national story. Gandhi had himself used religious myths, language and even practices to popularize the movement. Moorthy puts his "narrative technique" to similar use – the villagers are made to view this political conflict in terms of the eternal conflict between goodness and evil, enacted annually in Ramlila, on Dussehra and the stories of God coming on earth in human form to destroy evil. When the action is dressed in religious garb, every person, almost everyone, participates in the struggle as if it were a prime religious duty. The movement reaches all the sections of the village community. The faith in mythical conflict also makes the villages buoyant for they know that even if Ram had a humble army and fought against the mighty Ravana, truth and goodness will always win.

Niranjan, like Premchand, has focused mainly on the sufferings of the villagers in the hands of the moneylender and the zamindar, often the same person. Niranjan, a communist journalist, was working in a small village, Kayyur, in Kerala during 1942-43 when he saw four young village boys being publicly hanged, on 23 March 1943. They were involved in revolutionary propaganda, and were charged with killing a policeman. Though they were innocent of the murder, they were punished for the anti-British campaigning. A few years later Niranjan wrote in Kannada a fictional depiction of this historic incident, representing the surge of nationalist sentiments among the villagers, who were being exploited harshly by the Zamindar and the police. The four boys who are trained to spread awareness of rebellion among the villagers are Appu, Chirikandan, Kunhambu and Abu Bakra, who are young, innocent and disturbed by the suffering of their parents. Niranjan shows the villagers losing their land to the Zamindar, unable to feed their families, and losing hope altogether. A communist worker comes to Kayyur, begins to talk to the boys individually and then organizes the villagers to think of fighting against exploitation. The death of the boys fills the villagers with deep sense of anguish and anger, and they continue to resist the injustice meted out to them.

Chirsmasniye has the authenticity and immediacy of a novel based on an actual event. Such incidents occurred in different parts of the country. The villagers had started reacting against the cruel rule of the Britishers and were resisting the exploitation and oppression. They were now influenced by the political workers, who brought about organized rebellion.

With the overthrow of the foreign rule the country engaged itself in the reconstruction of the nation. Here again villages became important sites in the national drama. The planning for reform in the villages began at the level of Centre of political power, but for an awakened village populace the next step was to move towards its own reform and reconstruction. Gopinath Mohanty's novel *Mati Matal* gives a lyrical depiction of the small villages in Orissa, that began to get together to rebuild the village as a part of rebuilding the nation. The novel won its writer the Jnanpeeth award in 1966 for the inspirational depiction of the simple village people getting down to recasting their own small village, on their own resources, own planning, and their own labour. Ravi is a young man, who has been educated in the town, but is keen to work in the village, where he finds everything falling into pieces. He persuades people in the village to get together, men and women of all classes and castes and work for their own development. They now talk begin to about the Constitution of India, which takes the place of the scriptures. Ravi's unceasing hard work succeeds in bringing the villagers together, and they look forward to a modern state. This novel has an optimistic view that carries the Gandhian vision of the reform of villages through cooperative efforts. The villages thus reformed could then become socially and politically alert, and economically more self-sustaining.

Taking only four texts written with the village as a central protagonist, I have tried to draw out the diverse aspects of the villages shown by these writers. Each text represents a changing phase of village-life during the twentieth century. The villages have gone through many phases – sharing with the country its sorrows, struggle and the process of its remaking. The village has continued to change with changes in the larger landscape; it has continued to change after 1960s in significant ways. Novels depicting the impact of the new economy, new political equations and cultural re-mapping of village-life continue to be written in most Indian languages. The Indian village has so far retained its own self-directed thrust, refusing to become the city-in-miniature or be wiped out completely and has continued to be an ever-changing and thriving protagonist in the theatre of India's national life.

Notes

1. M.N. Srinivas discusses the reports written by British historians and sociologists about Indian villages in the early nineteenth century, which created a myth of static, insular, closed-in-the-shell minds of the villagers. See M.N. Srinivas "The Indian Village: Myth and Reality" in *The Village in India.* (Ed. Vandana Madan, New Delhi, Oxford, University Press, 2002, pp. 51-70).
2. Partha Chatterjee discusses the continuous history of peasant revolts in India since the seventeenth century, and its relationship with the nationalist movement. He believes, with Ranajit Guha, whose work

he discusses at length in "The Nation and Its Peasants" (1993), that the history of peasant revolts reflects the independent nature of the villages who "translated" even the ideology of the nationalist bourgeois political movement "to its own code" (160). Partha Chatterjee "The Nation and Its Peasant" in *The Partha Chatterjee Omnibus*, (New Delhi, Oxford University Press, 1999, pp. 158-172).

References

Chandra, Bipin. et al., *India's Struggle For Independence* (1987). New Delhi: Penguin, 2000.

Chatterjee, Partha. "The Nation and Its Peasants" (1993), in *The Partha Chatterjee Omnibus*. New Delhi: Oxford University Press, 1999.

Mohanty, Gopinath. *Mati Matal*, Hindi translation by Ṣhankar Lal Purohit (1974). New Delhi: Bhartiya Jnanapeeth Publications, 1989.

Nehru, Jawahar Lal. *The Discovery of India* (1947). Reprint, New Delhi: Penguin India, 1999.

Niranjan. *Chirsmaraniye* (1955), Translated into Hindi by Ravi Krishna Pandeya. Lucknow: Parikalpana Prakashan, 2000.

Premchand. *Godan* (1936), New Delhi: Prakashan Sansthan, 2001.

Raja Rao. *Kanthapura* (1938). New Delhi: Oxford University Press.

Srinivas, M.N. "The Indian Village: Myth and Reality" in *The Village in India*. Ed. Vandana Madan. New Delhi: Oxford University Press, 2002.

6

Villages in Crisis

A Comparative Study of Khushwant Singh's *Train to Pakistan*, Raghuvir Chaudhary's *Uparvas Kathatrayee* and Rahi Masoom Reza's *Adha Gaon*

AVADHESH KUMAR SINGH

I

Since the novels under consideration deal with villages and centralize them, in ways as varied as the novels themselves, I must at least roughly introduce the two terms 'centrality' and 'specificity' which I would be using while examining the concerned novelists' preoccupation with the village, its concerns and crises and their articulation in fictional terms. Of the two terms the former is characterized by intensity and latter by inclusiveness, which makes its use a little more convenient. It is expected that points of similarities and differences between the two terms, whatever they may be, deferred here, will come to surface by the end of this endeavour.

Whatever may be our discourse of villages – centrality or specificity as constructed by us – it would revolve around three keywords: creativity, environment and constituency. Creativity stands for ability or talent to create and its continuous and habitual use. Environment is constituted by those objects, situations and physical and social conditions that not only surround us but also influence feeling and development of those who live in it. Constituency is the area or region of a country chosen by the writer for his work. It need not always necessarily be a physical reality. Even a community or race or caste chosen by a writer may be his constituency. Creativity is related to environment in the manner the energy is to material.[1] A creative artist with his creativity does not operate in a vacuum but projects real or imagined, on the basis of his moorings in the real, environment around him. The elements of environment, after getting mingled with other elements like air and water, become the breath of the people in the concerned region and thereafter regulate, condition and govern their flow and even their duration. The elements of environment act as raw material for creativity, which receives material from the environment and thereafter, dissolving it with its energy, moulds it. But prior to that the writer or creator chooses his constituency which may be a village, region, state or country depending on the writer's sensibility, his concern and feeling for it, as would be reflected in their portrayal. Moreover, it will depend on a few factors: How the writer has seen his characters being influenced by the environment? How and to what extent the writer himself has been influenced by these factors and to what extent she/he is committed to his constituency?

The specificity, despite such generalizations, as attempted above, is a complex issue. However, in village-central novels, the specificity can be discerned in linguistic specificity, landscape specificity, cultural specificity and crisis specificity. The first three specificities leave their distinct imprint on a work and they are easily discernible to a sensitive or creative reader. But, if the writer over-stresses them indulgently, the work runs the risk of ending up as a tourist guidebook or at the most a readable documentary work. Keeping it in mind I have tried to consider the novels in the context of crisis specificity in particular, the way it operates in them and the way the village and its concerns become central in these works. It will not be incongruous for me to mention that these novels in three different languages were written in the three subsequent decades after independence, and deal with the villages of three different Indian states. Despite linguistic and cultural differences, there is an inherent similarity in them that brings them together, that they are concerned with that crucial period of transition of the Indian history when the tyranny of thraldom had come to an end and the new era commenced with the independence of the Indian sub-continent.

II

On the surface Khushwant Singh's *Train to Pakistan* (1956) seems to be a village-centred novel, for the events in this novel take place in Mano Majra, a typical Punjab village, smeared in dust, mud, values and culture of Punjab but almost untouched by the world around and from development also in whose name it has a railway station and a passing train with whose whistling the Mano Majrans have learnt to regulate and lead their lives.

Mano Majra, a small frontier village of seventy families, situated at the distance of half a kilometre from the Sutlej river, has, to good measure, shielded itself from the external world. Yet, the external events do leave their splashes on it. Ironically, the centre of the forces that shape the events in this village lies elsewhere. If these forces were the source of independence, then they were responsible for the partition also – of the people, families, villages and towns – without their consent. The partition disturbs the schedule of the train that brings dead bodies instead of passengers from Pakistan. This event turns Mano Majra a microcosm of the vivisected sub-continent, caught in the whirlpool of one of the cruellest, meanest and bloodiest events in the history of mankind that left ten million in flight and almost a million dead. Even then, this village has somehow saved itself from the flames of communalism and barbarism. It should, however, not mean that only angels of love, peace and mercy live in this village. If there is love among the people of the village, then, there are instances of occasional disputes and wranglings. But, whatever exists in this village is typically Punjabi in its character. Amid these developments, Juggat Singh, a scoundrel, falls in love with Nooran, the daughter of the Imam, and theirs remains genuinely Punjabi love to the very end.

The Hindus and Muslims are so entrenched in this village that they have nothing to do with political developments – the Sikhs and Hindus with Hindustan or the Muslims with Pakistan. The police sub-inspector tells the Deputy Commissioner:

> I am sure no one in Mano Majra even knows that British have left and country is divided into Pakistan and Hindustan. Some of them know about Gandhi but I doubt if any one has even heard of Jinnah. (133)

It is due to it that Imam Bakhsh says wiping his tears, "What have we to do with Pakistan, we were born here, and so our ancestors. We have lived amongst you as brothers" (126). The Mano Majrans are also unwilling to allow their Muslim brothers to leave the village. The Sikh Lambardar says immediately:

> Yes, you are our brothers. As far as we are concerned, you and your children and your grandchildren can live here as long as you like. If anyone spoke rudely to you, your wives or your children, it will be us first and our wives and children before a single hair of your head is touched. (126)

The Muslims leave the village only when compelled by the administration and the Mano Majrans allow them to do so only when they are convinced that the departure of the Muslims is in their interest. Imam Bakhsh states, "Alright.... if we have to go, we better pack up our bedding and belongings. It will take us more than a night to clear out of homes, it has taken our fathers and grandfathers hundreds of years to make" (137). The whole of Mano Majra is nonplussed at these unprecedented developments. "Not many people slept in Mano Majra that night. They went from house to house, talking, crying, swearing love and friendship, assuring each other that this would soon be over" (132), writes the novelist describing that night of separation.

The news of barbaric torture and killing of non-Muslims by the Muslims in Pakistan instigates the Sikh youth from other villages to retaliate, and they hatch a plot against the Muslims travelling in a train to Pakistan. Jugga comes to know of it. When the religious institutions do nothing but fan communal hatred, when a militate intellectual like Iqbal trembles with fear, when the administration sulks helpless and stands as mute spectator, the surging love of a *budmash* for his weaver girl rescues the situation. Jugga's beloved Nooran is likely to travel by the same train which is to be attacked by the Sikh youths who stretch a rope across the first span above the height of the funnel of the engine to sweep the people sitting on the roof of the train and then intend to butcher them. Sensing the danger Jugga stakes his life. Against all warning voices he climbs and succeeds in cutting the rope with his kirpan. The novelist describes the scene, "He went at it with his knife, and then with his teeth, the engine was almost on him. There was a volley of shots. The man shivered and collapsed. The rope snapped in the centre and he fell. The train went over him and went to Pakistan" (181).

The village centrality, it seems, enters the novels by the back door as a consequence of Khushwant Singh's admission to the feeling of a guilty conscience. As he himself has said in his essay "Compulsion to Write", "The partition theme was born out of a sense of guilt that I had done nothing to save lives of innocent people and behaved like a coward" (136). Further, it was a by-product of his disillusionment which he voiced thus:

> The beliefs I had cherished all my life were shattered. I had believed in the innate goodness of common men. But then the division of India had been accompanied by the most savage

> massacre known in the history of the country...I had believed that we Indians were peace-loving and non-violent, that we were more concerned with matters of the spirit, while the rest of the world was involved in the pursuit of material things. After the experience of autumn of 1947, I could no longer subscribe to these views. I became...an angry middle-aged man, who wanted to shout his disenchantment with the world.[2]

It was not possible for the novelist to articulate this disenchantment, disillusionment and sense of guilt through a stereotyped character. For that it was imperative to puncture the mouth of innate goodness inherent in man and thus re-assert that man is barbaric by nature. To project this, Khushwant Singh created a character like Jugga, "Number 10 budmash" possible only in a village like Mano Majra. Despite some inherent weaknesses there are some traces of goodness still left only in village characters like him, enough to rescue, at least symbolically, a village like Mano Majra trapped in transition, through his sacrifice.

In fact, the values held by it rescue that village. The novel is crisis-specific, along with its landscape culture and linguistic specificity – the last one carried over in English through the Punjabi culture and its code of conduct. Among its codes the most significant is its ideal or code of love. According to their code, honour and honesty were, and still are, all right but they were placed at much lower level in comparison to loyalty and faithfulness to friends and village-fellows. For friends one could tell a lie in the court and even cheat and no one would blame you.

Khushwant Singh tried to see through the claustrophobic catastrophe through Jugga's true love for Nooran, which is not the product of the shallow slogans like communal harmony of ideal love which are beyond Jugga's comprehension. What he understands is his uninhibited Punjabi love, which is the only and the brightest and the most durable patch on the altered clothes of humanity. The novelist has, with considerable success, delivered the village along with its humanity from the crisis for the time being.

That the village centrality has crept in the novel by its rear door must have been realized by the novelist also. Perhaps under this realization, he changed the title of the novel from "Mano Majra" to *Train to Pakistan* with an intention of developing "Train as an encompassing dynamic symbol of an otherwise static symbol of a village". Whatever may have been the writerly intention the novel does not end up merely as a document of a Punjabi village culture and its crisis specificity, for it articulation is not relegated to a subordinate position.

III

Uparvas Kathatrayee, a trilogy by Raghuvir Chaudhary, one of the novelists of much significance in Gujarati, is a "quest for public consciousness", in the words of the novelist himself, through three generations of the Anjana Patel community of North Gujarat in Sompura and villages around it. On the one end is the old generation for Doliman, Karshan and Pithu Bhagat in its evening, while on the other end is the generation of Narasang, Bheema, Wala, Chhana, Dhamal, Chehal and Kankoo sandwiched between the old generation and the new generation of Ghemar, Heti, Deboo, Lavji, Ranchhod and Madhoji among others, straining to emerge out of new compulsions and pressures.

In his trilogy Chaudhary has compared and contrasted three generations of Pithu Bhagat and Karsan, Pithu's family leads virtuous life marked by love, faith, pity and piety bequeathed to the subsequent generations. On the other hand, Karsan's family is rooted in ignorance, pride, wickedness and greed. Against the wickedness of Karsan's family, Pithu Bhagat sows seeds of values whose crop is reaped by his own family, his community, village and the entire region. Narasang, Pithu's son, forms a *Bhajan Mandal* in the village and begins classes of adult education, plays an active role in Seva Dal, establishes co-operative societies and library; and by employing new agricultural techniques and technologies he emerges as a progressive farmer. Though good in studies he gives up his study to support his father in farming for the sake of education of his younger brother Lavji. Even though at the familial level his small act is a severe blow to individualistic pursuits. It is because of such deeds that the village survives as a village and Sompura remains Sompura. Daboo is sensitive enough to perceive stasis lying beneath the surfacial prosperity of the village. He observes:

> Sompura is sick. Its dusty fields are now green. Tractors may be seen plying where bullock carts used to run earlier. The people who used to be happy with four annas and eight annas have got their accounts opened in the bank of Sarang. Even then...they are ignorant about the ground root reality. Continuously flowing blood of humanity in the heart of the village is decreasing. Everything appears to be healthy even then sickness prevails and knowingly and unknowingly the sickness is being treated in such a way that it increases in the process. (*Antarvas* 32)

The novelist has portrayed the condition of the village and change in the mentality of the people through Lavji, his dilemma and conflict. He oscillates between the village and the city. He is in love with his village but he is fated to live in a city. He is pained at being separated from his village and even more at the impending alienation in the city. He is torn between his wife Shanti and classmate Jaimini. In a sense they become symbols of cultures of village and city respectively. But, in Chaudhary's world, even this ossified culture is presented as an idealized culture. It may be termed as Chaudhary's purely Indian version of city culture. Due to his own love for village, the novelist makes Jaimini ask Lavji to get married to Shanti. And Lavji accepts it too. Not to be content with this, the novelist sends Lavji back to Sompura from Ahmedabad. These instances make Jaimini's character the most wonderful fiction amid other realistic characters. In a village-centred novel such situations as these appear as a pleasant change at times and on other occasions utterly unrealistic.

Lavji gives up his job and Jaimini's company as well in Ahmedabad to accept a job in the college at Sarang. His stay at Sompura marks the beginning of his disillusionment. He finds that all his endeavours to impose certain order on them are futile. The new generation, the source of his hope, fails his faith. In spite of being charged with corruption in the co-operative society, the corrupt party succeeds in appropriating power again. And after coming to power the new generation starts behaving like its old counterparts. In such a situation to live or not to live in a village is the biggest question for him. His dilemma comes to an end with an offer of an American scholarship by courtesy of Jaimini.

The novelist has tried to understand dilemmas and crises born out of social, economic and political changes in the post-Independent era in his own way. Hence, the novel celebrates lifestyle, language and culture of the Anjana Patels of North Gujarat and it accounts for landscape specifically, and cultural specificity evident in description of the village and lifestyle of its dwellers. As an instance the villagers are used to taking *khichari* (a dish of rice and pulse boiled together) with milk which is not the case with other parts of the country. Linguistic specificity has found expression in the original version but in its Hindi translation the novelist himself has replaced North Gujarati dialect of Gujarati with Awadhi. Crisis specificity may be seen in the way the novelist has voiced his concerns for the village, region and country. Like Mano Majra of Khushwant Singh and Gangauli of Rahi Masoom Reza independence has entered Sompura almost stealthily and the change brought by it therein disturbs the village in one way of the other, and they react to it in their typical manner, and try to participate in it as well.

After independence a new community of immoral opportunistic leadership whose speculation and execution suffered from dichotomy came into existence. An indirect contrast are

Pithu's family and people like Heerabhai who are seriously concerned at the erosion of moral, political and national values. Heerabhai puts it, "These people after becoming the party leaders intend to appropriate power. They are concerned neither with the party nor with the country". It accounts for people's disenchantment with the new leadership and they rightly ventilate it in their statements like "The Britishers went away and dyers have come" (623).

All these concerns, whether they are pertaining to the partition of the country, or to the movement for the statehood of Gujarat and its attainment, or to wars that India had to fight after its independence or to village development, have found space for themselves in the novel in different ways. These villagers have learnt to live with new centres of power like Delhi, Bombay and Ahmedabad. They have their own commonsense and wisdom with which they understand political motives, moves and crises. In the first part of *Kathatrayee* some of these crises have been mentioned but remain deals with the generations of Pithu and Karsan whose understanding of political and social issues was not as sharp as that of the subsequent generations of Pithu and Karsan whose understanding of political and social issues was not as sharp as that of the subsequent generations. These issues are taken up more seriously later in *Sahvas* and *Antarvas* – symbolically also. Pandit Nehru's death coincides with the fall of the banyan tree at the village crossroad. The nation and Sompura both become anxious at the sudden loss of patronage: "What will happen to them after Gandhi, Patel and Nehru? What will be the fate of the nation in the face of slogans like, 'We took Pakistan with smile and we'll capture Hindustan with force'." With these concerns and crises in the novel the crises specificity also finds expression for itself along with other specificities. But consciousness of crisis and its intensity are of different kind. While Khushwant Singh's *Train to Pakistan* depicts a village caught in turbulent crisis, *Uparvas Kathatrayee* is marked with a large number of tiny crises leading to a somewhat diffused effect. Further, these crises have not been examined from different angles the way Rohinton Mistry does in *Such a Long Journey* through his multiple narratives. Be it crisis perceived by the Parsee community or Lal Bahadur Shastri's death, or the Indo-China war or the Indo-Pak wars, every character of Mistry has a story or stories of his own to tell projecting light on the event or the crisis from different directions exhausting all possible versions which have been waiting for long to being told. Admittedly, Mistry's has his own way so has Chaudhary, and the critical intentions cannot dictate terms to writerly intentions but *Uparvas Kathatrayee* lacks in intensity of crisis-depiction.

Chaudhary has tried to present his trilogy as an autobiography of a village and Sompura as an epitome of India. He has succeeded also in his endeavours. But it would be correct to mention that the novel is village specific with community centrality. Among various characters from different generations of Pithu Bhagat and Karsan it is the Anjana Patel community that emerges as the real protagonist. Without questioning the authority of Chaudhary's statement if we accept *Uparvas Kathatrayeee* as the autobiography of a village then the trilogy is more of an odyssey of the Anjana Patel community in the post-independence era than that of the village. And the way this community has emerged as a protagonist is different from the centralization of the Parsee community and Shia Muslim community in Mistry and Reza respectively. One of the reasons for this is that Mistry's and Reza's characters find themselves more entangled in their tiny crises than those of their community. But, gradually, their and their community's fears and anxieties get integrated. Chaudhary's characters and their crises are also integrated with those of their village at one level, but Chaudhary has almost isolated his Anjana Patel community from other communities of the region. On the other hand, Khushwant Singh's Mano Majra projects social transaction in various communities like Sikh, Hindu and Muslim in relatively briefer space, and so does

Reza, even more intensely as he depicts relationship between the Muslims and Hindus with their sub-groups and castes and sub-castes.

The validity of comparing *Uparvas Kathatrayee* with *Such a Long Journey* and *Adha Gaon* may be questioned with justification because all three novels are also placed differently in the context of community, constituency and environment. The Parsee community is a minority community in the city of Bombay, state of Maharashtra and country India; the Shias are in majority in their village but in minority in the district Ghazipur, state Uttar Pradesh and country India; whereas the Anjana Patels are in majority in their village Sompura, region North Gujarat, state Gujarat and the country India also for they are part of the majority community Hindu. Hence, it becomes evident that the concerns and crises of the minority community have been more poignantly articulated by the writers, coming as they do, from minority community.

The point at which *Uparvas Kathatrayee* differs from other novels is the Anjana Patel community's understanding of post-independence problems of village, region, state and country, its strategy of development and participation in the process of development. It indirectly suggests the social process through which this community has progressed and thereby contributed to the progress of the region state and country. The novel charts out constituting elements of this strategy as self-defence – defence of the village by keeping vigilant watch by turns particularly by its youth, obedience to the instructions of the village head, establishment of organization like *Bhajan Mandali* to cater to religious and cultural needs, education – adult education and library, establishment of co-operative societies, and above all faith in the young generation. Whether Sompura has fully subscribed to this paradigm or strategy is difficult to say but whatever development of a village like Sompura and progress of a community like the Anjana Patel has taken place, or is possible, would rest on this model in its present or modified form. With its dilemmas and contradictions the way Pithu Bhagat's family of the Anjana Patel community is depicted as prescribing and following this strategy makes the novel community – central and village specific.

IV

Adha Gaon is a moving delineation of divided psyche of the Muslims, the Shias to be precise, of Gangauli village of Ghazipur district of eastern Uttar Pradesh, around the times of partition. Rahi Masoom Reza has heard the story of transformation of Gadipur into Ghazipur and of Gangauli's defiance of this process of transformation from the waves of "the great stream of filthy water" (10) called the Ganga flowing by the village. Weaving his story with linguistic landscape and culture-specific details the writer has seen Gangauli measuring itself and being measured by the standards of Ghazipur, Calcutta, Bombay, Kanpur and thereafter Karachi. Gangauli has its own world insulated from the world outside because in view of the Mians "the world came to an end with the court of Ghazipur so they did not know that what was happening in the world and what was not" (62).

With such *mians* as described above as characters *Adha Gaon* is a *shadinama* – marriage document or contract of Ganguali which has a 'full' hierarchy of relationships of 'half' a village. Earlier there were Gangauliwalas in Gangauli and the number of such people is on the decrease whereas the number of the Hindus and Muslims is increasing. Even among the Muslims there are sub-divisions as the Saiyads and non-Saiyads, and even further in Saiyads also there are Saiyads of Phatakwala, of Payjamawala and Lungiwala. Among women there are *bahoos, begums, dulhins, aziz dulhins,* and *nafis dulhins* depending usually on the amount of dowry brought by them. Human relationship in Gangauli is marked with profuse instances of flirtations and skirmishes and even here Gangauli has its own standards. One of its instances in the novel is the *lathaiti* (the quarrel between two groups or persons armed with bamboo sticks) between Phunnan Mian and Kunwar Pal Singh who attack each other after saying 'Ya Ali' and 'Jai Bajrang Bali' and wound themselves seriously. Mian cleanses the wounds of Thakur, puts him in his bullock cart and then falls down in it. In his last statement in the police station. Thakur deliberately saves Phunnan Mian, and breathes his last with the words 'Jai Krishna' on his lips leaving Phunnan "wailing and sobbing like children." (151) It cements the relationship between the two families forever.

On the one hand, Reza has integrated the Hindus and Muslims through the Ganga-Jamuni culture, while on the other he has shown emerging cracks in the hierarchy of relationships in one community through the new generation, though in all instances the characters seek energy for their action from their village. For instance, Migdad is high caste Saiyad whereas his beloved Saifunia is a low-caste barber girl. Despite opposition from his family, he is unflinching in his love for Saifunia and wants to get married to her. He asks her to leave the village and go to Calcutta to avoid the wrath of the Saiyads. Placing her love for her village above hers she says, "What do you say? Our relationship with this village is unbreakable. You get married elsewhere..." (189). At this Migdad retorts, "No... We will get married here only. Else we won't. Am I the only one left for that flabby daughter of my maternal uncle?"

> "Is it then this that you don't want to get married to her because she is ugly." Saifunia saw the magic of her dreams being broken into bits? "If this is the matter, then I won't marry you."
>
> "Won't you marry me?"
> "No".
> "Won't?"
> "No, No...No..."
>
> Migdad slapped here so forcefully that her face was turned to the other side. The slap brought down quite a few walls. She clung

to Migdad, and began to cry like a child and her tears began to mingle with Migdad's tears.

"Yes, I would marry you. If not to you, then to whom?" (191)

Reza has subverted vertical hierarchy of religion, caste and high-caste and low-caste considerations through the new generation of Migdad and Saifunia. Migdad and Saifunia get married and that too in Gangauli, and live there only. Gangauli, in fact, has enough courage and capacity to absorb such positive changes and even negative shocks. However, a few social, economic, political and emotional crises have shaken the roots of Gangauli. Incidentally all these crises are interrelated. Economic crises generate emotional crises. Troubled by economic problems, the young people of Gangauli leave Gangauli and go to some city, particularly Calcutta in search of some job, and Calcutta emerges not merely a name of a city but "the name of aspiration" for sons and daughters (2). The city torments daughters-in-law of Gangauli like their co-wives, and so they keep cursing the city for its villainous role in their lives and coming between them and their husbands. In this manner, the writer has placed village vis-à-vis city, and in very minute undertone has rayed the emotional anguish of woman in her different roles as a mother, sister, wife and daughter.

However, the people of Gangauli have learnt to live with new compulsions of life and time. But recent developments in the form of independence and its ancillary events are beyond their understanding, and though unpleasant it is difficult for them to ward them off. These developments have created disturbing ripples in their otherwise easy life. They were already plagued with unemployment and now they are to be deprived of their zamindari. It had not only intensified dark clouds of crises but the social system has also been subverted. Consequently, their servants and tenants do not behave well with their erstwhile landlords. Moreover, after becoming an MLA. Parsuramva became Parsuram compelling the hereditary landlords to bow down to him. Kammo's allopathic medical practice has threatened the *hakimi*, the traditional medical practice, of Hakim Saheb. And thanks to the increasing number of Hindus and Muslims, "Gangauliness" of Gangauli is in danger. On the other hand, with partition of the sub-continent, the Shias of Gangauli have to pay the penalty for a crime which they know nothing of.

A crisis such as this is unheard of in the life of Gangauli. It has posed a permanent question before Gangauli's existence and future. Due to the partition, half of this village is on the verge of further fragmentation. On the one hand is the political crisis and on the other the emotional. Admittedly, Calcutta was a villain in the world of Gangauli but its villainy was not so injurious as the devilish designs of Karachi which would eat up families and family members of Gangauli, whereas Calcutta used to spare people of Gangauli at least for *Moharram*.

Reza has developed *Moharram* as a religious, cultural, social, mythical and artistically integrative metaphor. Its social and cultural significance is that it brings together not only the Muslims of all ages and sects but the Hindus as well. It is a tragedy but Gangauli rejoices in it in abundance, for its separated children return to it to mourn. For the Saiyad family *Moharram* is in no sense less spiritual than Id. The novelist has hung the canvas of Ganguali and its people on the nails of *Moharram* fixed on the immeasurable walls of time. This canvas is generously sprinted with splashes of shades and colours of the socio-political and cultural events. Each splash contains multiple colours in it. If the *Moharram* is of religious and cultural significance, it is a symbol of mourning and separation. The Shias believe that Imam Hussain comes back to Hindustan during *Moharram*, and after it goes back to Karbala. After *Moharram* Gangauli seems desolate because with Imam Hussain's departure the young people of Gangauli also go back to Calcutta, their Karbala.

The partition is also another Karbala. The people of Gangauli have nothing to do with either Pakistan or Qaid-e-Azam. They are not concerned with the question whether

Aligarh stays with India or is annexed to Pakistan (242). The cardinal question is, "After the formation of Pakistan will you carry Urdu with you or leave it here?" (255). What shall be the ultimate face of Pakistan whose foundation, according to the people of Gangauli, is being laid on fear and hatred: Does the Hindustani Muslim not truly belong to this land? The Rajput Muslims of Dildarnagar and Gahmar are made of this soil too. Then why do they vote for the Muslim League? Why do they feel the need for a nation?... Do all those people who will vote for the Muslim League know as to what kind that Pakistan will be? Pakistan is not the God who should be believed in without seeing Him. For being written on the tongue of the people innumerable number of generations in between? What shall happen to the generations hanging in the air? These are a few questions asked by a young member of Gangauli like Tannoo. In the course of these questions the writer rejects the two-nation theory on the basis of religion, and prioritizes culture over religion (in its limited sense as it is used by some of the characters).

The questions of the innocent people of Gangauli may be motivated by their selfish interests but their questions and arguments cannot just be whisked away. Phunnan Mian does not understand the very logic behind the attacks on the Imambara in Delhi, and on mosques in Jallundhar and Amritsar. On being informed that this is being done to take revenge against the demolition of temples by the Mughal emperors, he counter questions what were the Hindus doing then. Why did they not beat the Mughal emperors? He is not ready to accept it. Why should they pay penalty for the misdeeds of the Mughal emperors? (302). In other words, the country is divided by the politicians and Gangauli and its people are the victims, as they are ground up. Out of their naivety they curse Gandhi and the Congress because they have lost their zamindari and influence because of them. In the next breath they curse Pakistan. For one thing Pakistan is the cause of their loss of zamindari because, according to them Gandhi said, "Well, Dear Mians, since you have got your Pakistan, then go to hell;" for another, Pakistan has snatched their sons and daughters. This is the reason why *Moharram* in its fullest meaning finds expression with the formation of Pakistan leading to division of houses and families in Gangauli. *Moharram* incarnate walks up to Gangauli whose people come to understand the real meaning of *Moharram* when the horseshoe called Pakistan becomes a noose put on their neck (299). The most horrible consequence of this new development was that half of their blood was in Gangauli and the other half was wandering in the streets of Karachi. For them now it is difficult to dream alone in the zigzag paths of dreamland. this is the reason why the flint-hearted people like Phunnan Mian, Kabir and Hakim Saheb break down and weep their unstoppable tears out over this *Moharram* after the partition, whereas they had to act and squeeze their eyes for a few tears on earlier occasions. These people abuse, curse, sob, weep and try. What else can these people do on the impending loss of the remaining reins of the horse called time. It is because of such agonizing portrayal of the partition that the novel earned praise of critics and creative writers alike: Mukul Kesavan, the author of *Looking Through Glass*, has called it the greatest novel written on the partition of the country (Kesavan 5).

Amidst the fluctuating relationships being defined in terms of concerns and crises the novelist has woven the novel with the unforeseen complexities of life caught in transition that the novel appears *nade Ali* the prayer in Arabic sung in the moments of crisis. It is *nade Ali* not by the Muslims only but by Gangauli and the whole of India. The author has tried to pour so many concerns and crises in the novel that it becomes almost impossible even for the novelist to bail them out or scrape them together on the part of a sensible reader. It is because Reza perceived his lifeline in Gangauli. Lifeline as usual if it is a vibrant one, defies authorial designs, however ambitious or meticulous they may be. So alive is Reza's lifeline that when he began to narrate its story, he could not do so and had to say in between, "The very task of saying whatever I have to is becoming more difficult with every word. Because the village and the people I speak of is my village and the people are my own people and I love them. This love stands as the wall in my endeavours to speak myself out" (296).

It is not merely authorial tactics or acrobating. Rather it is reality which speaks from each pore of the novel. The way Reza has listened to the story or stories of every pore of his village and then tapped them in with their intensity is a unique achievement in the whole range of literature. Equally notable is Reza's attachment and commitment to the village expressed at the levels of subject matter and its narration. The village remains the core of his concern which he expressed through Tannoo who tells Kali Sherwani "I am not a voter...I am a Muslim. But I love this village, because myself am this village. I love this godown of indigo, this pond and these *kuchacha* roads because these are my different forms. In the battlefield when I was very close to death, I used to remember Allah definitely but I used to remember Gangauli instead of Muazzam or Karbala-e-Mualla" (256). When Kali Sherwani opposes Tannoo's comparison of Gangauli with Mecca Sharif, he says again "Yes, I do...Gangauli is my village. Mecca is not my town. This is my home and Qaba of Allah Mian. If the God loves his home then can he not understand that we too can love our village in the same manner" (256).

The intensity with which this village-centrality at the level of voicing arises and the concerns of the village have been expressed in *Adha Gaon* is difficult to see elsewhere. It is the consequence of Reza's full commitment to his land and its soil, and of the fact that as a sensitive soul he himself lived fears and anxieties of the minority community. His love for his land is not amateurish, superficial but so strong that it keeps stimulating and energizing him page after page to express it again and again. When he finds Tannoo's fictional words inadequate, he himself intervenes in between the first and last chapter of the novel, and in the unconventional "*Bhoomika*" (Introduction) re-asserts it as a fact through his authorial authority:

> I am from Ghazipur. My relationship with Ghazipur is unbreakable. That is not a village only, that is my home also. Home! This word is in all dialects and languages of the world and in every dialect and language it is the most beautiful word. So I repeat it again. I am of Gangauli only because that is not a village alone. Because that is my home also. 'Because' how powerful is that word? There are innumerable other 'Becauses' and no sword is powerful enough to cut it apart. And till this 'because' is alive I, Saiyad Masoom Reza Abadi, shall belong only to Ghazipur. My grandfather may have belonged to some other place. And I do not hand over this right to anyone who tells me, "Rahi! You do not belong to Rai Bareilly. So leave Gangauli and go, for example to Rai Bareilly." Why should I go? I would not go at all! (296-97)

In *Adha Gaon* Reza's heart-song, is not only the whole of the village but the whole of India whose agonies have been skinned alive and rendered artistically in true Indian cultural terms. Within these cultural terms stands the temple of his Gangauli, and his home is the sanctum sanctorum of this temple. India, the village, the temple and its sanctum sanctorum are not made of bricks and walls but through a wholehearted subscription to the idea of belonging. Reza has examined this integrating idea from different angles - social, economic, political, religious, emotional and cultural. This idea of his is moulded by the grammar and vocabulary of culture, and whatever it is, it is Indian first. Religion, in its obtaining form and politics act as a divisive force whereas politics integrates and fights against designs of these divisive forces. It is with the cultural rudder that the people of Gangauli, albeit India, withstand the buffets of various crises.

I would court the risk of repetition or understatement by discussing landscape, linguistic and cultural specificities. The novel is so immersed in the last two specificities that Reza had to submit almost 69 notes to explain them. Of all these specificities, the crisis-specificity is of the greatest significance in the novel centralizing the community and village. The novelist has mingled the community and village specificities and their crises so snugly that the community and village specificities is and centrality come in existence simultaneously.

V

On the whole it can be said that *Train to Pakistan* is a village specific and not a village-centred novel, for the feeling and concern for the village, as they are articulated by Reza and Raghuvir Chaudhary in their works, are not voiced by Khushwant Singh. *Uparvas Kathatrayee* is a community-centred and village-specific novel whereas *Adha Gaon* is a community-centred and village-centred work in whose pages Reza poured his soul. However, these feelings, concerns and crises-consciousness are not limited to the concerned village or community only. At one level they transcend their community and village and strain to get integrated with feeling and concern for the region, and country, thereby facilitating, not so frequent, cross-fertilization of concerns and crises-consciousness in tense agonizing tales of villages.

Note: I am indebted to Dr. Kunwar Pal Singh, Reza's "Full" friend, to whom Reza dedicated *Adha Gaon* (Half of a Village) for sharing with me his incisive understanding of the novel, enriched and spurred by his involvement with the conception, gestation and creation of the novel from the closest possible quarters accessible to one other that the creator himself.

Notes

1. I use the term 'creativity' in the sense of its Indian Sanskrit counterpart '*Srajan*' or 'projection' as different from the Western

sense of the term 'creation' accordingly to which something comes out of nothing. '*Srajan*' is projection of that already existed. (Vivekanand, "The Vedant Philosophy" in *The Complete Works of Swami Vivekananda* (Vol. 1. Calcutta: Advait Ashram, 1969), p. 360.

2. Extract from the transcript of Khushwant Singh's talk for Australian Broadcasting Commission *Guest of Honour* programme on 5th April, 1964.

References

Chaudhary, Raghuvir. *Antarvas* in *Uparvas Kathatrayee* (Gujarati, 1976). New Delhi: Sahitya Akademi, 1982.

Kesavan, Mukul. "Interview" given to Kaveri, B. *Indian Express Magazine*, January 29, 1995.

Reza, Rahi Masoom. *Adha Gaon* (Hindi). New Delhi: Rajkamal, 1966.

Singh, Khushwant. *Train to Pakistan* (1956). New Delhi: Times Books International, 1990.

—. "Compulsion to Write", *Three Contemporary Novelists*. Ed. R.K. Dhawan. New Delhi: Classical Publications, 1985.

7

Plebeian Patricians in Premchand's Short Stories

AMEENA KAZI ANSARI

Literature, being a form of representation, is a way of imagining and structuring the world. In doing so, literature makes us aware of the ideological nature of writers' conception of reality. The vast corpus of literary creation down the ages embodies, besides other things, the multi-layered subtleties of the social fabric. Subjectivity dictates difference but the common thread that runs through writings is the explicit/implicit structure of social estates within which the creativity of each writer operates. The two broadest categories of this structure are grounded in, and go back to, the ancient civilization of Rome. That Roman society was quite clearly hierarchical is apparent in its basic contrastive classification of the 'patrician' and the 'plebeian.' The former represented the category/class of the Roman nobles, the aristocratic elite who, together with the Emperor, stood for ruthless power, brutal control and wealthy opulence. The 'plebeian,' on the other hand, represented ancient Rome's commoners, the base, ignoble, madding crowd, powerless in the face of power wielded by the patricians.

Premchand's short stories were written during a literary career that spanned the first three decades of the twentieth century. They are structured in a way that foregrounds the two estates – patricians and plebeians – of rural India. For Premchand, the village was a familiar site. Born and having spent his youth in Lamhi, a remote village or *dehat* in eastern Uttar Pradesh, the writer had his hand on the pulse of rural life. His short stories sensitively convey the subtle intricacies of this *dehat*'s ambience and milieu, its characters and their interactions, their concerns and their conflicts. The caste and class distinctions, economic inequalities, rigid conventions, especially those having to do with women, are all brought to the fore within a framework that underlines attitudes which are typically rural or urban.

I

Premchand's portrayal of this world tends to focus on the 'rural' plebeians, the downtrodden village folk who represent the stark realities of rural poverty, social classification, emotional segregation, and sexual politics. Drawn from the harsh depths of plebeian existence, these men and women in the short stories are bestowed a centrality which makes them 'patricians' in the fictional world of Premchand. In assigning them the role of metaphorical literary patricians, the power of these figures is shown to lie in the very powerlessness that assails their existence.

Indian peasantry often served as a convenient tool for the country's bourgeoisie in their struggle for political independence. This fictional reality only complemented the real one – an India groaning under colonial rule. The political, economic, social, and ideological domination of the British was exacerbated by prevalent prejudices, outdated values and beliefs. Ironically, this very same peasantry was not given much of a chance to cast aside and overcome the back-breaking oppression unleashed on it by the heartless upper echelons of rural society. Most of Premchand's short stories focus on the social predicaments arising out of the latter situation when a peasant struggles to face situations of ruthless exploitation and depravity created by the landowner. Implicated in the landowner/peasant dynamics is a kind of 'two-nation theory' of oppositional forces which, on one hand, mark the power/powerlessness of rural folk, and, on the other, symbolize the urban/rural divide.

The obvious theme that surfaces in Premchand's stories of the village is that "the quest for material gain has bred class distinctions...[and] a blighted reality...[in which] there lingers no afterglow of economic, social, or political hope" (Swan 122). The individual has to hold his/her own ground in trying to negotiate with the rigorous expectations or dictates of the village as a 'persona.' The village thus assumes a spatial-cum-human personality which Premchand's protagonists have to come to terms with. This coming to terms gradually turns into a conflict between values and concepts which cannot be explicitly seen but manifest themselves in various forms. The entire battle increasingly assumes the character of an inner conflict with little or no outward manifestations. Events "assume symbolic significance" and "become a saga of battles fought, won and lost within the confines of the personality of an individual" (Nagendra 104).

The Indian *dehat* is the backdrop against which these stories come alive. Premchand's depiction of this *dehat*, however, is far from idyllic. It is world of conflict, of tension, and of struggle. Premchand's village serves as a complex, unified identity or 'chorus' which has a personality of its own. It is a construct that assumes in each story a specific persona. As a spatial construct, it is a unit of geographical topography. But its more significant manifestation is its identity as a unit of human topography that juxtaposes the plebeians and patricians who exist within its confines. It thus becomes a microcosmic world of human encounter and interaction. As a space, it is imbued with an environment that broods over its inhabitants and binds them to conventions handed down from generation.

Yet, this space has macrocosmic dimensions as it comprises a set of individuals who stand for the continuities and conventions of yore. It is a multifaceted personality with attitudes and behavioural patterns that reflect manifold rural realities, especially the rifts that surface out of social and economic disparities.

In Premchand's short stories, the individual is usually pitted against the collective persona of a village. This persona of the village assumes multiple variants of personality. It could be a collective of individual(s), opinion(s), tradition(s), or even animals who symbolise a kind of diametrical opposition to the individual. The narratives usually unfold, along a set pattern, traditional forbearance of the plebeian, his/her unpleasant encounter with the village's powers-that-be, rebellion, punishment, and then back to fortitude and forbearance.

Premchand is wary of the liberal philosophy of individualism in which individuals pursuing their own good automatically contribute to the good of society at large. This philosophy underlines selfishness, acquisitiveness and self-centredness which become the heart of the matter in the writer's stories. In fact he rails against the restrictions and constraints that society places on individuals and thwarts their freedom. As a Progressive writer, Premchand seems to fall into the categorization of 'major novelists' whose works are significant in "terms of that human awareness [which] they promote; an awareness of the possibilities of life" (Leavis 10). He does so by mixing realism and truth, both of which foreground his didacticism.

Premchand's rural characters usually rise from the quagmire of straitened circumstances created by the persona of the village. They try to break free from the shackles of rigid traditions as well as social, economic and political oppression unleashed upon them by the persona of the village in the guise of landlords, moneylenders and upper castes. "Happiness" seems to lie in less in violent rebellion and more in "self-denial...which serves as an essential ingredient of fulfilment" (Nagendra 97). While the village persona conforms to the image of the oppressor, the rural characters "manifest not only the common traits of their class or social group but their own individualistic, almost private personalities which have distinct traits – a living, throbbing existence of their own" (Nagendra 101).

II

Under discussion are four of Premchand's short stories of the village. The village environment binds them all together yet each represents a different facet of village life and people. A different persona of the village presides over each of them. In the first story, this persona comprises the Brahmin and untouchable who come together to mete out raw justice to rival villagers. The omnipotence of faith in the environs and hearts of rustics shapes the village persona in the second story. The subsequent story revolves round a callous village which wreaks revenge on the victimizer only after the victim – a Brahmin widow – has lost her life. In the last story, it is through the tale of two bullocks that Premchand provides an insight into the innate cruelty that assails the human world of the village. These stories are representative because they portray four of the most outstanding realities of rural India – poverty, casteism, sexual politics, and cruelty to animals.

Mukti Marg ("The Road to Salvation") is the story of the daydreamer-turned-realist. When Jhingur, the peasant, saw his cane fields flourishing, his imagination painted a glorious picture of the future when he would sell his crop and aging bullocks, buy more land, and repeat the success that loomed large before his eyes. His pride in this vision had made him arrogant and quarrelsome, with the result that there was hardly a soul he had not quarrelled with in his village. His reverie was broken when he found Buddhu shepherding his flock into the very field that was going to make Jhingur a very rich man in the future. When remonstrations did not work, Jhingur took up his cudgel and hit out wildly at as many of the flock as he could lay his hands on. Buddhu remained a silent spectator but it was an eloquent silence. By the time Jhingur had the sensitivity to analyse it, it was too late. A fire, obviously set alight by Buddhu, raged in his fields, reducing all his dreams to ashes. By the time he came to terms with his own tragedy, a far bigger one unfolded – the fields of the entire village were destroyed in the blaze. In antagonizing Buddhu, Jhingur had antagonized the entire village populace which cursed him for their ruination.

As Buddhu's fortunes soared, Jhingur sought a way out of the situation by planning his own vendetta. He conspired with Harihar, the untouchable tanner. Jhingur was to convince Buddhu to allow the former's calf to graze with the latter's flock. In the midst of an elaborate feast that Buddhu had organized for the Brahmins who came to his housewarming, news came that Jhingur's calf lay dead. The feast for the upper castes was turned into a court which decided that Buddhu had committed a fiendish act by tying up a sacred cow. He was charged with murder – "Killing a cow is no less than killing a Brahmin" – and given a severe punishment – three months of begging, pilgrimage to seven holy places, feeding five hundred Brahmins and paying the cost of five cows. This punishment reduced the once prosperous Buddhu to a penury so severe that he and Jhingur ran into each other at a construction site. Both were now workers living a hand-to-mouth existence. In the drudgery of life, each confessed to being instrumental in the other's change of fortunes.

Jhingur's and Buddhu's pride came before their fall. All the fruits of their labours wilted away when they chose to rise from their plebeian roots to a prosperity they could not handle. In their one-upmanship against the other lay both ambition and rebellion. In seeking to outdo each other, they allowed their ambitions to soar to a point where they symbolically rebelled against their accorded places within society. In this vacuum created between their ambitions and their reality stepped in the persona of the village – in the guise of the tanner and the

Brahmins. In a strange intervention, the lower caste/outcaste and the upper caste came together to hasten the doom of two protagonists who till that point of time were outside the pale of the rigidities of caste/category. Economics eventually drove them to a bare survival in an urban world. Even their best efforts could make no dent in the persona of the village ranged against them. Centuries of demarcation between caste and community could not be wiped out. Their fate was also circumscribed within their very names – Jhingur, the insignificant cricket, and Buddhu, the stupid one.

Babaji ka Bhog ("A Feast for the Holy Man") is the story of the cost that Ramdhan, the poor farmer, has to pay in order to satisfy the hunger of a *sadhu* who wandered into his humble dwelling. It was a particularly tight situation that Ramdhan was in when the holy man appeared at his doorway – half the farmer's crop had been claimed by the moneylender, the other half by the landowner, and the remaining chaff had been sold to get the ox-trader off his back. Not a morsel remained in the house when the *sadhu* put in an appearance. Despite all his wife's protestations, Ramdhan made the woman hand over the measly amount of flour that she had kept aside for offering to the gods. The *sadhu* then let it be known that a little *dal* would be necessary to make the offering complete. Ramdhan's insistence got the wife to hand over some *dal* along with some salt and cowdung cakes to ensure that the *sadhu* would have at least the semblance of a decent meal. The *sadhu* then wheedled Ramdhan into providing a smatter of ghee to complete the ritual offering to a holy man. Ramdhan was despatched to the *banya* to procure this item as his wife argued that it was pointless to arouse the anger of a holy man just for a little ghee when they had already given away whatever little they had to eat. Ringing his bell and taking out a single handful as offering to the Lord, the *sadhu* enjoyed his meal, lay down on the threshold and went to sleep. The hungry Ramdhan and his wife warmed some watery leftover *dal* and drank it; there was nothing that remained to be cooked. As Ramdhan drifted off to sleep his only thought was that the *sadhu* was a far better man than himself.

In this story, the *sadhu* embodies the faith round which health and wealth of the rustics revolves. In the eyes of rustics across the board of caste and community, the *sadhu* symbolizes the spiritual. Ramdhan's capitulations to the *sadhu* stand for the sacrifices that are expected of mere mortals for keeping happy and contented a man who is close to the gods and can intercede on their behalf. The *sadhu*, thus, assumes another facet of the village persona. This time it is that of an emblem of faith, ritual and righteousness within the framework of which the helpless protagonist has to operate. Despite overwhelming poverty, debt and hunger, Ramdhan had no qualms about borrowing from the *banya*. After all, the silver lining to his otherwise cloudy existence was the realization that the *sadhu*, symbolizing divinity, could bring to Ramdhan the prosperity that had evaded him till then. This realization is the blind faith of the villager who is willing to suffer extreme privation in order to appease and keep the gods happy. Together with the money-lender and the ox-trader, the *sadhu* symbolizes the power structure that binds an Indian village. The story highlights the powerful spiritual facet of the village persona. As the plot unfolds, this becomes especially apparent – Ramdhan's responses to the wandering *sadhu* undergo subtle variations. His consciousness initially perceives the *sadhu* as a wandering holy man, then a *sadhu*, subsequently he is perceived as *babaji*, and finally is looked upon as a god who has condescended to visit Ramdhan. In this imaginative transition, a mere mortal becomes a god in the eyes of a simple rustic who is too humbled to bother about the callousness of a holy man.

Gharib ki Hai ('The Power of A Curse') tells the tale of Munshi Ramsevak's fall from grace in the eyes of Chandpur's inhabitants. In keeping with the family tradition, the Munshi was seen every day sitting within the precincts of the open-air small pleas court, his satchel crammed with papers. Though no one had ever seen him preparing a brief or arguing a case, he was renowned amongst the village populace for possessing the eloquence of Saraswati, the goddess of knowledge. Law gave the Munshi no income yet he was a rich man whose wealth accrued from the money that people gave to him for safekeeping. These were usually widows and rich old men who did not trust anyone with their wealth and handed it to over to the Munshi. Once Munshiji took charge of it he became tight-fisted. It was then extremely difficult, if not impossible, to get the money out of him. When the need arose, he would wriggle his way out by proclaiming himself a borrower and promising to pay by the evening which never came by. There were frequent wrangles and ugly scenes as owners came to claim their wealth but so formidable was Munshi Ramsevak's reputation for respectability that they usually went back empty-handed.

Munshiji met his match, however, in Moonga, a Brahmin widow of the village. She had entrusted to Munshiji the five hundred rupee compensation that the British sent her for her husband's services in the Burma war. For many years she had been eking out a living by begging back tiny sums from him. When several years had gone by and Moonga showed no signs of dying, Munshiji decided to declare that her principal was exhausted and he owed her nothing. For the poor woman, it was a shock and she accused him of having made off with half the amount that she had deposited for his safekeeping. The matter was taken to the panchayat but Munshi Ramsevak's eloquence won the day – not one councillor questioned the Munshi's integrity and Moonga lost her case. The loss haunted her to such an extent that she turned insane – a red-eyed, dishevelled, grimacing, screeching, emaciated creature from whom people slunk away. A mentally deranged Moonga finally became a squatter at Munshiji's doorstep. Cursing and screeching, she gave up eating and lay down at his threshold. One morning she was found dead, flies buzzing round her mouth. And it was her death that caused consternation in the village – it was the conscious murder of a Brahmin. In death, Moonga had extracted her revenge. Severe punishment and immeasurable disgrace awaited the man who had once been the icon of respectability in Chandpur. Munshiji and his family faced social boycott – the water-carrier, the washerman, the barber – all avoided him. Moonga's image haunted the Munshi and his family so much that they lived in terror of her reappearance. His pregnant wife, Nagin, died a delirious wreck and no one came to bear her corpse away. Munshiji had to cart it away for the last rites and the only other mourner was his son. Ostracized by the village, Munshiji became a *sadhu* and was consumed by flames when his hut caught fire. Not a hand went to rescue him. His son, Ramgulam, was caught stealing and the last that was heard of him was his incarceration at a reformatory.

The persona of Chandpur in this story evolves rather than remaining rigid and static. Its very evolution, ironically, is based on the centuries-old maxim that a Brahmin – no matter how wealthy or poor, powerful or weak, man or woman – has to be accorded his/her proper due in death. The village as whole, symbolized by the panchayat, had initially gone along with the humiliation and trifling that Munshiji meted out to the helpless Moonga. In the eyes of the village, the touchstone was respectability, even if that respectability was rooted in shameless guile. The word of a man held greater power, and his respectability was given precedence over the deceit and humiliation that he poured over a helpless woman. In life, Moonga was an object of the village's derision and scorn; it was only in death that the perception of the village underwent a drastic change, and this, too, was dictated by the fear of the circumstances in which she passed away. That a Brahmin should pass away in her wretched situation was enough to instil in the village a fear of the divine wrath that could descend upon them. It was to safeguard themselves from such retribution that they chose to cast aside Munshiji's influence and extract their own retribution. It took a Brahmin widow's tragic death to make the village change its views and transform Munshiji from victor to victim.

Premchand's *Do Bailon ki Kahani* ("The Story of the Two Bullocks") has the undertones of Swift's "Voyage to Hounhymns" as it inverts the village world of humans and presents them through the eyes of two bullocks – Hira and Moti. When their owner, Jhuri, sends them to his father-in-law's, Gaya, his brother-in-law, has a tough time herding them home. Hira and Moti only wish they could speak the human tongue to ask Jhuri why they were being sent away after they had served him so well. On the very first night in their new alien environment they decided to break tether and were found the next day by Jhuri standing at his trough. He embraced them and their return became the talk of the village. Jhuri's enraged wife perceived their return as defiance towards her parental home and had only dry straw given to them for eating. The next day Gaya turned up again, hitched them to a wagon, and drove them home. As punishment, they were offered dry straw while the other bullocks were given oilseed cake and ground lentils. Jhuri had never touched them even with a flower stem; at his in-laws place, however, they were severely beaten. When they were yoked to the plough, Hira and Moti decided not to budge a step despite Gaya's sharp blows. After a particularly nasty blow that Hira received, Moti's silent obduracy gave way and he took to his heels, smashing plough, yoke and harness. Moti felt like killing Gaya but it was Hira's gentle admonitions that stopped him in his tracks. Hard work, frequent beatings and dry straw became their staple diet of existence. The only affection anyone showed was Bhairon's daughter who herself was victimized by her stepmother. She would regularly smuggle out pieces of bread to feed them and, one night, she untied their ropes, giving them a chance to flee. They escaped even though Gaya gave them a long chase. Weakness and hunger made them dizzy but as luck would have it, they found themselves in a pea field and gorged with abandon. Just as they were settling down after the hearty meal, a threatening bull came into view. As master strategists, they were able to overcome the attacker who fled in the face of their onslaught. When they entered the pea-field again to appease their hunger, they were caught by the owner who had them confined in the village pound. There they were horrified to find many downtrodden animals like themselves. Each one seemed to have lost the will to live and seemed resigned to a fate worse than death. Hira and Moti again rallied their spirits and strength to bring down the wall of the pound and free their brethren. While the mares and the goats and the buffaloes galloped out to freedom, the two bullocks had to use their horns to push out the donkeys who were too indifferent to this opportunity for escape. While everyone else escaped, Hira and Moti chose to sleep within the pound. There was terrific commotion the next day in the human world when the clerk, watchman, and other officials saw what had transpired. The bullocks got a fierce drubbing and were securely tied up. One day an inspection was carried out and everyone went away, refusing to buy bullocks which looked like corpses. Then came a cruel-looking butcher who bid for them and bought them. As he herded them along, Hira and Moti felt that they were in familiar territory – this was the road to Jhuri's village. In a last ditch effort to get away from the butcher's knife they made a run for it. Jhuri was stunned to see them and find the bearded butcher claiming them. This time he stuck to his guns in claiming ownership. Hira and Moti threateningly lowered their horns when the butcher persisted and succeeded in driving him away. Excitement gripped the village on their return. Oilseed, bran, hay and grain were offered to them and Jhuri's wife came out to kiss them on their foreheads.

The animal world in this story is created as a satirical reflection of the human one. The bullocks are animals but are perceived as having been men in their previous incarnation. This perception of a village boy is transmuted to a reality that mirrors the repressive social hierarchy of the human world. The village pound assumes the persona of village society with its clearly demarcated caste/category distinctions. The order in which the animals flee the pound after Moti brings down the wall underlines this. The escaping horses, buffaloes, and goats symbolize the upper castes; the fatalistic donkeys, representing the downtrodden lower castes/untouchables, have to be pushed into gaining their freedom. Hira and Moti believe that they represent the dharma of their community and are, therefore, bestowed with an enlightened consciousness that rightfully places a premium on freedom and equality. In the rigid human world of caste hierarchy, the bullocks evoke a spirit of activism to break from the repression and control of humans. In this particular instance, Premchand portrays a society divided against itself, where exploitation and injustice are an accepted way of life.

Premchand's is an art of sympathy born out of his sensitivity to man's inhumanity to man. Most of his short stories centre round the individual who endeavours to struggle and break out from the social mechanism that binds a village hierarchy. It is the persona of individual that takes on the collective might of the village persona and the writer seeks an objectivity to appropriately convey the subjective states that form the framework of each story. In his 1936 Presidential speech given at the Progressive Writers' Conference in Lucknow, Premchand spoke on *Sahitya ka Uddeshya*, the objectives of literature. He called for a change in the "standard of beauty" which had hitherto seen the artist "fixing his gaze on the women's inner quarters and on palaces and bungalows." Bemoaning the fact that "Mud huts and ruins were not worthy of his [artist's] attention" and "he considered them beyond the pale of humanity," Premchand had made sure that his own writings carried a strong aroma of the rural world of the rustic (Oxford India Premchand, Appendix). In this scheme of things, society became literature's courtroom in which social realities were presented with perception and sensitivity. It was this propensity that makes him an "idealistic realist" (Swan 49). He depends on reality but defamiliarises it by shaping it into an independent fictional existence.

His narrative begins with ripples of disturbance in an apparently placid rural world in which discontent simmers just below the surface. While the individual symbolizes the disturbance, the populace of the village symbolizes an apparently placid world. The latter's equilibrium is shattered when the individual seeks to break free from the rigours of caste and custom. The climax comes with the creation of new equilibriums which destroy and take the place of the old ones. This pattern is reflective of the social and political change that was manifesting itself in the first quarter of the twentieth century. It arose out of the dissatisfaction with the feudal, hierarchical, caste-conscious, deferential society of the past, and the emergence of a more egalitarian outlook inspired by the spirit of national dignity and individual self-respect that marked the country's freedom struggle. Premchand is the rural insider who does not have the "distanced objectivity of the urban outsider" (Orsini ix). He presents his fictional plebeians in a manner that makes them the story's patricians. Though he exhibits a strong social conscience inclined towards socialism and embodies an inclusive view of the Indian nation, he also foreground "a fragmented society which has a long way to go before it can become a nation" (Sharma 133). The persona of the *dehat* in his fiction takes on a much larger dimension. It comes to symbolize the realities of nation which still has to come to terms with poverty, casteism, and the denigration of women.

References

Leavis, F.R. *The Great Tradition*. London: Penguin, 1962.

Nagendra. *Premchand: An Anthology*. Delhi: Bansal & Co, 1981.

Orsini, Francesca. 'Introduction,' *The Oxford India Premchand*. 2004.

Sharma, G.N. *Premchand: Novelist and Thinker*. Delhi: Pragati Publications, 1999.

Swan, Robert O. *Munshi Premchand of Lamhi Village*. Durham: Duke University Press, 1969.

8

Ritual as a Defining Point

Saratchandra Chatterjee's *Palli Samaj* and *"Abhagi ka Swarg"*

BANDANA CHAKRABARTY

> We human beings in all our practices, engage in rituals everywhere, in all parts of the globe and in all types of society. Some rituals are construed as an attribute of culture, collective action in common spaces. Other rituals seem to be personal inventions, carried out in private settings.
>
> (Meyer and Smith 1994)

Recognized by historians of modern Indian culture as one of the most significant personalities in twentieth century literature Saratchandra Chatterjee (1876-1938) brought Bengali literature to the masses. His novels appealed to people of all walks of life. When his novels are being repeatedly translated into all other Indian languages one can judge the continued fame and popularity of Saratchandra which are unparalleled on the Indian literary history.

Ranked as 'Novelist of the Century' by an online poll conducted by an Internet literary journal *Meghdutam*, Saratchandra wrote classics like *Srikanta, Charitraheen, Datta, Grihadaha, Palli Samaj* and *Pather Dabi* in the decade between 1916-1926. Inspired by his writings Vishnu Prabhakar, himself a great name in Hindi literature, wrote the biography of Saratchandra titled *Awara Masiha* (1998). It is a literary masterpiece which sheds new light on the life of Saratchandra Chatterjee. In the preface to his book Prabhakar writes, "There is no doubt that Sarat wrote great literature but his life, too, was nonetheless great" (9, trans. mine). It was his encounters with life as a country youth that provided him with the inspiration, material and the storylines for his life-like characters. No Bengali novelist has received the same kind of love and affection that Saratchandra so naturally commands.

This paper attempts to explore the significance of rituals with reference to religious law or social custom in Saratchandra's *Palli Samaj*[1] and *"Abhagi ka Swarg"*. The centre of the narrative structure in both the novel and short story is the ritual. *Palli Samaj* is the story of a caste-ridden village dominated by superstitious social conventions and rituals and Ramesh's attempts to bring about changes in that society. "*Abhagi ka Swarg*" also depicts a rigid social structure in which ritual does not bind but rather disrupts an individual's social life leading the protagonist to identify attainment of salvation with ritualistic practices of the Brahmins. A village is not just a physical space or a settlement of a group of people. As Vandana Madan in her introduction in *The Village in India* says, "Social life in a village is organized along definite ritual and secular principles such as those of caste, kinship, economy, politics and religion" (13).

The performance of rituals is an integral part of religion and the personality of the village is to be seen in its rituals. Rituals are stylized and usually repetitive acts that take place at a set time and location. They involve the use of symbolic objects, words and actions. Irrespective of who we are or where we live, rituals form a basic part of our lives. We see rituals being performed and we also participate in them. Rituals are physical actions which are performed because they help us achieve what we need in order to proceed to the next step in our daily lives. They are repetitive and ceremonious and often work within prescribed codes and patterns. Meant to inculcate feelings of devotion, they are aimed at bringing about divine orientation of human life. Ritual is often the most 'visible manifestation' and ritual practices are not static of religion and ritual is not static (Salamone 2004). They have varied enormously over the course of human history and across cultures and are instrumental in defining kinships, communities and religions.

Palli Samaj (1916) depicts the story of a village commune near Tarakeshwar in the Hooghly district in West Bengal. The time is apparently towards the end of the nineteenth century when village life was dominated by superstitious social conventions and caste prejudices and social power was wielded by the richer section of the society namely, the landowners, money-lenders and the Brahmins as well. The rigid social structure in the village had reduced the existence of the low-born and the poor to an almost subhuman level, pushing them to the periphery in all progressive movements and keeping them out of employment.

The opening event of the novel is a death and it brings in its wake many quarrels and questions that have no answers. The book opens with Ramesh, a young Roorkee-trained engineer who returns to his village to perform the last rites of his father, Tarini Ghoshal. When a person is dead, the rituals performed must effect transitions at three levels of meaning and experience. The dead body (corpse), the soul of the deceased and the community at large all have their status thrown into question by death. These categories come into social interplay through rituals. Death may be an end for an individual but the living, the kith and kin, the community continue as a group. The death ritual does not end with the elimination of the body. Relatives have yet to see to the safety of the soul. An eleven-day ritual called *shraddha* is performed to ensure the passage of the soul during its journey to the other world.

In the novel brahminhood is brought out by rituals performed according to prescribed rites. According to *Manu*

Smriti the Brahmins have emerged from the mouth of the god Brahma. They have a right to the performance and use of sixteen sacraments or rituals. Of these sixteen, *Svargarohana* or funeral ceremonies or obsequies to forward the entrance of the spirit into *svarga* or heaven is the last and final ritual. This ceremony involves status, expenditure and has the element of a feast, specially if the deceased is from a well-to-do family and past the prime of life. The very private is made public, the religious is made social. How the dead body is disposed, who follows, who mourns, how richly the brahmins are fed, all these define the salvation and the status of the dead and the devotion of the family.

In Tarini Ghoshal's *shraddha* all the villagers are invited for lunch after the ceremony is over. In fact this is part of the ceremony and Ramesh has made elaborate arrangements for it. In Kuanpur nobody else had arranged things on such a grand scale before. "Confectioners had been brought from Calcutta" (11). Ramesh says, "I have no enmity with anyone. So I feel Aunty that I should invite the entire Brahmins and the Sudras without any discrimination without taking note of the factional disputes" (29). But Aunt[2] Bishweshwari tells him, "But it's not a simple question... One whom the society shuns, mustn't be invited that way ... In a village the most difficult job is to decide who's to be invited and who's to be left out!" (29). Rigidity in the enforcement of caste rules was highest among brahmins.

Everyone uses the choicest words to flatter Ramesh but soon this funeral ceremony becomes the arena of rivalry and animosity amongst the villagers. Amongst the invitees is a widow, Sukumari, and her mother. Their presence spoils everything for the brahmins and the brahmins threaten not to partake of even a drop of water in that house and "One by one a number of persons placed their wraps on their shoulders and stood up" (34). Saratchandra observes that they knew very well which move would be the most advantageous in a situation like this. The entry of widows would pollute the sacrosanct precincts of a brahmin household. A widow tends to be a highly marginalized person in a village and receives very little support from anyone.

The object of *antyeshti* or the post funeral rites which are carried out for twelve days after the death is to soothe and give peace to the troubled spirit but the funeral ceremony, in the novel, ends in a fiasco. Sheer wastefulness is part of this final ritual, that is, the funeral ceremony. Bhairab tells Ramesh, "Big ceremonies often witness fights and also bloodshed. But after some time everything settles down." Distributing pieces of cloth is part of this ceremony but here too the difference between the high caste and low caste is made evident. Govinda Ganguly, a brahmin leader of the village says, "Distributing clothes to these low-caste fellows is as good as pouring ghee on burnt-out fire. A pair of *dhotis* to each adult Brahmin and a piece to each Brahmin child would have brought him more fame" (15).

Durkheim, the eminent philosopher, was of the opinion that rituals enhance social cohesion because they convey the collective values of society to the ritual participant. In *Palli Samaj* rituals instead of being cohesive are actually disruptive. They fragment the village community into upper caste and lower caste, the Hindus and Muslims and the married and the widowed. This happens because instead of helping the bereaved to come to terms with their grief, the rituals become a basis for the display of wealth and social discrimination, thus subverting the role of a ritualistic performance.

Food which is an inextricable part of life is even more so in Bengali culture. Usually the eldest woman of the house keeps control over the storehouse or *bhandar*. But during this *shraddha* there is a lot of wastefulness. Though Bishweshwari Devi belongs to another family and is Ramesh's aunt she cannot witness the wasteful expenditure. She takes over control of the storehouse and sees to its management. When the dispute over the entry of the widow, Sukumari, and her mother took place in Ramesh's house someone from the crowd spoke, "Where else will you get sixteen pieces of *luchi* and four pairs of *sandesh* to take home? That too after a sumptuous feast?" (36). Partaking of food is an essential ritual whether it is the birth ceremony, the *annaprashan* or feeding the first rice ceremony, the *upanayan* ceremony or the death ceremony. When the ceremony of feeding the first rice to Bhairab's grandson was taking place Ramesh was surprised to see that Bhairab had invited everyone in the village except him. It was clear to him that he had been ostracized by the village community. Just as Sukumari and her mother were not welcome in a brahmin household similarly Ramesh, being ostracized by society, is not welcome in Bhairab's house. Social and economic inequalities on a group basis are defining characteristics of the Indian village. As Madan observes, "Caste divisions are regarded as divinely ordained and are hierarchically graded" (353). Adherence to traditional forms is considered not only desirable but also necessary in the village. It is an exaggeration that the village is a utopia of perfect integration.

Other rituals performed by brahmins are alluded to throughout the book. When Ramesh and his childhood friend Rama, a widow, meet at Tarkeshwar temple Rama invites him for a meal. Sitting down for the meal Rama objects to his not sipping water before starting the meal. Ritual sipping originally *gandush* in Bengali is one in which brahmins are required to take a sip of water after chanting some sacred chants before any major meal. When they meet at the temple Rama enters the temple but Ramesh does not offer prayers. As a widow in the orthodox Hindu society, Rama could not marry Ramesh as there was no place for such a union in the Hindu society of the day. Consequently "the lives of these two noble souls became infructuous" (Mukherjee xiii). When Ramesh wishes Rama a long life she reminds him, "You ought to know that wishing me a long life is as good as cursing me. Among the Hindus no relative ever prays for the long life of a widow" (74). Saratchandra had to bear bitter and hostile criticism from the conservative section of society of the day. He was vehemently attacked for depicting extra-marital love but Saratchandra had the courage and conviction to portray in literature a woman's steadfast and unwavering love. He said, "I do not belittle the value of chastity, but consider that it is a superstition to make a fetish out of it and treat it as the be-all and end-all of a woman's life" (qtd. by Mukherjee xii).

Madan is of the view, "Often rituals or secular events would require transgression of boundaries, for instance, service of all castes are required at the time of the worship of the village deity. Fairs, festivals and other similar celebratory ritual also widen the ritual space of a village" (14). In the novel the celebration of Durga Puja every year on a grand scale in Rama's house is another ritual activity in which not only the Hindus but also the Muslim tenants of Pirpur came in large numbers to partake of the consecrated food that is the *prasad* (121) but after Ramesh is sent to jail and Durga Puja celebrations are on in Rama's house, after the first day's worship is over the vast courtyard of the Mukherji house was nearly deserted. All those who loved and respected Ramesh had boycotted the Puja. The strangest thing was that the Hindus and Muslims had joined hands. Social and ritual events play an important part in the life of a community.

When Ramesh saw the difference in the conditions prevailing in the Hindu and Muslim villages his distaste for the caste system increased. He devoted himself completely to the opening of a new school at Pirpur for the Muslim boys and regained his peace of mind. Education and progress were viewed with suspicion. Education becomes an oppositional process and this conflict is the cause of dislocation of Ramesh's authority in the village.

A crucial event in the life of the orthodox upper caste Hindu male is an initiation *(upanayan)* ceremony which takes place for some young boys between the age of six and twelve to mark the transition to awareness and adult religious responsibilities. This ritual is seen as a new birth – a rite through which a child is initiated into the vows of the guru. The three strands of thread are symbolic. The upanayan marks the dawn of a new era in the life of the initiate. Sarat's novel portrays the manner in which social and religious rituals become oppressively demanding and go on to create barriers and divisions instead of bringing people together in a gesture of solidarity. This happens when Jatin's (Rama's brother) sacred thread ceremony is to be performed. When a brahmin boy attains a certain prescribed age he has to undergo a religious ceremony for his initiation into brahminhood. He is invested with a sacred thread which is the symbol of his brahminhood. As Rama has been excommunicated by the village elders, no one comes to attend the ceremony and Jatin's ceremony is boycotted.

Palli Samaj begins with an arrival and ends with a departure. It is the arrival of Ramesh to Kuanpur and the novel ends with the departure of Rama and Bishweshwari Devi. Both of them embark upon a pilgrimage to Benaras. It was believed that there is one other way to achieve liberation – that is, to die within the city of Benaras on the Ganges. Death elsewhere feared becomes a rare spiritual goal in Benaras and death is welcome there. At the end of novel Rama, who is critically ill, leaves for Benaras with Bishweshwari Devi to attain salvation. Between the arrival and departure is encompassed a whole world of rural life and its rituals. Pilgrim centres were also a place of refuge for the rejected members of society. Rama's departure is an escape from facing the consequences of her emotional attachment to Ramesh as well as a break in the all controlling circumference of the village.

Before Ramesh returned to Kuanpur he had an idyllic view of Bengali villages believing that "the real wealth of the Bengalis was to be found intact in the sympathetic hearts of the villagers as a whole"(66) but when he actually saw the disputes and jealousies he was shocked. He felt, "Where's that living religion in our old sequestered village ...The unfortunate members of the village community are clinging with all their might to this disfigured and discoloured corpse as the thing itself" (67).

Chhoto Babu, that is, Ramesh has changed everything for the poor villagers at the end of the novel. They are no longer in awe of the brahmins like Beni Ghoshal and Govinda Ganguly. The villain, Sanatan Hajra tells Beni, "No one becomes a Brahmin simply because he has a few threads hanging down his shoulders" (127) and also "No fisherman will henceforth come to a Brahmin's house for a meal" (126). Rituals like the husk of a seed preserve the life of religion and make it germinate. It is only when the rituals are separated from the faith and assume an independent existence that they become mechanical and lifeless. Change is dynamic. Ritual, if used with discretion, can be the process to unshackle your life from superstitions.

Sarat's short story "*Abhagi Ka Swarg*" also begins with a death – the death of the wife of Thakurdas Mukherjee, a Brahmin. The cremation journey of his deceased wife is witnessed by the whole village. The writer of the story comments that it appeared like a celebration. It appeared "as if the lady of a rich family was going to her husband's house after about fifty years"[3] (6). The death of a rich Brahmin's wife becomes a spectacle to be devoured by all the villagers. Kangali's mother is a silent observer of the last rites of this rich brahmin lady. She watches the ceremony from a distance because she was an outcaste and a poor woman. Doubly marginalized the poor woman, as she sees the smoke rising upward, tells her son, Kangali, "See, son, the Brahmin mother is riding the chariot to heaven" (7). She has a deep yearning to be cremated in the same manner. She tells her son, "If you light my funeral pyre, son, I, too, shall go to heaven like the brahmin mother" (11).

Kangali's mother obsessed by this dream of salvation takes to her bed, fades away and dies. The son, in turn, is now loaded with his mother's dying wish. He traces his missing father, the father who had discarded them long ago. He also makes desperate attempts to gather wood for the funeral. With this in mind Rasik, the husband, begins to cut down a tree to provide wood for the dead body but is forbidden to do so.

Kangali runs from pillar to post to arrange wood for his dead mother's cremation but he is showered with only abuses and humiliation at the hands of the upper-caste brahmins and the Zamindar. The eldest son of the Mukherjee family says, "See Bhattacharya Mahashaya, these boys want to become Brahmin-Kayasthas" (17).

An untouchable is so called because if he comes into contact with persons of the upper caste he pollutes them, and some form of ritual cleansing is essential before the polluted person is fit again to perform his normal acts. When Kangali goes from house to house and person to person in order to receive justice, with the dead body of his mother still lying in the house the Zamindar growls at him, "If mother is dead, go and stand downstairs. Who's there, throw a little cow-dung and water here. What caste are you?" (13). At the end of the story Kangali gives up all hope of giving his mother a decent cremation. He simply digs up the earth near the river and lays down his mother. Kangali's mother's wish is partially fulfilled. The son touches the mother's mouth with a burnt stick of grain and immediately removes it. Gradually Kangali and the villagers cover the body with dust as it is done in the case of the low-born and untouchables. As the smoke emanates from the cowdung smouldering in the shallow grave Kangali, in his turn, imagines his mother's soul rising to the heavens.

The corpse becomes a metaphor in both the stories. The corpse keeps lying unattended in *Palli Samaj* when Dwarik Chakraborty dies and nobody comes forward to touch the corpse because "the prescribed expiatory rites weren't performed before his death" (68). For want of money the corpse keeps lying untouched in *Palli Samaj* as well as in "*Abhagi ka Swarg.*" In the short story Kangali cannot fulfil his mother's last wishes because of extreme poverty. In *Palli Samaj* the funeral ceremony of the rich Brahmin, Tarini Ghoshal, is performed with great fanfare, similarly Thakurdas Mukherjee's wife's funeral ceremony is not an event of mourning but it is an act of celebration "as if a festivity was going on" (5). Even the dead body of a Brahmin enjoys prominence whereas the dead body of a poor or lower caste person is always subjected to insult and humiliation.

In both the novel and the short story it is rituals which play the most dominant role in differentiating between the brahmins and the lower castes. The caste system was the chief impediment to change and growth in rural India. In fact ritual behaviour has not undergone much change. Looking at the social and ritual distinction between the castes, one can understand that there is hardly any change in the relationships between those at the top and those at the bottom. To Saratchandra goes the credit of awakening our social conscience from the slumber and lethargy of centuries by his deeply sympathetic portrayal of the unmerited sufferings of the victims of social justice. He was writing at a time when the nationalist movement was gaining momentum together with an awakening of social consciousness. He found the novel an appropriate medium for depicting the turbulence in society and it became a powerful weapon of social, political and religious reform. Saratchandra Chatterjee criticized and gave a healing touch to the malignant sores which were vitiating the social fabric and gnawing at its vitals. Not only does he critique ritualistic acts, he goes a step further by using these very rituals as a narrative force which become the site of the contestation between tradition and change, and also a way of holding the various strands together in a cohesive structure.

Notes

1. Prasenjit Mukherjee in his translation of *Palli Samaj* has chosen the title *The Homecoming*.
2. Mukherjee in his translation has used 'aunt' for Bishweshwari Devi. She is the 'Jyathima' or father's elder brother's wife. The word 'aunt' for '*Jyathima*' falsifies the kinship pattern.

3. The English translations of the quotations from "*Abhagi ka Swarg*" have been done by me from the Hindi version of the story.

References

Chatterjee, Saratchandra. "*Abhagi Ka Swarg*" (Hindi). New Delhi: Satsahitya Prakashan, 2002.

—. *Palli Samaj* (1916). Trans. Prasenjit Mukherjee as *The Homecoming*. New Delhi: Rupa, 1989.

Durkheim, Emile. *The Elementary Forms of Religious Life*. New York: The Free Press, 1954.

Knowles, Ralph L. "*Rituals of Place.*" University of S. California, 1999.

Madan, Vandana. *The Village in India*. Delhi: Oxford University Press, 2002.

Meyer, Marvin and Richard Smith. eds. *Ancient Christian Magic: Coptic Texts of Ritual Power*. New York: Harper Collins, 1999.

Prabhakar, Vishnu. *Awara Masiha* (Hindi). Delhi: Rajpal & Sons, 1998.

Salamone, Frank. ed. "Introduction" *Encyclopedia of Religious Rites, Rituals and Festivals*. London: Routledge, 2004.

Srinivas, M.N. *India's Villages*. Bombay: Media Promoters and Publishers Pvt. Ltd., 1955.

9

"[Wo] man is Not Made for Defeat"

Vignettes from Village Narratives

USHA BANDE

> Home has to have a touch of the pastoral, even when poisoned village has caused the homelessness. Home is 'natural' womanly nurture in a rediscovered village.
>
> Ashis Nandy

A narrative of the village is incomplete without its peasant community and the farming community is incomplete without its womenfolk. In literature, farmer woman often stands as a symbol of strength, conducting herself with dignity despite the various handicaps of her situation - illiteracy, poverty, gendered identity and the stranglehold of dead customs and traditions. Unaware of the concepts like women's liberation or feminism, impervious to externally induced changes in urban India, she subtly de-emphasizes the connotations of femininity without breaking away from its cultural definition, and in redefining her identity, she shows what Ashis Nandy terms the "commonplace paradox" of "social interpretation of the Indian woman" (Nandy 1980: 43). Discussing woman and womanliness in the Indian political culture, Nandy opines that since in the Indian society norms for traditionally undefined social situations come from mythology and folklore, integration of feminine identity with masculine norms is acceptable and as such when some of the male qualities like aggression, power and activism are associated with women, they are neither questioned nor thought of as aberrations. That does not, however, indicate that the peasant women have successfully transcended the mechanism of patriarchal control, winning the battle that their sisters are still fighting, but it does signify that in some situations, peasant women have shown remarkable ability to turn their powerlessness and invisibility into resoluteness and positions of control. That during crisis the peasant women have responded with great enthusiasm is corroborated by sociological studies of peasant struggles. In their paper "That Magic Time," Vasantha Kannabiran and K. Lalitha show how women "achieved major gains" during periods of social dysfunction.[1]

The aim of this paper is to study Mulk Raj Anand's Gauri (*The Old Woman and the Cow*, 1960)[2], Kamala Markandaya's Rukmani (*Nectar in a Sieve*, 1954), and Yogini Joglekar's Rakhma in her Marathi short story 'Pazar' (Pazar, 1976), to see how during times of trouble, these peasant women, docile and meek otherwise, show superhuman courage, will-power and presence of mind. It may be clarified here that the problems depicted in these fictional renderings are not of social or national dimensions, they are just personal/familial. But the dominant mood in these portrayals is of the will to survive. The authors have not painted "exotic and spectacular pictures of idyllic Indian village that glorify naïve rusticity as supreme innocence" (Satchidanandan 1999:93); instead, they have tried to give textual visibility to the women in portraying the truth of rural life. While Gauri, Anand's heroine, suffers because of the male-dominated tradition-bound social order before she takes the extreme step of leaving her home and husband, Markandaya's Rukmani and Joglekar's Rakhma fight against the ruthless forces of nature – famine, water scarcity, and the quirks of fate. Both stand as strong support to their husbands and seem to epitomize Hemingway's dictum (with variation) that "[wo] man is not made for defeat."

Both *Gauri* and *Nectar in a Sieve* appeared in the early post-independence period when the villages were witnessing fast changes. Markandaya's novel focusing on a South Indian village was her first whereas Anand had already written ten novels before he wrote Gauri, three of them were on the village life and the peasantry of Punjab – *The Village* (1939), *Across the Black Waters* (1940), and *The Sword and the Sickle* (1942). The decade in which this trilogy appeared (1935-41) was a period of "social flux" when the cross-currents of the spirit of socialism, new liberal values and modern ideologies were sweeping across the country. By the time *Gauri* was written (1960), the Punjab villages were witnessing socio-economic transformation, though the social ethos was not much changed. The author who had incorporated his ideologies of village upliftment, social reforms and economic and social justice to the poor in his earlier works with focus on the male victims of an unjust social order now shifts his attention to a peasant woman in a patriarchal society. In 1957 Anand wrote in *Apology for Heroism*:

> It seemed to me that precisely because modern commercial society had forced the writer into isolation, it was necessary for him to link himself with the disinherited, the weak and the dispossessed, as a human being and as an artist with special talents, to help transform society. (Anand: 81)

The author sets his story in a small village of Punjab. The village is backward and orthodox; and the heroine Gauri is illiterate and comes from a poor background. These two facts are important to understand Gauri's troubled life – wagging tongues, nagging elderly females like Kesaro, beatings from the husband, a callous mother who sells Gauri to get back her cow, and the male lust that makes existence insecure. What redeems Gauri is her inner strength, which she displays during her march from silence to rebellion. It is then that she decides to look the "world in the face."[3] Transformed from the meek and gentle cow to the angry Durga, as her name Gauri signifies, she discards tradition, rejects her husband and ignores the society. She is "transformed from the gentle cow's acquiescent visage of the time she had arrived in Panchi's house, to that of a woman – with a will of her own" (264). It goes to the credit of Anand as an artist that he does not allow his heroine to fall from grace. The decision, though exigent is not an easy one and as she leaves her house her "heart palpitated with every step" (264). It is her boldness coupled with her tenderness that leads critics to extol her as "the modern Mother India."[4] Meenakshi Mukherjee sees a new beginning for the Indian novel in this unique work "in rejecting rather than extolling the time-honoured womanly virtues of patience and submission" (Mukherjee 1971:159). Anand paints his Gauri with tender touches and sympathetic understanding and calls the novel his tribute to the Indian womanhood.[5]

Before assessing Gauri's final decision to challenge the social mores, it is vital to trace her life since her marriage. Panchi is fascinated by the "comely and innocent" looks of his bride and finds her like a "cow, very gentle and very good." But, his immediate thought is highly gender specific when he thinks of her as a "prize of a girl – a girl whom he could fold in his arms at night and kick during the day" (11). This is exactly what awaits her and what she undergoes silently because she has internalized such expressions of male power. Even her mother has exhorted her to "be like Sita" (30) thus enjoining on her the task of upholding the Sita ideal. It may be added here with some advantage that this is an oft-repeated counsel prevalent in all classes, all over India. Gita Hariharan's Devi receives such instructions oft and on and Shashi Deshpande's Mira bursts out in verse:

> Don't tread paths barred to you
> Obey, never utter a 'no'
> Submit and your life will be
> As paradise, she said and blessed me (Deshpande 1992:83).

After the marriage, Panchi exercises his patriarchal authority, beats her at Kesaro's behest and warns her to be patient with Kesaro. Gauri resists it once with vehemence, "Patience, how long can I go on being patient against the nagging of that woman and your shoe beatings on her behalf" (44). Her angry outburst cautions Panchi that it was wrong to take her as the gentle cow because she "had an uncanny grasp of things" (49); he takes refuge in the traditional wisdom to justify his action that it is "the role of a husband to chastise his wife if she goes wrong" (51). At this point the reader realizes that Gauri has the nerve to defend herself without being unduly aggressive. She values the traditional norms of husband-wife relations and easily settles into the role of a loving and caring wife and despite Panchi's mood swings she remains patient and obedient.

The author pursues the Sita myth up to this point before he reverses it. He seems to suggest that the same ending as of the Ramayana story cannot be relevant here. As Meenakshi Mukherjee points out it is the "negative use of myth" "intended to indicate that the same ending is no longer possible (or desirable) in our time" (Mukherjee 1971:133). After her encounter with Seth Jai Ram Das and Dr. Batra, she sheds the Sita image and becomes Shakti or Kali, her namesake; she protects her self-respect vigorously as if "from an plumbed depth there arose in her...Kali, the energy of sheer negation" (165). Earlier, when Kesaro comes to Rafique Chacha's house with her usual "hate campaign" and passes derogatory remarks on Gauri, the latter confronts her boldly. Her fiery beauty overwhelms Panchi as she looks on at "the sudden flashing power that had come into the gentle Gauri, turning her into her other incarnation, Kali, the divine destroyer herself" (95).

Gauri is not a destroyer, though. That Gauri who is carrying life within her should have Panchi uppermost in her thoughts and that she should wish to go back to him and win his love is ample proof of her naïve faith in him. She "was willing to wait like Hindu wife and go patiently through everything to get to the source of that antagonism and distrust and hatred which he showed to her" (100). Gauri realizes soon enough that it is futile to expect reasonableness from Panchi. He is not only weak and cowardly but is also jealous, egoistic and irresponsible with no capacity to think on his own. Gauri could tolerate his beatings but she would not take the aspersions on her chastity. Dr. Mahendra has taught her to be self-reliant and have a positive self-esteem. When Panchi ill-treats her, she takes a quick decision and resolves to make a fresh start. She flagrantly throws him out of her life as she says, "I shall go and work in Daktar Mahendra's hospital and have my child there. And I will not come back again" (263).

As Gauri decides to work out her own destiny, she acquires a new vibrancy. In challenging the traditional ethos Gauri gains individuality and an independent will. Compared to her Panchi pales into insignificance. Gauri is no Sita for whom the earth will open up, but she does not want to hide herself into the bosom of Mother Earth. She wants to face the world, to give a distinct personality to her child and to make him/her a good human being. Not cowardly like his/her father. Obviously, Anand wants "women to be bold, courageous and capable of taking extreme decisions, if they find that their lives have become dwarfed by the burden of obsolete traditions" (Dhar 1998:84). Whether Gauri goes back to Panchi or not is a debatable question. Nevertheless, her journey is an epic journey and it is creditable for a woman of her social status and rural background.

If Gauri is called "the modern Mother India", Kamala Markandaya's Rukmani is termed "Mother Earth" – so great is her patience and tolerance. Though both these novels are set in post-independence Indian villages – one of the North and the other of the South – the rural traditional culture does not seem to have undergone much change, nor has the economic realities turned for the better. Fortunately, Anand's village is spared the agony of abject starvation, which Markandaya's unnamed village suffers. Anand is not so much concerned here with the upliftment programs and industrialization of villages as he had been in his other works, but Kamala Markandaya tackles almost all the vital issues at the cost of her art. There are occasions when her Rukmani appears an unconvincing figure despite the dignity with which she handles trying situations of life.

Life for Rukmani is as difficult as it is for Gauri with the difference that Nathan treats her with due respect and care. A tenant farmer, Nathan appears to be over-awed by Rukmani's family standing and her claim to education, whatever it be. Interestingly, Markandaya exploits her educational abilities to the full towards the end of the novel, creating a highly improbable situation. Nathan is placid and quiet but he is the man of the house and he exerts his authority sometimes. One particular occasion is the birth of their first child a girl. He makes it clear that he wants sons to work for and with him on the land. In desperation, Rukmani also broods "... what woman wants a daughter for first-born?" (14). Paradoxically, this appears pathetically comic coming as it does from a landless farmer.

As the narrative progresses, we see the young Rukmani coping with changes – at familial, social and personal levels. She has had a long and happy married life with Nathan. They have had storms, floods, famine and starvation. They saw deaths of their sons and also suffered their sons' exodus to the cities in search of employment. Together they witnessed, endured and withstood it all. The novel opens with Rukmani remembering her dead husband with tender feelings. "Sometimes at night I think that my husband is with me again, coming gently through the mists, and we are tranquil together. The morning comes, the wavering grey turns into gold, there is a stirring within as the sleepers awake, and he softly departs" (p.1).

When *Nectar in a Sieve* was published in 1954, it was hailed as a genuine novel of rural India. Hari Mohan Prasad termed it "an epic of the Indian life at the grass-roots, a full view of the village world where peasant grow and live, suffer and endure and emerge more dignified, more human in their elements with their tattered rags, their dying moans and their obstinate clinging to the soil like the stump withered all over but its roots delved in the earth." (Prasad 1984:98). The novel is told from Rukmani's point-of-view. She recasts her life from her marriage to Nathan, a landless farmer who was "poor in everything but in love," till his death in the city and her return to the village to her son. Between this span of a hard life Markandaya weaves the picture of village life: the hardships, the sufferings, the transitional period, the villagers in their unmasked behaviour and the end of innocence as the tannery and the urban values take roots in the village. The story is enacted in an unnamed South Indian village. The locale does not throb with life as in R.K. Narayan's Malgudi, but the village has its own life pattern. The villagers are tradition-bound, following blindly the conventions and superstitions; most of them are illiterate or semi-literate; they have their tiny joys of life, a touch of humour despite misery and problems of daily life. Among them we encounter good human beings like the Old Granny, the greedy ones like Biswas, the Bania and the troublemakers like Kunthi, however, despite their human failings, they are all god-fearing, simple human beings and not despicable villains. Their over-all characteristics can be summed up by what Kenny says about them. Calling them "Acquiescent imbeciles" (114), he retorts "I work among you when my spirit wills it...I go when I am tired of your follies and stupidities, your eternal, shameful poverty. I can only take you people... in small doses" (71).

The Indian peasant is conditioned to accept life and work without hope, to leave everything to fate and to God's Will. He suffers mutely and has not learnt to protest even when there is injustice meted out by the dominant group. Kenny voices the Western pragmatic view of life when he snubs Rukmani for her self-effacing philosophy, "Never mind what is said or what you have been told. There is no grandeur in want or in endurance" (113). Kenny here becomes the representative of the author. He argues against the value-system that teaches not to crave for betterment like Anand's Dr. Mahendra. Whatever Kenny's views, Rukmani does not counter him though she has her own philosophy. She broods on Dr. Kenny's exhortations thus: "O, well, and what if we gave in to our troubles at every step! We would be pitiable creatures indeed to be so weak, for is not a man's spirit given to him to rise above his misfortunes" (105). With this spirit, Rukmani and her ilk face life, and the novel becomes a saga of courage in its most seminal form.

Thematically, the novel revolves round the questions of poverty, economic deprivation, social taboos and traditional outlook. Underneath this broad pattern run the tiny currents of allied problems. There is a muffled indictment of some of the social norms – the craving for sons, the disregard of the girl child, illiteracy and the government's apathy towards the condition of the villages and the poor. A first person narration, *Nectar in a Sieve* gives a long rope to Rukmani to record her life. She recollects the events of her life with Nathan with due warmth and clarity. However, the semi-literate protagonist donning the mantle of lofty ideas, philosophical thoughts and psychological probing appears unconvincing. The story is "somewhat tampered" says a critic, asserting that "action is subordinated ...to an individual's thoughts and feelings" (Niroj Banerji, 1990:123).

Markandaya has had the experience of living and working in villages when she was involved in social work. In making Rukmani the authorial voice of the novel, she has fulfilled a significant purpose that of giving a first hand picture of a typical farmer woman – strong, hard working, uncomplaining, tolerant and able. Rukmani has often been compared to the 'mother earth' and to shakti. She is resolute and once she takes a step, she sticks to it as is revealed in the first few paragraphs of the novel when she upholds her decision to bring the leper boy, Puli with her from the city, "what is done is done, there can be no repining" (1), she says. The novel takes off from this point and a reflective, benevolent, affectionate but strong Rukmani recounts her life and through her the village community is revealed to us.

It is, in fact, Rukmani who holds the sway all through the novel. She sustains hope despite hopelessness, she is all forgiving when Nathan betrays her trust and her son flings aspersions on her; she is as tender towards the Old Granny and the stranger Puli as towards her children. In her recent work on South Asian women writers, Shoshana M. Landow assesses the value of suffering in Nectar in a Sieve as a cultural construct and extols Rukmani and Ira for their uncanny ability find sureness and inner peace in suffering. There are, however, certain new values that the author upholds. She is all for girl's education and takes pains, through Rukmani's case, to show how education can be a support in times of adversity. Rukmani takes medical help for herself and for her daughter's conception instead of turning to superstitious practices. She educates her sons and gives them an edge over their illiterate counterparts. When in need, Rukmani earns a livelihood by writing letters for the illiterate city people. All this is good enough, but as Margaret P. Joseph points out it is difficult to convince the readers that a village girl can not only write but write so well that she can earn her bread by writing letters for the illiterate males. The entire scenario appears contrived and incredible.

Modernity perceives progress as synonymous with industrialization. The tannery comes to the village with the new message of hope of employment for the youth and the opening of new avenues for the village economy. The villagers, however, who look at all modern and urban things with disdain and suspicion, are not much enthusiastic about the establishment of the tannery but they do not resent it as do some of the heroes of Mulk Raj Anand's novels who look at industrialization with distrust. Markandaya's villagers just criticize the tannery, feel fearful of its effect on their lives and on the young generation and wait for the worst to happen. True to their apprehensions the tannery proves a curse for Nathan and

Rukmani and many others as their sons leave the traditional work of tilling the land and become unskilled labours.

The depiction of village life is not completely negative. Rukmani and Nathan enjoy the beauty of the Earth when the harvest is rich. Rukmani feels fulfilled to see her vegetables grow plentifully. She is thrilled to be in touch with the soil. The bliss of a farmer's life is described with all its opulence and glory. In a paragraph loaded with the English Romantic imagery and Indian philosophical reflections, Rukmani expresses the happiness of gleaning a good harvest rather elaborately:

> The sowing of seed disciplines the body and the sprouting of the seed uplifts the spirit, but there is nothing to equal the rich satisfaction of a gathered harvest, when the grain is set before you in shining mounds and your hands are whitened with the dust of the good rice; or the very act of measuring – of filling the measure, and topping it with a peak, careless of its height because you can afford to be, and also because you know in your prudence that the grains will see to it that you are not too generous, and slip and tumble down the sides of the measure if that peak be too tall. So many handfuls of measure, so many measures to one sack: one after the other the sacks are filled and put away, with rejoicing and thankfulness. (104)

This picture of a rich harvest is, in fact, too good to be true because year after year the farmers in the area see destruction due to natural calamities. The younger generation of Arjun, Thambi and Raja has seen nothing but want. They therefore, do not subscribe to the value-system of the elders. They do not want to suffer hunger and want and turn to the city or other places in search of livelihood. The problems that the simple, uneducated youth face in the cities are depicted by Kamala Markandaya in this novel but have been elaborated upon in *A Handful of Rice.* Away from their familiar value-system and the usual milieu, the young men fail to settle and many a time go astray.

One of the new ideas that the author wants to implement through Rukmani is family planning. The concept of family planning in its present form was not yet popular in the early 1950s but Markandaya, living in England and being aware of the small family norms imposes it on the village ethos. Rukmani often broods that it was difficult to feed so many mouths in so meagre an income. In the village value-system, no mother would ever think of her family as large for fear of the nemesis. But, without Rukmani's direct intervention, Markandaya cannot succeed in drawing our attention to the fact that craving for sons and a large family accounts for many problems that Nathan and Rukmani face. The author also wants to convey that the practice of considering a barren woman an accursed presence is erroneous and that with medical expertise the problem of barrenness can be cured. Moreover, only a woman cannot be infertile, man can also have some debility. That men do not admit the fact or accept the blame is borne out by the domineering attitude of Ira's husband. The village value-system is so entangled with the author's Western educated view that sometimes the village and the villagers appear unnatural. This flaw has led many a critic to call the novel contrived and meant for the Western readers only. Shyamala Venkateshwaran points out:

> One gets the impression that Kamala Markandaya is not reacting to a specific village in India but to the Western audience's image of an Indian village. The poverty of the villagers, along with their ignorance of modern agricultural techniques, is stressed – there is the long talk of Rukmani, the village woman who is the narrator of the novel, about the use and misuse of cow-dung... Rukmani details the various uses cow-dung is put to in the village (which precludes it being used as a fertilizer as Kenny wants), and one feels that Markandaya is playing tourist guide" (Venkateswaran 59).

Rukmani and Nathan make an ideal couple. There never arises the question of ego between them. Rukmani is the traditional wife and she respects him as the master of their home. Rukmani remembers with relish his immense patience in dealing with her, "What patience indeed my husband must have had, to put up with me uncomplainingly during those early days of our married lives! Not one cross word or impatient look, praise whatever small success I achieved." (8) Rukmani gratefully admits that though poor, her husband was rich in love and care for her. As Rukmani recalls her story, she appears a contented and fulfilled wife.

On the first day of her marriage, she is disappointed to see the mud hut in which she was to spend the rest of her life, "This mud hut, nothing but mud and thatch was my home... I sank down. Nathan's face filled with concern as he came to hold me." Such sentiments pass off soon and Rukmani adjusts to life with all its ups and downs. While Nathan is at times desperate and broken, Rukmani holds her calm. She suffers with her man and she often shows courage and presence of mind to find ways and means to come out of the situation. She shows more awareness than Nathan. When they are evicted from the land and are forced to take shelter in a temple in a town, Rukmani sustains and supports a broken Nathan by her ingenuity and courage. She is not only Nathan's companion through thick and thin, but is also Mother Earth for her children and later for Puli, the orphan she adopts. When her daughter gives birth to an illegitimate child, it is she who swallows all pride and gives emotional support to the unfortunate woman and infant. Despite all odds, Rukmani remains a pillar of strength for the family.

Yogini Joglekar's Marathi short story "Pazar" has a limited scope, however. It records the events of just a fortnight or so and concentrates on one aspect only, that of a dry spell in Maharashtra where water level has gone down during a period of scanty rains. The travails of the farmer are matched by the encouragement and faith of the woman who sustains hope and it is because of her active support that ultimately the couple is able to strike water and feel jubilant. The earth is parched and unyielding; there is no water inside the earth's belly. For days together they dig without success. All financial resources have dried up and the man is on the verge of despair. He wants to abandon the work, for he is defeated, but not his wife. Rakhma and their little daughter Manjula stand by him – encouraging him, persuading him and cheering him. Rakhma sells whatever meagre jewellery she has. Ultimately, the day comes when water oozes out and the well is filled to the surprise and admiration of the villagers who were skeptical of their success. The denouement comes when even their daughter comes with her silver anklets and asks her parents to offer them to the Goddess who has given them water. The man's eyes well up with tears of joy and gratitude, that is Pazar, the spring/spout of water and tears (spout of water). Here again is the picture of a strong-willed woman. She does not accept defeat; she decides not to back out. She is the daughter of the soil and she has faith in the benevolence of Mother Earth.

This does not mean that these farmer women are insensitive to feelings or that they are above social norms. That would mean an unrealistic presentation, a picture blown out of proportion. On the contrary, novels depicting the peasant women place them within the immediate environment of their community and the society in general. Gauri in Anand's novel goes through social indictment, ridicule and anger. She suffers as much due to the wags of her village as because of Panchi's feeble-mindedness. She encounters lechers like Dr. Batra and the Sahu; she learns how greed can turn a human being into monsters; but she also sees goodness in the world in people like Rafiq Chacha and Dr. Mahendra. In Nectar in the Sieve, Rukhmani faces derision from Kunthi and other women for her visits to Dr. Kenny, she has also gone through the pangs of pain of infidelity of Nathan, she has experienced her son's bitter remarks and Dr. Kenny's indictment. But she too is patient, all forgiving and supportive. Both Rukmani and Gauri are women of deep feelings; they love their husbands despite their weaknesses but when time comes to take decision they both are discerning and remarkably courageous and independent.

The authors have made the farmer women representative of change. They are the women of determination and can be harbingers of change. Whether they be from the North like Anand's Gauri, or from the South like Rukmani, or from the East like Bhabani Bhattacharya's farmer women facing the drought or from the West like Joglekar's Rakhma, the farmer woman is an epitome of robustness, strong will-power, self-respect and fortitude.

Notes

1. Vasanth Kannabiran and K. Lalitha record that though the peasant women in Telangana were generally passive, secondary and oppressed, during the Telangana Movement most of them found opportunities to assert themselves. "Suddenly, the four walls of the household seemed to fall apart and structures of feudal oppression, so unchanging and permanent in the past, were not only being questioned but were also challenged in practice.... It is only in such periods of social dysfunction, with the breakdown of constant surveillance and the mechanism of discipline that normally objectify them, that women rush forth to grasp the opportunities for response and growth that become possible." See *Recasting Women: Essays in Colonial History*. Ed. Kumkum Sangari and Suresh Vaid (Delhi: Kali for Women, 1989), 180-203.
2. *The Old Woman and the Cow* was published in 1960 but was renamed *Gauri* in subsequent editions. In this paper, the title will be referred to hereafter as *Gauri*.
3. T.N. Dhar has used these words as title for his paper "Looking the World in the Face: The Changed Women in Anand's *Gauri*." See Naresh K. Jain, ed. *Women in Indo-Anglian Fiction: Tradition and Modernity* (New Delhi: Manohar, 1998).
4. Used by S.C. Harrex in *The Fire and the Offering: The English Language Novel of India*: 1935-1972. Calcutta: Writers Workshop, 1978.
5. The blurb on the Indian edition of Gauri records Anand's words that Gauri is his "offering to the beauty, dignity and devotion of Indian women."

References

Anand, Mulk Raj. *Gauri.* First published as *The Old Woman and The Cow.* Bombay: Kutub Popular, 1960. New Delhi: Arnold-Heinemann, 1981.

—. *Apology for Heroism.* London: George Routledge and Sons, 1942.

Bande, Usha. "Her Country's Joy and Pride", *The Tribune*, Chandigarh, 4 May 1997.

Banerji, Niroj. *Kamala Markandaya: A Critical Study.* Allahabad: Kitab Mahal, 1990.

Deshpande, Shashi. *The Binding Vine.* New Delhi: Penguin, 1992.

Dhar, T.N. "Looking the World in the Face: The Changed Woman in Anand's Gauri." *Women in Indo-Anglian Fiction: Tradition and Modernity.* Ed. Naresh K. Jain. Delhi: Manohar, 1998.

Joglekar, Yogini. "Pazar" in *Pazar* (A Collection of Short Stories). Pune: Sanjay Prakashan, 1976.

Joseph, Margaret P. *Kamala Markandaya.* New Delhi: Arnold-Heinemann, 1980.

Landow, Shoshana M. "Value of Suffering in Kamala Markandaya's Nectar in a Seive," *South Asian Woman Writers: Another Approach to Feminism.* Ed. Ranjini Obeysekere. Princeton: Princeton University Press. 1989.

Markandaya, Kamala. *Nectar in a Sieve.* Bombay: Jaico, 1956.

Mukherjee, Meenakshi. *Twice Born Fiction.* New Delhi: Arnold-Heinemann, 1971.

Nandy, Ashis. *At the Edge of Psychology: Essays in Politics and Culture.* New Delhi: Oxford University Press, 1980

Prasad, Hari Mohan. "The Fictional Epic on Indian Life: A Study in Theme and Technique of *Nectar in a Sieve*," *Perspectives on Kamala Markandaya.* Ed. Madhusudan Prasad, Ghaziabad: Vimal Prakashan, 1984.

Satchidanandan, K. *Indian Literature: Positions and Propositions.* New Delhi: Pencraft International, 1990.

Vasantha Kannabiran and K. Laitha. "That Magic Time," *Recasting Women: Essays in Colonial History.* Ed. Kumkum Sangari and Suresh Vaid (Delhi: Kali for Women, 1989),

Venkateshwaran, Shyamala. "The Language of Kamala Markandaya's Novels." *The Literary Criterion.* 9.3 (Winter 1970).

10

Power Politics from Class to Caste

Premchand and Limbale

VEENA JAIN

> Every village is a political power centre. Political power in a village community operates both at micro level and the macro level. However, our consciousnesses are formed in such a way that many of the operations of power become invisible.
>
> (Kancha Ilaiah 36)

The movement away from Premchand to Limbale mirrors the movement from imagination to experience. Premchand's writing is undoubtedly Marxist in its social commitment and secular stand. It presents the grinding poverty of peasant millions, so powerfully depicted in his short stories like "*Kafan*" and "*Pus Ki Rat*" and novels like *Karmabhumi* and *Godan*. But his world is the world of the entire peasant community fighting against the zamindari system. This is dealt with at the macro level. There is another system of power operation operating within the village community – that is of the dalits against the savarnas. This is the micro level which, though not completely ignored by savarna writers like Premchand, Mulk Raj Anand and Siya Ram Sharan Gupt, is unacceptable to dalit writers as unrealistic and incomplete in its portrayal of dalit experience.

The perspective of non-dalit writers is one of a reform that contains within it sympathy and compassion. But dalit literature has now found its own voice, and refuses to be in the position of the 'other' as a recipient of pity and sympathy. It has its own experience of untouchability fraught with pain, fear, degradation, inhuman treatment, resentment and anger to be expressed. It is a grim picture of reality, and of a discrimination that needs to be addressed. The focus of my paper will be on the play of power politics as depicted in the works of Premchand, who was of an upper caste and Sharan Kumar Limbale, who is a dalit. The two writers offer insights into the different ways power structures come into being and the manner in which they affect village people in their work.

In all the village narratives where power operations are at work, the writer unfolds a tale of social truth that bespeaks its own historical reality. Right from Premchand to Sharan Kumar Limbale, a period of about eight decades, in all the narratives, where community acts as an agency of change or control as in Raja Rao's *Kanthapura* (1938), Phaneshwar Nath Renu's *Maila Anchal* (1954), T.S.S. Pillai's *Chemeen* (1956) and Khushwant Singh's *Train to Pakistan* (1956), it is power politics that comes to the fore. It may be a tale of misery and suffering where an individual is crushed by oppressive forces as in Premchand's *Godan* (1936), or Pillai's *Chemeen* or an entire community fighting for its rights against an inhuman social system as in Limbale's *Hindu* (2004), or Premchand's *Karmabhumi* (1932). The play of power that these works portray manifests itself in either a negative and debilitating force or a positive force of solidarity that carries the potential for a revolution. The village then becomes a site for reform. The forces of power in both cases that control human lives need to be analysed. There has been a shift and a great change in these portrayals from passive resistance (in Premchand's *Godan* and Pillai's *Chemmeen*) to an active opposition (in *Maila Anchal*) and finally to an aggressive stand (in *Hindu*).

While *Godan* is a true representation of the Indian peasantry fighting against the zamindari system, *Karmabhumi* portrays an idealistic community solidarity that brings about reform as a consequence of its struggle. The backdrop of the novel is the struggle for independence. The revolutionary zeal either to enter the village temple perforce by Harijans or refusal to pay the levy, makes its mark felt in the novel. When we move a little ahead in time in *Hindu* (2004), the present scenario of a village is no more encouraging. Caste struggle is important, but the community is no longer the same. The sa̍varnas and the dalits are looked in a direct confrontation and when dalits raise their voice, politics is used to divide and silence them. It has now become imperative for forces playing the game of politics to keep alive the tension within a village. Caste has now become a potent factor in changing the face of politics of the country, and the village has become the centre for any political movement.

Hailed as a spokesman for the downtrodden and downcast, Premchand's humanitarian approach was what drew him to Gandhian thought and Marx. He questioned exploitative capitalism that destroys economic equality. Whereas *Godan* is based on individual Anarchism, which insists on individual autonomy against authority and coercion, *Karmabhumi* libertarian socialism. Both the approaches stress class divide and social disparity as the basis for their struggle. *Karmabhumi* is a fictionalized version of the satyagraha movement. There is no intercaste rift or segregation within the lower class groups. Their revolutionary force is an outcome of their united secular front. Group solidarity in a village narrative is exemplified in *Karmabhumi*. Foucault's concept of knowledge and power gains validity when applied to this text. He says:

> We should admit rather that power produces knowledge, that power and knowledge directly imply one another, that there is no power relation without the correlative constituency of a field of knowledge, nor any knowledge that does not pre-suppose and

> constitute at the same time power relations. (Foucault 1977, www.google.com)

When revolt and rebellion lead to reform, it is an awakening. Realization of one's condition leads to a necessity for change and this brings a knowledge of one's potential for power. In *Karmabhumi*, we have a curious blend of the middle class reformist idealism with its sharp reaction against the British rule and the capitalistic forces which take the form of a nationalistic movement. The working class is made aware of its group power to bring about reform.

The entire narrative is inspired by Gandhian ideology where the protagonist Amar Kant, an upper caste educated youth, rebels against his father and leaves his house and his family to work in a village of harijans where he imparts education and knowledge. He heads the movement against the British government who levies lagaan on the farm products. He is sent to prison. His wife Sukhda is similarly inspired to work for the lower caste people and the labourers when she emerges as their leader She is successful in inciting the "chamars" with a fiery zeal to gain entry into the village temple land. The educated middle class is inspired by one another's sacrificial attitude and right from Lala Samar Kant and Renuka Devi to Saleem and his father join the resistance movement. The narrative is full of incidents that portray high nationalistic feeling of the thirties. Munni's rape, the murder of two British sepoys by her and the triumphant procession are temper building devices. Groups are organized into powers of rebellion. The temple entry movement ends in success though many lives are lost. This ideal-oriented realism and the break from Gandhism was replaced by social realism in *Godan*.

In *Godan*, which is Premchand's classic novel there is no ideological compromise as the focus shifts from the enemy outside to the enemy within.[1] The enemy is no more the absentee landlord, the British official or the rich moneyed class. It is the Gram Panchayat, the Biradari, the upper caste priests and Karindas acting on behalf of the rich peasant. The stronghold of ritualistic religion, traditional beliefs, customs and belongingness to the community are other deterrent factors that act as the inside enemy.

> He could not imagine a life outside the fold of community. The feeling that there could be no integration of life without the community, that marriages, religious rites ceremonies and death had meaning only within the community. Outcasted, he'd just disintegrate. (*Godan 97)*

Hori refuses to be outcasted and is instead ready to pay a fine of rupees hundred as a punishment for keeping the pregnant Jhunia in their house. Even Gobar who is a model for the village youth brimming with new ideas, shows defiance against the moneylenders, is caught up by social norms. He runs away from the village after making a promise of marriage to the pregnant Jhunia. Orthodoxy and the rigid social set up with its caste barriers cast their net on the individual.

The portrayal of Hori as a tragic character, as a living symbol of the colonial peasant struggling against a helpless social order also hints at "the total collapse of the peasant utopia" (Joshi 55). Hori's movement from the "kisan" status to the "majoor" is the result of the moneylender's grip on him. The farmer who yearns for a cow and small piece of land makes all compromises to realize the dream of his life, but remains unsuccessful. The suggested donation of a cow to a Brahmin to secure a place in heaven carries the ironical sting in the form of its title.

A few incidents of defiance by individuals or by groups act as dislocation of power holds, but they are few. Dhania fights for the pregnant Jhunia against the entire society. This gives her emotional support and this makes them bond as sisters. Selia outcasted is again taken in by Dhania in spite of regular threats by the villagers. The Harijan community avenges itself on Mattadeen for illtreating Selia who is his mistress. They force a piece of bone down his throat, thereby making him an untouchable for the rest of the Brahmin community. These acts of defiance are a step towards self assertion.

The 'swang' (masquerade), enacted by Gobar on Holi is another device for disrupting power. In the second item a peasant is shown holding the feet of Jhenguri Singh. After much pleading the Thakur agrees to loan him ten rupees. The necessary formalities take place: he hands the man five rupees. The peasant is taken aback.

> "These are only five rupees, my master."
> "They are ten. Go and count them again at home."
> "No sir, they are five."
> "One rupee goes for my gratification. Right?"
> "Yes, sir"
> "One for the paper itself. Right?"
> "Yes, Sir"
> "One as my interest. Right?"
> "Yes, Sir"
> "Five rupees in cash. That makes ten. Right?"
> "Better keep these five too with you"
> "Nonsense!"
> "I mean it, Sir. One rupee as my gift to your younger wife. One for the elder. One rupee to buy betel leaves for the elder wife. And one for the younger. That makes four. The fifth rupee is for your funeral rites." (*Godan* 174)

Such incidents of mimic, jibe and jokes bring the village farmers together and the congregational gatherings of the reading of Ramayana, Allah and Kajri songs are group activities that provide entertainment and oneness.

Another group of characters from the urban centre stand as a contrast to the village narrative. Though progressive ideas of growth and development and a period of change and transition are hinted at in the idealized characters of Mr. Mehta and Malti, the onslaught of "Mahajani" culture and capitalistic society is depicted in the characters of Mr. Khanna, Mr. Tankha and Rai Sahab. They are indirect parasites preying on the villagers and are full of hypocrisy, deception and lies. They lead a life of luxury with wine and women.

Even the language of Premchand with its fluidity, ironical tone and satirical bent is able to bring out different shades of meaning in power projection and power disruption. There is coercion, flattery, light hearted raillery and an inflection in the indirect barb used by Premchand. Hori tells Dhania, "When your neck is being trampled under the tyrant's heel the safest course is to keep on tickling his feet" (*Godan* 5). On another occasion, Gobar questions his father, "why do you humiliate yourself so often ... How does it help us to fawn on him?" (*Godan* 16). The village thus becomes a closed space with no opening or outlet for Hori, while Gobar's shift towards the town shows a release from the clutches of the "enemy within".

Premchand was one of the first storywriters in Hindi to have portrayed the life of untouchables with their state of being and problems of life (a whole village of untouchables exists in *Karmabhumi*) specially in the last phase of his writing. In *Karmabhumi* important incidents occur like the skinning of a cow, the aversion expressed by Amarkant, Munni's stay with a lower caste family as their family member in spite of being a Rajput herself, Saloni's reluctance to part with her land which is so precious to her as the rest of the characters are all landless people.

Similarly, in *Godan*, the Seliya episode is important where she refuses to go back to her family members in spite of inhuman treatment by Mattadeen. These incidents undoubtedly depict the progressive attitude of Premchand and his reformist zeal but are an outsider's view, the view of a higher caste Hindu who is unfamiliar with many aspects of the lives of lower castes, who has not lived the experience of a dalit.

Against the idealistic picture of power gained by solidarity moves in 1932 in *Karmabhumi* and the class struggle sensitively portrayed in *Godan* is the dismal picture of reality that cannot be explained or formulated by Marxist theory.[2] The divide here, is not between the rich and the poor, or the peasant and the landlord, where money power forms the basis of division. It is a deep rooted social malaise within the Hindu community that divides two groups on the basis of birth. The experience of untouchability – of pain, indignity, oppression and hatred binds them together. This lower class group, when it gradually gains power in Limbale's *Hindu*, is weakened by political moves.

It is a dalit text written by a dalit writer about the forces in politics that weaken their 'Andolan' Limbale writes in the Introduction:

> There is a change in the environment. The Hindu of today is no longer tolerant. Communal violence, social tension and insecurity are the bane of today's life. Political terrorism has changed the secularism of this country into bloodshed. To postmortem the difficult patterns of Hindu society and its ugly caste system-this novel was written.[3] (*Hindu* 9)

The harsh reality around us – of a dalit basti being burnt, women raped and paraded nude, forcible entry into temples, mass conversions all are woven into a tale simmering with explosive power. The injustices perpetrated on dalits are many-faceted. The hegemonic patterns may be less visible with the dalits gaining entry into politics and all other fields of life due to reservation. Their social mobility has increased, the solidarity of caste as a group is on the rise, but in villages the upper castes refuse to acknowledge them as equals. Hence there are persistent assaults both visible and invisible in the form of political maneuvers on the dalit community.

In Premchand's *Karmabhumi* the harijans are supported by the upper castes – Sukhda and her family – in their fight against the upper class. But in Limbale's *Hindu*, the upper castes (Manikchand and Gopichand) are mere agents motivated by an eye on political gain and economic benefits. They donate huge sums to the dalit cause. According to Ram Ahuja:

> The relation between caste and politics may be analyzed at two levels... identification of castes with political parties; influence of castes on political affairs; actual participation of castes in politics ... effect of castes on voting behaviour etc. On the other hand, effect of politics on caste may be perceived as to how politics is used by a caste in rising social scale and/or achieving its goal. This has been described as the process of politicization of caste.[4] (Ahuja 332)

In *Hindu* both the levels work together. Caste is used as a tool for gaining political power. The upper caste village Patel is about to complete his term and in accordance with the reservation rules, the next Patel has to be a dalit. The narrative begins with the murder of Tantya Kamble an active dalit leader and the most likely candidate for the post and ends with the murder of Prabhakar Kavle who was the assassin of Tantya Kamble. Acquitted of the murder charge, a procession is led to celebrate the victory of upper castes. Kabir Kamble is filled with rage and frustration and kills Prabhakar. The revenge plot is thereby complete, but the forces that operate in between are what the writer is interested in.

The murder of a dalit activist provides ample opportunity for drawing political mileage out of such a situation. Politics works at different levels. For the twin brothers it provides a lucrative business deal. For the dalit workers it gives them a chance to gain prominence through the media. For the ex-minister and voluntary organizations it provides an opportunity for starting developmental projects of building houses, roads, lights etc.

Nemichand and Gopichand silence the voice of Milind Kamble as a witness to the murder of Tantya Kamble. He is threatened with a murderous attempt on his life and is rewarded for his silence. The brothers rape a dalit bride hiding in the jungle and the narrator is unable to oppose them, as they often include him in their licentious acts. The narrator's objective appraisal of the whole situation, of which he is a part, exposes many hidden imperialistic structures.

The twins, with their power of money, control the dalit movement. They have a hold on Milind who is an active member of the dalit cause and they control the life of people like Sadanand Kamble, a tool in their hands for gaining power and popularity. Sadanand Kamble is the brother of Tantya Kamble (the murdered dalit leader) and he is unable to protest. He is again silenced by the offer of the post of a Panch. Throughout his life, he licks the heels of the two brothers and ultimately becomes the minister. He even withdraws his case against Prabhakar Kavle.

Achalpur becomes the hub of politics after the murder incident. Rahul Bansode insists on the body being taken to the Collectorate. He leads the procession. Temporary houses, then Pucca houses are built and electric poles are installed after the basti has been set on fire by the Shivshakti workers. The youths of Shivshakti and Bheemshakti confront each other. They are incited to keep the political tension alive. "There should always be tension in society. Riots are a must. Or else, how are we, who are the members of peace committee to get any importance?" (*Hindu* 32).

Every move by dalits to gain equality of status is countered by the savarna group. The elections of Gram Panchayat give the opportunity to the two brothers Nemichand and Gopichand to play politics. After Sadanand is made the Sarpanch, the upper castes refuse to acknowledge him as one and stop him from hoisting the flag on Independence Day. Similar incidents of confrontation occur when dalits try to gain equal power and dignity. Dr. Ambedkar's lesson is destroyed from all the textbooks when the teacher tries to teach them. The two brothers act as peacemakers. Draupadi is called a sorceress when she refuses to satisfy the lust of the temple Pujari. She is paraded nude for her crime. Mass conversions are announced. Climax reaches the narrative with procession of victory for Prabhakar Kavle and subsequently his murder by Kabir Kamble. Milind the narrator, considers himself an eunuch having lost his manliness and power to protest.

The revenge of Kabir Kamble for his friend Tantya Kamble by the act of murder mirrors the power to hit back, and the expression of anger, resentment and rage of the lower castes who are no more mere recipients and objects of sympathy and compassion but have acquired a voice and are in the process of gaining individual dignity that diminishes the position of the "other". They find a space for themselves in the village.

The house or land becomes a metaphor for space in the village narrative. It is used both by Premchand and Limbale. In *Karmabhumi* Sukhda's struggle is for acquiring land from the municipality for building houses for the lower caste group. She fights to give them space. Amarkant, and those associated with him (Salim and his father), make the village of lower castes a site for reform. In Limbale's *Hindu*, it is the group of Bhimshakti workers, the youths of lower caste who fight to find a space for themselves, when their entire basti is burnt by Shivshakti workers after the murder of Tantya Kamble – a lower caste activist. The destruction of the basti is an effort on the part of the savarna group to efface the identity of lower caste. When new houses and a street named after Tantya Kamble are built away from the village, the lower caste is still dependent on the upper caste for survival.

The sensitive portrayal of the relationship of Sonali and Rohit and their impossible union is an indication of the deep rift aroused by caste barriers. In the darkness of the night she dares to go to his basti to reach out to him. She is followed and taken back to the house. Similarly his anguished cry to see her in the courtyard of her house proves futile.

The small skit of Rajhans with the wild pigeons, the tame ones and the hunter is full of political innuendoes. The tame ones betray the wild ones to the hunter. The dance, songs and social plays are replaced by skits with an underlying message for rebellion. Laughter rings with sarcasm. The language of Limbale is direct. There is irony of situation. Crudeness is combined with satire and frankness with self-introspection.

Caste, according to Rajni Kothari, "provides to politics on the one hand a structure of divisions and accommodations and on the other hand a cohesive element which absorbs tensions and frustrations" (Kothari qtd. by in Ahuja 336). It thus works with its two way paradoxical process that of (i) integration (ii) division. A village narrative thus becomes the centre for all political activities. It forms alliances, groups and organizations. But it can also decentre certain oppositional groups. Biradaries can thus give support and can also act tyrannically by ousting an individual. The village then, today is a far cry from the Arden of Shakespeare or the Arcadia of Philip Sydney. With its expansion towards industrialization and growth and growing politics, it is likely to lose its autonomous identity and merge into urban centres or turn into small towns. The village narrative reflects this reality, and warns us of such a danger.

Notes

1. This idea is expressed by P.C. Joshi in his article "Munshi Premchand and the Indian Village".
2. According to Limbale, in his book, *Towards an Aesthetic of Dalit Literature*, "Marxism cannot evolve without taking into consideration the unequal social order created by Hinduism, because inequality in Indian society is not the consequence of Capitalism alone ... there can be no movement forward unless the place of caste, morality and truth in Hinduism is evaluated" (62).
3. The original text is in Marathi. The English translation from Hindi is mine, as no English translation of the text is yet available.
4. Ahuja feels that Rajni Kothari's observation that electoral system in India has given a new lease of life to caste identifications has important relevance. But the "entrenched castes" he mentions do not get importance. The castes, which are numerically larger, are the determinants of politics (337).

References

Ahuja, Ram. *Indian Social System*. Delhi: Rawat Publications, 1994.

Foucault, Michel. "Power, Knowledge and the Body", *The Birth of the Prison*. New York: Pantheon, 1977, www.google.com

Ilaiah, Kancha. *Why I am not a Hindu: A Sudra Critique of Hindutava Philosophy, Culture and Political Economy*. Kolkata: Samya, new ed. 2005.

Joshi, P.C. "Munshi Premchand and the Indian Village", *Premchand Our Contemporary*. Ed. Shivkumar Mishra. New Delhi: National Publishing House, 1986.

Kothari, Rajni. *Caste in Indian Politics*. New Delhi: Orient Longman, 1970.

Limbale, Sharan Kumar. *Towards an Aesthetic of Dalit Literature*, trans. from Marathi by Alok Mukherjee. Delhi: Orient Longman, 2004.

—. *Hindu*, trans. from Marathi by Surya Narayan Ransubhe. New Delhi: Vani Prakashan, 2004.

Premchand, Munshi. *Godan*, trans(1936), into English by Jai Ratan and P.Lal. Mumbai: Jaico Publishing House,1979.

—. *Karmabhumi*. Delhi: Manoj Publications(1932), 2005.

11

Contradictory Images of Nature in *Pather Panchali*

MADHURI CHATTERJEE

Bibhutibhushan Banerjee is recognized as one of the most important novelist of the post Tagore period whose remarkable masterpiece *Pather Panchali* (1928) is acknowledged as one of the greatest Bengali novels. It is a vivid and authentic portrayal of village life seen through the eyes of two children of a Bengali Brahmin family. The village Nischindipur is not idealized, it is not explained or commented on, it is presented as it is, objectively at times but more often subjectively, by the people who live in it and in particular by the two children.

In a lifetime of literary work Banerjee attempted to present the face of village Bengal as it had been during the pre-independence days. He has authored more than a dozen novels and two hundred and fifty stories apart from literature for the adolescent. He rarely forgot the cosmic background of man's destiny and yet a sense of excruciating pain and pity for the suffering of humanity seems to excite his creative centre. His unique and incomparable vision comes through in his three great works – *Pather Panchali*, *Aparajita* and *Aranayak*. The novel *Panchali* is in two parts – the first part lingers upon the past and hearsay accounts, it focuses on the old aunt Indir Thakrun and the second part vividly captures life itself and the playfulness of Opu and Durga. Opu is born in Part One but is not old enough to participate consciously in the life of the world around him until the first chapter of Part Two. There are abrupt transitions from the present to the past and back again to the present, and many of the episodes narrated are laconic in brevity. The events in the story are separated from one another in time, in places by only an hour or so and in others by a lapse of years, but Opu and his sister Durga still walk on, growing continuously in character and experience and in the changing nature of their dreams and their hopes for the future. The meaning of the novel is not conveyed by the sequence of events but by cluster of images and states of mind that occur at different points of time. They encounter other travellers on their journey, some of whom go with along them several stretches of the road, others whom they meet only once, but all leave their mark on the lives of the principals and strengthen the emotional impulses that drive them on.

The earlier chapters, preceding Opu's birth, are a link with the past, where the history of Horihar's family is traced and the narrative continuity emphasized. Indir Thakrun's past reveals the village past – excruciating poverty, sorrows, child marriages, kulin marriages, gender divide, zamindari system, religious rituals, births, marriages, deaths – and yet all these contradictory images are woven in the texture of the world of nature. Indir Thakrun's life bears all the pain, isolation and degradation of poverty and widowhood. She recollects her past beside the river Ichamati "My husband only came to see me about three times. It all seems like a dream now. Bishveshvari was two then...." (37). Her images are fluid as her memory. In the process of recollection, the perception of nature is sorrowful. "Sometime after that a man arrives at the house... one of my uncles read the letter.... They made me take the bangles off my arms, and the silver wristlets my father and mother had given me.... I knew then I was a widow" (37).

Indir Thakrun is a very distant connection of Horihar (Opu's father) on his mother's side. The villages inter-household support system helps her to survive. She depends on many for her sustenance and survival. She even loses her daughter at an early age. Only much later, she finds a place at Horihar's household as he sets up a house in Ramchand's place. The acquisition or loss of land is taken as a criterion of economic stability. In Durga, she finds her joy and "the hunger of a life now almost at its close... the road of her life was an old road. She had walked along it since childhood and now even the slightest bend in it made her happy" (27).

The principal characters in *Pather Panchali* are Opu and Durga (the two children), their parents (Shorbojoya and Horihor) – and their poor and dilapidated home and the village Nischindipur. There is a galaxy of other subsidiary characters, all of whom are vividly portrayed – Opu's Vaisnava grandpa, Proshonno the schoolmaster, the desperately unhappy widow of Tomrej, the callous Onnoda Ray, and the pathetic little Gulki. The place seems to have plural faces – presenting a different reality to different people. However, it is nature that is portrayed as a personified being – the trees, fruits, flowers village paths, bathing steps, jungle open country, birds, sky, clouds and the sun. The novel is the most lyrical evocation of the theme of nature. *Pather Panchali* reminds us of life's vibrancy. Every morning, every season comes to Opu and Durga like a gold-bordered invitation card. Nischindipur offers its marvellous dawns and lovely evenings, its first drops of rain, the exciting rail road and the picnic in the *shorbon*. The children know every leaf and fruit of the village soil and every bird/beetle by its name. Bibhutibhushan draws nature with a Keatsian sensuousness:

> It was a dark night. The air was damp with dew and there was a touch of autumn in it and heavy with strong scent of the *chatim* flowers. Towards midnight the waning moon rose above the tips of the bamboo trees, and its pale light sparkled on the

> dew.... There was a strange mysterious magic in the play of light and shade which filled the forest. It looked like a fairyland asleep. Suddenly a gust of wind stirred, and the branches of the *shondali* tree began to sway and the *telekuncho* bushes trembled....
>
> Opu used to wake up, and when he did he thought about the Goddess, the divine *Bisalaksi*, the forgotten founder of the village..... she knew the bushes where the *bashok* flowers lay hidden, the secret recesses of the forest were the *chatim* blossoms slept in the shade of their trees, the cluster of green reeds by a bend in the Ichamoti where the indigo and *holmi* huddled together, and the thorn trees where the baby tailor birds had got woken up in their little nests of straw. The whole forest glowed with the light of gracious loveliness.... Nobody, since Sarup Chakravorty had ever seen her. (160)

The village Nischindipur has its own deity – Bisalaksi who is the protector of the village. Every caste participates in the annual propitation of the village deity, providing their traditional services without the social hierarchy transgressed. The author expresses this joy of expansion in his novel and believes that the obstacles of life which debar us from discovering the path bring joy in a different way which is provided through small little incidents and tiny little happenings. Opu lives more on the imaginative plane while Durga remains rooted to the concrete objects of Nischindipur. Opu is forever distracted by things beyond his reach and in the process loses his hold over the present but Durga's pleasures are all earth-bound.

The vivid and sympathetic realism of portrayal, the naturalness and faithfulness to detail seems, in large measure, large measure, to have been derived from the autobiographical foundations which underlie its conception. The element of self-reflexity allows him to recount events of the past. The author was able to live through Opu and make him so convincing primarily, because, in a true sense, he was Opu. Opu's childhood was a reflection of his own and Opu's environment a reproduction of that in which he himself had grown up. Banerjee spent his childhood in Barrackpore famous for its indigo plantations. His father earned a precarious living like Horihar and his mother Mrinalinidebi became the model for Shorbojaya who bore throughout their lives the burden of the crushing poverty. The author's own marriage was short-lived and his personal loss and isolated life helped him discover his creative freedom. The quiet and peace of the silent forest gave a cosmic dimension to his literature. It was here that he composed *Pather Panchali.* He began writing the book in 1926 and completed the work in April 1928 and he admits that nature had coloured his vision with so much beauty and ecstasy.

The interesting feature of *Panchali* is that the author has found words to describe the most subtle shades of feeling, the most rare and yet perfectly natural sensation of how little Opu wakes up in the middle of the night and finds his mother fast asleep. Their thatched hut is drowned in darkness and the pattering of the raindrops can be heard amidst the rustling of the wind. The child is confused by these mingling noises and the surrounding darkness, a confusion which finds a home in his memory to be recalled years later. Sometimes a new experience echoes an older one (Durga, old Brahmin in Benaras). Sometimes the old images are relived in memory in a new situation and sometimes the author himself connects the present to the future. Sisir K. Mukhopadhaya believes that the novel is without a rival in the expression of significant moments. These memorable moments in the village of Nischindipur captured through Opu's inner mindscape reflect his harmony with nature. Opu's predicament becomes the predicament of the common man of the village.

The novel does not speak so much of man, Opu's childhood experiences did not embrace the complexities of life. But religion and superstition alone keep the village kinship alive by reaffirming the importance of the relationship between deities and the common man. Often, as though in a soliloquy,

Banerjee communicates with the reader and speaks of the lord of life "Jiban Debata". Biru Ray, Horihar's predecessor, had notoriously acquired money by secretly murdering the Brahmins. He gets his due punishment by an invisible judge when from the corner of the tall grass a crocodile dragged his son into the river and an invisible judge awarded his verdict:

> Biru Roy had been a fool; but he know now by bitter experience that the unseen arbiter of right and wrong is not cheated of his retribution because the deed lies buried under the dark grass of a lake. His way is light even in Darkness. (33)

There is an invisible power working behind this cohesiveness. The villagers are supposed to be in harmony with the deities and incompatibility with the people and the land. Horihar is the eldest son to survive the curse of God which brought Biru Ray's sons and others to a premature death.

In Nischindipur the villages generally appear impoverished, in many ways fatalistic – being often physically isolated and at the mercy of the elements – yet self-contained having a sense of control over their lives. Durga dies of malaria, just prior to Durga Puja, and her intended marriage, though never sermonized, becomes archetypal as death leads to her impending departure and separation. She even gets strange premonitions of departure as she watches the ferry ghat, the trees, the rain and the road under the *gab* tree with sadness and apprehension. Like the idol of Goddess Durga, the little girl is also immersed with the elements of the nature.

The topography and ecology of the village seems to be idyllic yet there is exploitation and deprivation everywhere. Amidst this, the children move around in the resplendent woods and forests, enjoying the cycle of seasons:

> Day by day, as the years of his childhood passed, Opu had walked with Nature. When one season went and another came, the trees, the sky, the wind, the singing of the birds told him about it. His heart leaped within him to behold the seasons

> touch the changing face of the Ichamoti with new beauties. He knew so well what changes the maturing year would spell out in the trees, on land and water, in the sky, and in the fruit and flowers. He loved them all as if they were his brothers and sisters, and he could not imagine a life without them. (283)

The chapters in the novel are blended by reference to changes of season, and Opu's growing up is marked in terms of the summers, rains and winters he goes through. Durga and Opu gather pleasure picking mangoes and berries from *Shona Mukhi*, they sit and play under the *bokul tree* with the fruit seeds and kories taste the bamboo fruit, catch a fish or two and steal coconut and fruit from other orchards. In her toy chest, Durga collects mangoes, mirrors, beads, sindoor box, shiny weeds of wild flowers. She represents the sensory world of nature. She also incurs the wrath and curse of their mother Shorbojoya. "I wish I could have you taken to the *chatim* tree" (89). The *chatim* tree grows in the village cremation ground. Also half-way through the story Durga, mother throws away her chest "It is like a ritual ending of Durga's childhood". In the heat of the mid-day sun, nature gets infused with mythological beauty. Opu could see in the distance where near the banyan tree the sky leant down to the earth:

> Karna the mythical hero, the object of a pity which could never end... it was Arjun who slew his hapless foe with a bolt loosed from his chariot; but his was not the victory. Karna was the victor; Karna it was who lived on in the tears of countless generations, ever present where love is born of human pain. (76)

It is not just natural calamity that causes deprivation, even mistaken religious beliefs bring this about. Horihar is afraid of performing puja in the house of lower caste people for his livelihood. Nischindipur, like any other village is both a society of equals and of non-equals. The hierarchical solidarity is ritually constituted. Interestingly religious ceremonies and festivals – Chorok festival, Chariot festival, Festival of Holy pond, Festival of Goddess Chandi and Durga puja seem strongly interwoven with the elements of nature and are recurring measure of time. In the festival of Holy Pond the sisters pray for their brothers: "There was a small square pit in the yard. Some days before Durga had planted pulse and peas in it, and already the shoots were showing in the damp soil. She had also set some banana suckers outside the pit, and when Opu found her she was tracing pictures round them, lotuses, birds, bundles of rice, and the rising sun," and Durga prays "Oh, holy pond; oh, holy flower! I worship you neath the noon-day sky. A maiden's purity is my dower; My brother lives and blest am I" (92).

Banerjee is a believer in the spirit of man. Yet the shared life of the village of Nischindipur is a product of several events some mythical rooted in sacred tradition, and some in reminiscences. Both of which colour the perception of the villagers themselves and others. The strains of the change coming in with modernization are not very evident. The children's first encounter with industrialization happens when Opu and his father visit the railway track. Pillars of metal joined one to another by long lines of string. And "the pillars went on and on, indeed as far as his eye could see there were white pillars and strings stretched between them" (135). In their childish mind, the railway track defines the boundary of the familiar world. It is only after Durga's death that Opu has the opportunity of travelling by train. It is an act of betrayal and desertion as the spirit of Durga lingers on in Nischindipur who even when unwell had inquired: "Will you take me to see the train one day?" (249). But Opu moves on and is once again reassured by the author, who looks into the future, "You are going on a journey. You have no notion what you are likely to see as you travel on" (135).

The last chapter of *Pather Panchali* is significantly entitled Akrur Sambad (words of the wise). It signals the death of Opu's childhood dreams and the stirrings of the birth of new dream of a larger life. Opu leaves Nischindipur, his quiet garden of Eden, to begin a new life. He misses his sister Durga but is assisted by the presence of his mother and father and his youthful innocence. His thirst for life is evident in the midst of suffering, poverty and struggle. But one can't forget the wonderful sense of assurance at the end of *Pather Panchali*. The continuity of life and the eternity of Nature intermingle. The deity of the eternal road smiles benevolently and asserts:

> You silly boy, my road has not ended in your village bamboo grooves, under the people tree of the thug Biru Rai, or near the ferry. Beyond the pasture ground... on the after side of Ichamoti, by the side of lotus infested Madhukhali Swamp.... the road proceeds on endlessly from one country to another, from sunrise to sunset, from tomorrow to the unknown, months, years ages, time, space. I have given on your forehead the invisible mark of the wanderer and brought you out of your home....Now let us step forward! (312)

The novel ends with Opu leaving Nischindipur with his parents and bidding farewell to his home and village and yet there is sense of continuity. The novel may have an episodic structure and abrupt transitions but emotionally it is coherent. The title *Pather Panchali* has been translated variously as *Song of the Road, Wayfarer's Song, or Bends in the Road.* as it retains the symbolism of road broken into series of stretches divided from one another by bends which conceal what lies ahead. Meenakshi Mukherjee has further elaborated on this, "*Panchali* also refers to a devotional narrative song which continues for a stretch of time without any obvious climax and where the story does not follow a rigidly sequential order" (Mukherjee 131). As the characters walk along the road – some of the stretches are lush with grass, fruit flowers and song of the bird but others are hard and strewn with thorns, lashed with storms, and hot with the summer heat. Yet there is a hope that it will be less arduous further on and despite the discontinuity in the narrative of the chapter – the road is one, in spite of changes of mood, scene and incident. The debut film of Satyajit Ray retained this ending in the film version, which depicts a continuity and secured a place in people's psyche with its lyricism, freshness, realism and humanism.

Bibhutibhushan perceives the unity of man and nature. Nature heals our wounds and awakens us to greater perceptions and ideals. Our restlessness is quietened and our nerves invigorated. He confesses in *Aranayak* that he dreams of God and Nature "not as a dictator or all powerful judge of things but as wise and deep philosopher. When I looked at the beauty of red cluster of clouds... or the expanse of bare ground in moonlight, I thought of God as a poet, painter and a lover... a unique creator" (213).

Thus, Banerjee's entire literary output testifies to this great realization of the essence of time. It seemed to him that man and nature had a embryonic existence in time Eternal. Bibhutibhushan reveals Bengal and the post war Bengali literature turned to Marx and Freud returns back and discovers its inherent truth in nature and to the simple man of the village.

References

Banerjee, Bibhutibhushan. *Pather Panchali* (1928). Trans. T.W. Clark and Tarapada Mukherji. New Delhi: Rupa Paperback, 1990.

—. *Aranayak.* Calcutta: Seagull Books, 2002.

Mukherjee, Meenakshi. *Realism and Reality: The Novel and Society in India*. Delhi: Oxford University Press, 1985.

12

The Film Version of the Village Fair

Site for Counter-Cultural Resistance

VRINDA MATHUR

"Dharti sunehri amber neela
har mausam rangeela
aisa desh hai mera ...."

[*Veer Zaara* 2004]

Welcome to the world of colour and celebration of the village fair in Hindi films.

Fairs and celebrations are a distinctive feature of the Indian cultural heritage. As magnificent representations of fun and frolic, gaiety and charm they are a complex phenomena embodying man's basic instincts of enjoying in a group. As live theatres they are vibrant, exciting forms of public welfare and public entertainment and therefore have a direct connection with man's social, cultural and emotional gratification.

In the course of human events the significance of this complex phenomenon remains shrouded in mystery. One wonders as to what exactly the village fair is? Is it therapy or is it escape – (specially for the village women who go to it to escape the dull drudge of their daily grinds) – is it ritualistic valorization or is it a combination of all these and much more? An indepth study of the fair reveals how the perceptions of people who visit it vary from person to person. An urban couple going to the village fair thinks about it differently as compared to a rural couple. A sociologist who is going to the fair for a sociological analysis has totally different views of it as compared to the historian who is studying it from the historical and cultural point of view. Its therapeutic and economic significance has its own rich implications. Thus, this complex cultural landscape offers inviting and challenging grounds for scrutiny to establish its credentials as a special place meriting special attention.

Having humble beginnings in primitive man's collective celebration of the awe-inspiring natural phenomenon, the village fair today has evolved into a potpourri of treasures and pleasures and wonderful ways to pass the time – regional and seasonal, cultural or religious, the village fair overshadows other forms of entertainment in excitement and size. The myriad of stalls, games of skill and chance and the hustle bustle of activity add a wonderful dimension to the fair's personality. A general classification of the fairs reveals that the seasonal one's like the Teej fair at the onset of monsoons, or the Gangaur fair and the Baisakhi fairs held in the harvest season are very popular and internationally famous. The Surajkund Crafts Fair of Haryana exhibits breathtaking exhibits of artists, craftsmen, painters and sculptors. People throng the Pushkar pilgrimage centre of Rajasthan to see the annual religious and cattle fair. Trades and parades and race competitions are held for the camels, horses and cows. The entire fair is a big draw. The biggest cattle fair of Asia takes place at Sonepur in Bihar, annually. The Hindus actively participate in Kumbh Mela held once in every three years either on the banks of river Godavari in Nasik, Shipra in Ujjain, Ganga in Haridwar or at the confluence of the three sacred rivers namely Ganga, Yamuna and Saraswati. This auspicious fair of the Purna or Maha Kumbh is celebrated once in every twelve years. The delightful festival of Dusshera also sees several fairs in most villages where people participate with zest and enthusiasm. Taken as a group these fairs seek to advance an understanding of a substantial expanse of the socio-cultural landscape.

Hindi films, too, are a powerful medium of public entertainment. The magnitude of their canvas directly and significantly impacts the socio-cultural values of their viewers and thus accounts for their mass-appeal. The use of the fair in films as a device, as a motif to foreground and highlight several issues along with the valorization of the rich cultural heritage is indeed a triumph of the Hindi films in the twenty first century. When the lights of the cinema hall dim and the projector rolls, the narrative gets concentrated and the one single factor which binds the audience together as a nation is the effusive spirit of the fair in the village. Reflecting the vibrancy and the multi-hued traditions of the people in the village the village fair brings to the fore the cultural sentiments of the village populace. The myriad hued culture manifests itself in the eruption of colour and music. The entire environment resounds with festivities and excitement and brings about a magic in the air.

Hindi films have a strong impact on the minds of people and the village fair with all its colour and celebration provides the framework for focusing the attention on several significant contemporary issues. The village fair in Hindi films becomes a direct and straightforward form of nationalist artistic discourse overwhelming all other tender shoots in the cinematic environment which are muffled by a dense monoglossia (that is to say that all other themes become insignificant). The village fair in Hindi films becomes a powerful and illuminating model – a vibrant symbol of the social fabric of the country with a resonance that reverberates through the rhythms across the country from Kashmir to Kanyakumari; from the rural heartlands of Punjab to the Bihu beats of the North East.

Starting from the mould set by the Dilip Kumar-Nargis starrer *Mela* (1948) to the Raj Kapoor hit *Jis desh mein Ganga behti hai* (1960), to the Rajesh Khanna-Mumtaz *Dushman* (1970) to Nasiruddin Shah-Rekha's *Astha* (1997) (famous for its animal fair) to the more recent *Veer Zaara* (2004) and *Mangal Pandey* (2005) – the village fair has come a long way. If in the early films the village fair represented the twin brother sister lost and found formula or leering cheering dacoits and kidnapping contexts or the blossoming of young love in the revelry of the fairground themes today the village fair has assumed slightly different dimensions.

Moving from obvious themes and jaded rhetoric to a new form of patriotism the village fair today represents a very significant socio-cultural phenomenon. This is Manoj Kumar's *'desh ki dharti'* with a difference. Here, there is no contentious, venomous politics, only culture and traditions; no blood or terrorist bombs – only singing dancing and *balle-balle*; no vitriolic *'dooriyans'* only rejuvenating *'nazdikiyans'*.

The village fair as a significant socio-cultural phenomenon serves several purposes. Whether it is a religious fair, seasonal fair, entertainment fair, or business fair or agricultural fair (where the trade of animals takes place – as in Rekha's film *Astha*) or any other, it represents a strong social, cultural and economic context.

Given its scope and complexity this socio-cultural phenomenon of the village fair in films largely remains undiscovered territory. In this paper, I seek to address a fairly large component of this enigma, offering it a contemporary comprehension, viewing it as a platform for influencing the common people and most important focusing attention on its foregrounding in films as signaling of a significant trend. In this paper today I choose to present the village fair in Hindi films with all its colour and celebrations as a special site for counter-cultural resistance. Intense and earthy, carrying the fragrance of the soil, the village fair today is important as an antidote to the ongoing process of global standardization and westernization. It is a source of indigenous cultural resistance of an indigenous society in the grip of western cultural hegemony. It is simultaneously also a vehicle of a non-western society to regain control over its actions, celebrations and environment. It is as Jasbir Jain pointed out in her keynote address,[1] a revolution starting from the village. It is in this sense that I see the village fair assuming the connotations of a counter culture.

As the lights of the cinema hall dim and the projector rolls, the colours magnify the landscape and the village fair becomes a powerful and illuminating model for carrying forward the indigenous traditions and culture of our country. The village fair scene of the recent celluloid hit *Veer Zaara* is a case in example. The reverberations of the beating drums through the lush green fields find an echo in the national cultural ethos and the attention gets focused on the festivity, revelry and hospitality of a Punjab village – Ranjeetpur – in this case. The entry into the village via the village fair to the accompaniment of music and song, the words of which categorically define indigenous values, provides an outlet for us to connect with our culture, our traditions and our heritage.

The identity that emerges is a liberal, pluralistic, passionately national identity which is co-terminus with the individual's ethnic identity, state identity and linguistic identity. I may be a Punjabi, Bengali, or a Keralite but I am an Indian. This pluralistic pan Indian identity bears the hallmark of the Indian national essence and thus becomes a symbol of the social fabric of the country. This plurality is central to the Indian national ethos. The country has over the years constructed a socio-cultural system which enshrines this pluralistic identity as a virtue. So also the village fair with all its culture, traditions, colour and celebrations, becomes the one single factor which binds the audience to their seats, binds us together as a nation and most important shifts the attention of viewers from meaningless gyrations to the rhythm, style and merry beat of folk music and folk dances.

Today, we are living in a world in which the forces of globalization are sweeping identities aside to create an integrated market for consumerist capitalism. The village fair with all its colour and celebrations therefore poses a strong challenge to this dangerous phenomenon. Not just this, but the vibrancy and effusiveness of the village fair with its indigenous skills of nat ka khel, tight rope walking, the crafts of the village like clay pottery, colourful weaving, fine handicrafts, dancers, singers and other performers, also constitutes a concrete bulwark to the modern idea of expertise, to the technocratic rule of scientists, bankers and other development experts. The indigenous skills of the village are a counterpoise to the steam rolling effect of westernization and global uniformization. Thus, the village fair in Hindi films is taking us back to our roots.

One very revealing example of this is the village fair scene in *Mangal Pandey – The Rising*. The scene is set in 1857 in a village in Satara. Throughout the scene the song of the chorus '*Jaagi hai dharti ...*' foregrounds and felicitates the theme of socio-cultural renaissance. However one more aspect of the village fair makes itself strongly felt in this scene. It is revealed that as the words of the song signal socio-cultural awakening simultaneously the camera also constantly focuses on the pathetic slave-sale context of the village. Communicating the plight of the slave girl the village fair highlights the pathos of the situation. Thus, in this sense, the village fair serves a pedagogic function in addition to its performative one.

I understand that counter cultural resistance runs the risk of leading to parochialism and communal self enclosure. The village fair in this sense also becomes crucial for not only carrying forward the indigenous traditions of society but also for salvaging the humanistic meaning of development and providing a bulwark against cultural isolation and self enclosure. Charles Taylor in a recent essay on multiculturalism underscores this aspect of the village fair. Taylor points out that "stories of cultivation and self formation in premodern times were embedded in shared ways of life which were interpersonal by definition: Given the fragility of shared life forms in modern times the link of interpersonal mutuality has to be deliberately cultivated" (32-33).

The village fair is this link of interpersonal mutuality. With all its festive spirit it acknowledges this need of the modern times. Answering this need with its dialogical character the village fair establishes its credentials through its rooted dialogical philosophy – where the imposition of one point of view or the adoption of a superior standpoint is not the essence of growth but the forging of a common universe of discourse in the encounter among people is the spirit of enriching sustainable development. It is this reaching out aspect of the village fair which I wish to emphasize. Even if we are to view the village fair, vis a vis the fair in the cities in films as in the Twinkle Khanna-Aamir Khan starrer *Mela* (2000), we would find that in the village fair the focus is on the nationalist sentiment whereas in the urban city fair the focus is on exotic memorabilia and artifacts.

Thus the village fair becomes the platform where liberal, pluralistic identities are formulated and safeguarded. The bewilderment that one sometimes feels in being overwhelmed or swept aside by the global forces gets checked. As the exuberance of colours and reverberations of rhythms offer healing companionships the atmosphere of benumbing self centred interests gets shattered. The spontaneous celebrations of the village fair successfully translate benumbed compassion into vibrant effusiveness. As the spirits soar, the excitement rises and Hindi films succeed in presenting the village fair as a symbol of solidarity, hope and unity. The colourful chaos, with the dust, dirt and ogling eyes notwithstanding obliterates many super imposed western ideas and notions and the village fair becomes a significant cultural frame for social transformation.

The words of the song '*Dharti sunehri amber neela*', during the journey of the village fair become a metaphor for the nationalist sentiment. The hero who sings the song is a rescue pilot with the Indian Air Force. Sqdn. Leader Veer Pratap Singh is a 'Son of the Soil' who has grown up in the village, gone out and become successful and is coming back to his roots to valorize them to a guest.

Evidence from other movies like *Hum Aapke Hain Kaun* (1994) in which the colour and celebration of the village fair corroborates the feelings of de-ja-vu of the star couple who are passing through it, also highlights a fascinating characteristic of the village fair, which creates its own 'village fair universe' – with its own dynamic connotations. The village fair with its color, celebration, singing, dancing and exhibition of indigenous skills and expertise offers counter-cultural resistance to the western mainstream culture at both the levels of culture – the surface level culture as well as the deep culture. At the surface level, culture manifests itself in the language, dress, arts, crafts, music, dance, food and other visuals and at a deeper level, it manifests itself through values, norms, assumptions and expectations which shape attitudes and behaviour.

As the embodiment of indigenous polychronic culture the village fair in Hindi films today displays values where relationships and interactions are more significant than arbitrary schedules. Here the multiple happenings and interruptions as a way of life are focused upon as against the west's concentration of one thing at a time theme. In the Indian village the philosophy of time as fluid and flexible is highlighted as against the west's time is precious, limited commodity philosophy. Here there is plenty of time for work and pleasure and these are usually mixed up with a focus on building and maintaining relationships. If for the west time is money the village fair announces that when God made time he made plenty of it. In western culture the focus is on independence and individuality but in the indigenous culture of the village fair the emphasis is on interdependence and group orientation. If for the west each person takes responsibility for himself/herself and identity as individual comes first then the village fair foregrounds group feeling, where people feel most comfortable as part of a group and seek others to share work, *needs* and experiences. Here identity as part of a family or group is significant rather than as an individual. Against the 'I, me, myself' culture here there is the 'we' culture. In the western culture the individual's life is compartmentalised but in the indigenous culture it is holistic: here everything, including work and personal life, is interconnected whereas in the west there is separation of work from personal life. In western culture, different parts of one's life – roles and relationships are viewed as separate and often kept private but here in the culture of the village the person, his job, work, appearance, family, friends, social life are all connected. To separate these would seem artificial or at least confusing.

Western culture is often viewed as being result-oriented but indigenous culture is process-oriented. Here one takes care of relationships along the way. The process of getting to a destination or goal is just as important as achieving the goal and this is being significantly emphasized in the words of songs and actions of the village fair scene on screen in today's Hindi films. In western culture communication is explicit whether spoken or written but the village fair highlights that in the indigenous culture communication is implicit. Here one gives and receives information in multiple ways: what is said, not said, implied not implied, verbal and non-verbal messages are all just as significant. The most important point on which the village fair in Hindi films offers counter cultural resistance is the valuing and valorising of the past, of culture and of traditions. This valorising is a direct challenge to the west's 'Past is over and gone' theory and philosophy.

Thus, we see that the village fair in Hindi films today with all its colour and celebration, special reference to films like *Hum Aapke Hain Kaun* or the latest *Veer Zaara* and also Ketan Mehta's *Mangal Pandey – The Rising,* along with several others is signaling a significant trend. Located just outside the village, it symbolizes a two way negotiation of space – from dense enclosures inside to at least breathing space outside and from festive revelry and merry making of the fairgrounds outside to the roots inside with a rejuvenated, revitalized identity.

In this journey of discovery the village fair in Hindi films today represents the hospitality, spontaneity, sense of camaraderie and light heartedness of traditional India. It becomes an exuberant and vibrant reflection of the multi-hued traditions of the Indian people. Serving varied purposes, whether it is religious pilgrimage, ethnic shopping, ethnic delicacies, animal trades or foregrounding the spirit of bonding, the village fair with its colour. celebrations and festivities resounds the whole environment with excitement and succeeds admirably in passing on the traditions to the new generation – the generation X of metropolitan standards which is looking for anchors to hold on to in the modern deluge of commercial westernization and the resultant acute identity crisis. In this journey of discovery the village fair in films attempts to create a passionately national identity – an identity which values its indigenous tradition, culture, skills and expertise – An identity which is redefining the xenophobic, flagwaving patriotism of the past and is gently persuading us to explore who we are and who the other is.

Note

1. This paper was originally presented at a seminar, "Village as Protagonist: The Centre of the Periphery" where Jasbir Jain introduced the seminar theme.

References

Banuri, Tariq. "Modernization and its Discontents: A Cultural Perspective on the Theories of Development." *Dominating Knowledge: Development, Culture and Resistance*. Ed. Fredrique Apffel Margin and Stephen A. Margin. Oxford: Clarendon Press, 1990.

Nandy, Ashis. "Cultural Frames for Social Transformation: A Credo." *Political Discourse: Explorations in Indian and Western Political Thought*. Ed. Bhikhu Parekh and Thomas Pantham. New Delhi: Sage, 1987.

Panikkar, Raimundo. "What is Comparative Philosophy Comparing?" *Interpreting Across Boundaries: New Essays in Comparative Philosophy*. Ed. Gerald J. Larson and Eliot Deutsche. Princeton: Princeton University Press, 1988.

Talcott, Parsons. *The Structure of Social Action*. New York: McGraw Hill, 1937.

—. *The Social System*. Glencoe, IL: Free Press, 1951.

—. *Politics and Social Structure*. New York: Free Press, 1989.

Taylor, Charles. "The Politics of Recognition". *Multiculturalism and the Politics of Recognition*. Princeton: Princeton University Press, 1992.

13

Awakened Rustics in Renu's *Maila Aanchal*

NEELAM RAISINGHANI

The realities of life in post-independence India are so complex and multidimensional that no single novel can claim to circumscribe them in its limited space. Therefore, the urban and rural lives are depicted at different levels. Most of the novelists have seriously and closely observed the changing attitudes as a result of political instability, degeneration of social values, confrontation between selfish ends and growing intellectual sensibilities. Rural life of twenty-first century is different from what it was in the decades of forties and fifties of the last century.

Regional novelists like Phaneshwar Nath 'Renu', Nagarjun, Rajendra Awasthi, Rahi Masoom Reza, Shri Lal Shukla, Ramdarash Mishra, Vivek Rai and Himanshu Joshi have keenly observed the changing political social, religious and economic values in their writings and depicted these changes in a distinct colour. Contemporary rural life is portrayed in *Maila Aanchal, Parti Parikatha, Varun Ke Bete, Jangal Ke Phool, Adha Gaon, Alag Alag Vaitarni, Raag Darbari, Jal Tootata Hua, Kagar Ki Aag* and *Ratinath Ki Chachi*.

In his preface to *Maila Aanchal* 'Renu' admits that he chose Marygunj, a small village in District Purnea of Northern Bihar because it represents the backwardness and underdevelopment of Indian villages. Named after the dead wife of a white businessman Mr. Martin, Marygunj lacks the values of social justice, liberty and scientific advancement, which are very dear to western society. Martin's wife Mary died of malaria due to lack of medical facilities in the village. Since then he had been trying to establish a Malaria Centre in the village but his failure led him to insanity. His dream could be materialized years later by the altruistic efforts of Dr. Prashant, a medical graduate from Patna Medical College, who chooses Marygunj for his researches and experiments on malaria and black fever. The opening of this Malaria Centre is like a new wonder of the world for the ignorant and superstitious villagers. They are even scared of the officials who survey the land for this centre. Although no freedom movement has ever reached the village but their knowledge of military atrocities based on rumours has frightened them so much that they mistake the Malaria Centre officials for military personnel. Even the educated *Tehsildar* of the village goes to meet these officers with a fear in his heart. The illiterate villagers are unaware of the political change that has taken place after independence. Considering these officials to be the representatives of the British government, the rustics try to appease them by presenting before them an enchained *'Suraji'* leader Baldev, who always says *"Jai Hind"*.

Dr. Prashant, who had refused to accept a government scholarship to study abroad, faces a lot of resistance from the people in the beginning. It is rumoured about him that he would inject poison into their veins and defile their wells by sprinkling insecticides into them. With the help of Baldev, Kalicharan and the Tehsildar, Dr. Prashant disinfects all water bodies in the village at the outbreak of cholera. Kalicharan and his socialist party members help him in inoculating the ignorant villagers forcibly. Gradually they realize that the doctor is their saviour and without proper medical aid they would have been devoured by the epidemic of cholera.

'Renu' has not only portrayed the fears, doubts, ugliness, the many questions and desires of the poor and illiterate people of this backward village, but he has also works through images of humanitarian sensitivity. A general assumption of freedom struggle was that after independence, a process would start that would break the caste system. But new political culture was quick to prove this hope false. A new kind of caste system is institutionalized, which is different from the traditional caste system. In the traditional system people knew their limitations as they were socially conditioned to accept their lot and did not react to it. But in modern post-independence India, there is a hope that independence would bring about casteless society. They have a reason to believe so because scientific advancements and growing industrialization have weakened the age-old values and led to the awakening of the backward classes. Despite the provisions in the Indian Constitution towards equal rights the caste system still continues to exist, possible in a more sinister form than ever before.

'Renu' has exposed the class-consciousness, untouchability and poverty of the lower classes, which is an eternal existential reality since times immemorial. Lower caste people of this backward village of Bihar are shown to be entangled in sub-human social existence, abject poverty, economic exploitation, in fact an entire sub-culture of submission and powerlessness. R.P. Dewan, in his work or untouchability, has observed:

> Centuries of continuous misfortunes have suppressed their heat of anger and they patiently handle their miseries. They have withstood the psycho-economic pressures of social conformity for centuries. (Dewan 66)

Sexual exploitation of the lower class women is a very common thing. In the dark hours of night the powerful landlords forget their religion, caste and social status and only allow their lust to surface. *Brahmins* and *Rajputs* have a superior air and bluntly refuse to mix with the lower classes. Yadavas who have recently emerged as a new political power, are still unacceptable to the higher castes as their leaders. Hargauri, a Rajput youth condemns Baldev, a Yadav Congress worker:

> *Aap to leader he hoge. To aaj kal Congress office ka chowka bartan kaun karta hai? Arre bhai sabhi Kashi chale jaoge? Pattal chhatane ke liye bhi to kuchh log rah jao. Jail kya gaye Pandit Jamahirlal ho gaye.* (19)
> (You have now become a leader. Then who takes care of the Congress Party's kitchen and other routine household chores? Will all of you go to Kashi? At least some of you should stay back to lick the leavings of food. Went to jail and started imagining yourself to be Pandit Jamiharlal!).

Entry of Gandhiji and B.R. Ambedkar into Indian political scene witnessed a total transformation of the code of conduct enforced by the upper-caste groups. Glen and Johnson, in their work, *Main Currents in Indian Sociology*, have pointed out:

> The role of ideas as an agent of change is notoriously difficult to assess, but it is clear that Western concepts of political and social equality imported, primarily to the elite caste Hindu society through education in Britain or on the British model substantially influenced that perception of caste and untouchability by the caste Hindu leaders and some untouchables as well. Gandhiji's crusades on behalf of untouchables, for example, rested on a curious blend of Western egalitarianism and Hindu reformism. (65)

The new look of the Congress, its determination to shift politics from the drawing rooms of the educated elite and the businessmen to the huts in the countryside and to the tillers of the soil could not fail to attract the attention of the villagers. The Congress promised *'Swaraj'*, if the people would follow their programmes. A new spirit of boldness and confidence inspires the people of Marygunj under the leadership of outsiders like Dr. Prashant, Baldev and Bawandas.

'Renu' has raised his voice against the class discrimination prevalent in the village society. He holds this evil responsible for the exploitation of the *'dalits'* and the downtrodden. Kalicharan seems to be the spokesman of 'Renu', who believes that the traditional hierarchy of caste structure is breaking up and now there are only two classes – the rich and the poor. He raises his voice against the rich and sympathises with the individual as well as the united rebellions by the poor against their rich exploiters. He further hits the caste system by planning matrimonial alliances between the high castes and untouchables. Marriage of Prashant and Kamala deviates from social norms and ridicules the traditional caste system.

Dr. Prashant is an outsider but he is genuinely interested in the welfare of the community. He had come to Marygunj to conduct his scientific research on malaria but the direction of his research changes when he confronts the harsh realities of life. His priorities change from now on his whole concentration is on improving the conditions of life for the landless labourers and to create for them conditions of human dignity. He writes to Mamata:

> *Kya karega wah sanjeevani booti khoj kar? Use nahin chahiye sanjeevani. Bhookh aur bebasi se chhatpatakar marne se achha hai malignant malaria se behosh hokar mar jana. Til-til kar ghul-ghulkar marne ke liye unhen jilana bahut bari krurta hogi... yahan insan hain kahan? ... Abhi pehla kam hai, janwar ko insan banana.* (175)
>
> (What will he get by discovering an elixir for malaria? He does not want the elixir. It is better to let them die of malaria than to make them wallow in abject hunger and poverty. It would be a cruelty to vivify them for dying by small bits and to waste themselves to death. Where are human beings here?... My first priority is to transform these animals into human beings).

The central theme of the novel is the rebellion by the aliens – Santhals, who had been working for the landlords for generations. The news of Bihar government's resolution to abolish zamindari came to the villages. Those who have cultivated the land for three consecutive years are supposed to be the owners of that land. But Santhals do not own even the huts in which they live. In 1937, an English officer had tried to improve their lot, but he had been transferred before he could achieve much. Now the new law gives them courage to rise against their masters. They claim their right to the land they had been cultivating for years but they are placed in a minority a handful of santhals and their females are unable to confront two hundred villagers. Four Santhals are killed, seven are wounded. Their women are sexually harassed. But still they are able to kill Hargauri, the new Tehsildar and nine other rustics. Twelve villagers are badly wounded and thirty others are hit by their primitive weapons – bows and arrows. They have to pay a very heavy price for this rebellion. The men are all sent to jail. Their women have to sell their ornaments to fight a legal battle. The only relief these poor people get is that they are not awarded death sentences. The landless primitive tribals are in jail on the eve of independence.

Kalicharan is another rebel, who joins the socialist party and lectures:

> *Yeh poonjipati aur zamindar, khatmalon aur machharon ki tarah sosakh hain. Khatmal ! Iseeliye bahut se marwariyon ke naam ke saath 'mal' laga hua hai.* (176)
> (These capitalists and landlords are bloodsuckers like mosquitoes and bugs (*khatmals*). Therefore '*mal*' is suffixed after the names of most of the *marwaris*).

Dr. Prashant endorses his revolutionary ideas and equates freedom with political awakening:

> *Jis din dhani, zamindar, seth aur mill walon ko rah chalte kodhi aur paagal samajhne lagenge usi din, usi din asal suraj ho jayega.* (275)
> (The day people begin to treat these wealthy people, landlords, capitalists and millowners as lepers and mad people, that day the real sun will rise.)

Kalicharan, the socialist, is arrested by the police on the charge of having links with murderous dacoits, while Dr. Prashant is declared a staunch communist and arrested for his alleged involvement in provoking the Santhals. But the spirit of the age triumphs ultimately. Despite all the atrocities rustics awaken from their stupor and assert themselves. Lower-class people constitute their separate panchayats and raise their voice against their rich and upper-class exploiters. They resolve to protest against their women's exploitation by their rich masters. They decide to penalize those husbands who send their wives to their masters. Even Tatma, Paswan, Dhanuk and Kori women, while playing their annual farce 'Jat-Jattin' to please the rain-gods, give vent to their repressed anger by abusing their exploiters playfully. Jeevesara chamar refuses to sweep Thakur Ramkirpal Singh's courtyard where a cow's corpse had been stinking for many days. The village barbers unite an act which is overtly visible from the unshaved faces of the Rajputs. Kalicharan subverts the religious hierarchy to support the 'Devdasi' of the 'Math'. Chalittar Karmakar, a 'Chamar' becomes dacoit and creates terror. *Rajputs* and *Brahmins* start feeling a threat to their existence. They cannot tolerate the insolence of the lower caste people. It is beyond their imagination to appease the untouchables.

Phaneshwar Nath 'Renu' has directly or indirectly criticized the contemporary social, political and capitalist economic systems. He has also portrayed the conflicts of the colonial and postcolonial India. He has reconstructed collective consciousness of those groups, which constitute society. He has portrayed their values, attitudes, inspiration and motives.

In spite of all the horror and misery that Marygunj has gone through, the villagers preserve their rich cultural heritage and language that exert a powerful influence over their lives. This background is a mixture of popular philosophy, tradition, history, myth, folk tales and folk songs. It is not possible to draw a line between these. The old epics of India, the Ramayana, the Mahabharata and other scriptures are widely known among the illiterate masses and every incident, story and moral in them are engraved on the popular mind. They know hundreds of verses by heart. It is amazing to see the literary turn given by the villagers to Bidapat Ka Naach, the tale of Suranga - Sadabrij. Religious kirtans are turned into Suraj Kirtans, festivals like Sirwa, Satuani, Satyanarayan Ki Puja, and Holi revive these villagers with a new zeal. They have a vivid picture gallery in their minds drawn from their culture, rituals, oral traditions and festivals.

Through these folk songs 'Renu' has satirized the hypocrisy of the high-class brahmins, who do not drink water touched by untouchables but do not mind having sexual relationships with their women. Comrade Mahantha flagellates the upper class people's hypocrisy in his folk song *'Bhadonwa'*, which is sung on the occasion of Holi. The folk songs do not spare even the selfish politicians. In a *'Jogida'* they satirize all political parties. Not only *'Jogida'*, *'Faguas'* are also sung to instil the sprit of patriotism and glorify our great national leaders like Mahatma Gandhi, Rajendra Prasad, Jawahar Lal Nehru, Vallabh Bhai Patel and Jai Prakash Narain. Romantic folk songs like *'Jhumar Barahmasa'* enchant Dr. Prashant so much that he forgets to write case histories. 'Renu' has portrayed through various rural myths the imaginative sweet dreams of rustics, to sharpen the sensitivities of the readers.

'Renu' has tried to create a new form by integrating the rural folk style, narrative art, rural nautankis and traditional oral literature with modern novel form. As a result of this a bridge is established between traditional-modern values, rural-urban values and attitudes. His commitment to his native rural life is evident from his language. To convey this love for rural life he has used rural Hindi. The regional language of Purnea is a mixture of Maithili, Angika and Bangla. Characters of *Maila Aanchal* speak the kind of Hindi and pronounce English words as usually the rural people from lower social stratum speak. This language depicts their close social association. This vernacular brings them closer in their struggles as well as cooperation. It enables them to adapt themselves to their rich cultural heritage. His language is innovative, which facilitates him to portray the traditional modern and rural urban culture and social changes.

The final impact is of optimism, the writer is optimistic about the future of the rustics wallowing under the *'Maila Aanchal'* the soiled mantle of rural *'Bharath Mata'* Mother India. He is confident that there will be smiles on their shrivelled faces with a revival in their faith in their own potential. Love and non-violence would enlighten the lives of the villagers. He has immense faith in humanity, a faith indestructible in its innate strength.

References

Dewan, R.P. *How to Erase Untouchability*. New Delhi: R.P. Bookwala, 1979.

Glen, M. and Johnson, S.B. "Social Mobility Among Untouchables", *Main Currents in Indian Sociology Part III Cohesion and Conflict in Modern India*, Ed. G.R. Gupta. Delhi: Vikas, 1978.

'Renu', Phaneshwar Nath. *Maila Aanchal* (Hindi, 1954). Delhi: Raj Kamal Paperbacks. 2004.

14

Aesthetics of a Decentred Narrative *Train to Pakistan*

SAROJINI

A literary text not only creates meaning but also contextualizes the meaning. Khushwant Singh's story *Train to Pakistan* works through a post-partition narrative to explore the history of a nation. The novel written in 1956, less than a decade after the partition of the country, is amongst the earliest to go back to the traumatic happening which brought conventional communities living in harmony face to face with the incomprehensible reality of the partition. Mano Majra is located on the border between the two countries, a border that was slow to come into formation. This paper proposes to examine the double action of the spatial dynamics – one is its gradual polarization along religious line, the other is the expansion of this village to become a metaphor for the nation. Working through this the question of the shifting protagonist is taken up. Who is the protagonist? Is it the village? Juggat or Iqbal? Or the magistrate who is the arm of the administration? Or the army, which forces the politics of exclusion? The visible and invisible forces which are at play in the novel are instrumental in decentring the narrative.

The partition was a long time in the making – the thirties and the forties went into building up the frenzy – but was quick to happen. The British government advanced its date of withdrawal from the country from July 1948 to August 1947, thus compressing all political decisions into a shorter period. Ten million people were in flight, one million were reported dead. This was a singular civil war, as Arjun Mahey observes: "There were no borders, no assigned forces, no plans, only a spontaneous, visceral ferocity, whose possibility was unanticipated and whose legacy is more than evident even today" (138). This terrible cataclysm was constituted in the first instance by the passivity of the British government and a total breakdown of law and order. There was an administrative vacuum as M. Asaduddin has observed: "That which essentially was a human problem, and needed an imaginative and sensitive treatment, was sought to be solved by a single stroke dividing the land" (124).

Khushwant Singh in *Train to Pakistan* takes up for its subject the life of the people of Mano Majra, who despite the unrest around them continue to live in a self-contained would and in a state of communal harmony.

The spatial dynamics of Mano Majra make for an idyllic village. Situated on the bank of the river Sutlej, it was a place of exceptional scenic beauty. It was a favourite haunt of the bureaucrats who went there for a weekend hideout at the Officers Rest House by the riverside. They spent their time fishing or shooting pheasant in the marshes. At the time of the partition, the district magistrate made it his headquarter to monitor the law and order situation of his district.

Mano Majra had a special significance due to its magnificent railroad bridge that spanned the river. On its eastern side was a small one-track railway station, on the western side a pond ringed by keeker trees. Beside the pond, under a keekar tree stood a three-foot slab of sandstone – the local *deo* (deity) that united the villagers – Hindus, Muslims, Sikhs and even Christians.

Through graphic description, the reader is told of a cluster of flat-roofed mudhuts, with narrow lanes, surrounded by fields, which belonged to the Sikhs. At the centre of the village was a triangle with three brick buildings and a peepul tree. One of the brick structures belonged to Ramlal, the moneylender; the other two were the mosque and the Gurudwara of the village. Most of the collective activities centred around this area. It served as a refuge in times of distress. Mano Majra consisted of about 70 families of Muslims and Sikhs – almost equal in number. Absence of a hierarchy characterized the village. There was a perfect understanding between the two communities, who had lived together for thousands of years, complementing each other, "The Sikhs owned all the land around the village; the Muslims are tenants and share the tilling with the owners" (10). A lone Hindu, the moneylender and a few families of sweepers, who were Christian converts, completed the structure of the community.

What gave a unique character to Mano Majra was its railway station. The daily routine of the villagers was regulated by the arrivals and departures of various trains. The trains formed an integral part of their lives. The mail train rushing to Lahore at daybreak was like the clarion call to the villagers. The drivers of the engine would invariably give two blasts of the whistle and in an instant all Mano Majrans woke up. The crows began to caw, the bats returned to their perches in the Peepul, the Mullah at the mosque sounded his sonorous prayer – "Allah – ho – Akbar"; the priest at the temple followed with his bathing ablutions, intoning his prayers in monotonous sing song to the splashing of water. By the time the 10:30 morning passenger train from Delhi went through, life at Mano Majra would have settled down to a dull daily routine – men in the fields, women in the kitchen and the children out grazing the cattle by the river. By midday when the express train passes by, all Mano Majrans stop to rest. Men and children come home for their meal and the afternoon siesta. When the evening train comes in from Lahore, everyone goes to work again. The cattle are rounded up and driven home to be milked, the women cook the evening meal. Later they all gather on their rooftops where they sleep during summer. Sitting on the charpoys they eat their supper of vegetables and chappaties, and sip hot creamy milk out of large copper glasses and idle away the time till the goods train steams in. It is like saying goodnight. The Mullah again calls the faithful to prayer, "God is great", and the Sikh murmmers his prayers to drowsy men and women. The life in Mano Majra is stilled to sleep, lulled by the goods train as it rumbles off over the bridge.

The unlettered, rustic villagers had imbibed, over uninterrupted time, a composite ethos of a shared, meaningful mutually enriching community life. Indo-Muslim culture had become an inalienable part of their experiential world and social consciousness. Independence meant little to them. They held that freedom was for the educated people. For them it would make little difference. Earlier they were the slaves of the British, now it would be the educated Indians. For them freedom would be meaningful if it gave them more land, more buffaloes, and no debts.

The moral code of the community, although baffling to a western educated man like the communist activist, had evolved on the basis of community loyalty. Everyone in the village was related to each other. Hence for them the universal values on truth, honour, and financial integrity were placed much lower down the scale than being true to one's self, to one's friends and fellow villagers. For friends you could lie in court or cheat. No one would blame you. In fact you became a *nar admi,* a he-man who had defied authority (of the magistrate/police) and religion (taken an oath on the scripture and lied) but proved true to friendship and loyal to your village. Meet Singh, the Sikh priest, is critical of Jugga, the village gangster who is arrested as a suspect of the moneylender's murder. Had he killed someone in the neighbouring village, Meet Singh would probably have appeared in his defence, and sworn on the holy Granth to prove his alibi, but as he is suspected of having killed a fellow-villager, his crime becomes unforgivable. So the villagers are not sorry that Jugga and Iqbal, the Communist are arrested, although it turns out later that they were not the real culprits.

Jugga and Iqbal are arrested on trumped up charges and lodged in the lock-up at the Chundunagar police station. Iqbal's identity is intentionally falsified to frame him as a communal informer. The police, acting as the arm of the government, try and provoke both Jugga and Iqbal to violence. Mali and his accomplices, while being discharged from the lock-up are encouraged to pass provocative remarks about Jugga's Muslim girlfriend. Jugga turns violent and savagely attacks Mali. All this happens in the police station. Spatial dynamics play a major role in inciting communal discord.

After the murder of Ramlal, the moneylender, the villagers sense a premonition of impending calamities. They read the signs in the timings of the trains going wrong. Not only did the trains become more unpunctual but many unscheduled trains started running through Mano Majra at night. This resulted in throwing the whole pattern of the villagers' lives out of gear. Instead of the Mullah giving the first call for prayer, he waited for the Sikh priest to make a start; people stayed in bed late, without realizing that the mail train might not run through at all. Children did not know when to be hungry, so they clamoured for food all the time. In the evenings everyone was indoors before sunset as the goods train had stopped running altogether. There was no train to lull them to sleep at night. All this disrupted the lives of the villagers.

The train is a prominent metaphor used in fiction. In the context of displaced refugees, images of long kafilas of people moving with their loaded bullock carts has become a metaphor for the longest human migration in history. The train too has been used by many writers; in Krishan Chander's short story "Peshawar Express", Bhisham Sahni's "We Have Arrived in Amritsar", and in Mali Rai's "Kichas" the train has been used to articulate the fragility of life. It not only records incidents of blood and brutality, but he train becomes a vehicle of corpses of refugees and a reporter of tales of horror and rumours. In *Train to Pakistan* the train is an important metaphor. In peacetime it sets the tempo of life of the Mano Majrans. At the time of the holocaust it not only brings the corpses of the massacred Hindus from Pakistan but also brings home the uncertainty of the Muslim refugees of being able to reach their destination. It clearly symbolizes the body of the nation being torn apart. Jugga and Hukum Chand stand for love and the human spirit that triumphs in the end.

The intuition of the villagers was validated by the arrival of a train from Pakistan loaded with corpses of massacred Sikhs. Shocked and stunned by the sight, stilled in deathly silence by the odour of burning flesh, the villagers did not react in a frenzy of irrational revenge. Though they bemoaned the madness of their countrymen, they did not join the mad dance of communal violence. They faced the unfortunate outcome with equanimity – the refugees were adjusted in the Gurdwara. The hospitality, the care and concern of the Muslims of Mano Majra was commendable. They made the Sikh refugees from Pakistan feel at home and welcome. The skill of crisis management of the villagers was unexceptionable. But the government had its own plans. Hukumchand, the DM ordered the evacuation of the Muslims to refugee camps as a precaution. The Mano Majrans were in a dilemma as the Hindu Mano Majrans had expressed their solidarity to their Muslim tenants. But the government anticipated riots to spread all over. Hence all precautions were taken to prevent any incident. The Mano Majrans resolved to stand by their Muslim brethren, promising to look after their property. They believed it was a temporary dislocation. Things would soon return to normalcy. They strove to maintain a composite ethos; having imbibed true culture within themselves which had the capacity to be all-encompassing. This innate capacity was foreclosed by the advent of communalism, perceiving the difference as the "other" and therefore as a threat.

Hukumchand stands as a foil to the village as a protagonist. His bias is evident as he tells his confidant, the sub-inspector "No, Inspector Sahib, whatever our view - and God alone knows what I would have done to these Pakistanis if I were not a government servant - we must not let there be killings or destruction of property. Let them go out, but be careful they do not take too much with them" (32). Hukumchand's complicity is evident in his order releasing the criminal elements, Mali and his gang, absolving them of all blame and legalizing their loot and plunder of the properties of the Muslims of Mano Majra by appointing them as their caretakers.

The Mano Majrans felt helpless to prevent the external forces from violating their norms and disrupting the peaceful communal life. Numerous gory events failed to shake their faith in communal harmony. There was another ghost train, which brought bloody tales of massacred Sikhs and Hindus. Nature too showed its fury: The rains caused the river to rise - the river which had been their life support, became a vehicle of transporting the debris of the carnage taking place upcountry. Thousands of corpses along with carcasses of horses, bullock carts floated down the river on the banks of Mano Majra. The baggage of calamities got heavier as the carnage got more fierce. The village became one large graveyard. The Mano Majrans, however, at no stage, participated in the communal civil war. They desperately tried to remain neutral.

Humankind is buffeted again and again by overwhelming forces. This is pessimistic determinism at its worst. It cannot be denied that the vision of the powerlessness of individuals in the face of circumstances is particularly appropriate in recreating the tragedy of the partition. However, the author is intentionally pointing at the sharp divide between human beings and their environment. The village (protagonist) never displays the harsh side of life - feelings of anger, selfishness and revenge are always located outside them, and so is religion.

The powerful militants pressurized the villagers to retaliate and avenge their fellowmen. But the villagers stuck to their moral code. Meet Singh, their spokesman argues – "What have the Muslims here done to us for us to kill them in revenge for what the Muslims in Pakistan are doing? Only people who have committed crimes should be punished" (171). The militants had plotted to ambush the train to Pakistan carrying Muslims from Chundunagar and Mano Majra. The villagers refuse to kill their fellow brethren. They are conscientious objectors in the true sense. It is again the external forces – the refugees and Mali and his gang, the criminal elements who volunteer to attack the train. The Mano Majrans are not men of action. They do not act but are acted upon. They are not heroes in the way Juggat Singh is – plunging headlong into the fray. It is, ultimately, his supreme sacrifice that succeeds in foiling the seditious plan of the militants.

Upon learning about the plot of attacking the train at Mano Majra, Hukumchand was confronted with human reality at a personal level. While at the Rest House outside Mano Majra, he had got emotionally involved with a young innocent prostitute, Haseena. She reminded him of his daughter, who would have been the same age had she not died. Hukumchand's personal history is intertwined with national history. He plans to prevent the catastrophic event and uses Iqbal, the social worker, and Jugga, the dare-devil, as his agents to put his plan into action. He not only wants to save Haseena and her family who is going to be on that train but other innocent people too. Jugga too has his sweetheart, Nuru, the Mullah's daughter's welfare in mind. When he reaches the village and learns about the plans of the militants, his love for the girl is aroused. At this time religious hatred is brushed away, yielding place to a more nobler love of humanity. He succeeds in foiling the plans of the militants at the risk of his own life. Just as he succeeds in cutting the rope at the nick of time, before the train passes Mano Majra, he is shot down. But his sacrifice does not go to waste. Thousands of people on the train are saved as the train to Pakistan speeds past Mano Majra, unharmed. It symbolizes the triumph of the human spirit and the defeat of the destructive forces.

Pamela Rooks in her 1997 transference of the novel into a film has slightly deviated from the novel. But the film version, which was apparently approved by Khushwant Singh, sharpens the human element. It too has no central protagonist and works with space, this laying bare the skeletal framework of the novel with its emphasis on the anguish of dislocation, the helplessness of the prisoners, and the failure of ideology in the face of the supreme human sacrifice which often the self offers for the sake of the loved one.

References

Asaduddin, M. "Against Forgetting: Memory as Metaphor in 'Dream Images'". In *Translating Partition*. Eds. Ravikant and Tarun K. Saint. New Delhi: Katha, 2001.

Khushwant Singh, *Train to Pakistan*. (1956). New Delhi: Ravi Dayal, 2001.

Mahey, Arjun, "Partition Narratives: Some Observations", in *Translating Partition.* Eds. Ravikant and Tarun K. Saint. New Delhi: Katha, 2001.

15

Time and Space in Khushwant Singh's *Train to Pakistan*

RAMA RANI LALL

Thousands of trains cross thousands of bridges every day. But some crossings are possible only after a ritual sacrifice, some crossings take their passengers towards death and despair, while others towards life. In Khushwant Singh's novel the train's journey to Pakistan, at a time of hostility and hatred, is made at the cost of a human sacrifice which seeks to reverse the trend of ghost trains crossing from one country to another in 1947. In those days trains full of corpses, or trains which began their journeys never to reach their destination were common.

Singh's novel was written in 1956, less than a decade after partition riots and at a time when the wounds had not fully healed. Srinivas Iyengar in his history of *Indian Writing in English* (1962) has commented upon the difficulty of writing a novel on, "The events so recent, so terrible in their utter savagery and meaninglessness" (502), and of converting them into fiction with aesthetic dimensions. Its reception and four decades later, the film version in 1997 by Pamela Brooks has confirmed its status as a classic. Arthur Lall in his 'Introduction' to the novel has also commented upon this.

The important question then is, what goes into the making of a classic? It is not mere authenticity or the recording of history; it is also not merely the juxtaposition of ordinary lives with power politics, or stylistic reinforcement through images. A classic is ordinarily that which can transcend the limits of its contextuality, and move beyond the particular to encompass the universal; in fact that which can simultaneously appeal both to reason and to emotion, probing into the human consciousness in order to evoke an enlargement of a specific happening. In short, a piece of writing becomes a classic through its aesthetics.

This paper proposes to explore the spatio-temporal dimensions of the novel, the interaction of the past and the present and the reproduction of national conflicts in the story of a village. Mano Majra is a village on the newly defined border between India and Pakistan. Its sole significance is seen as a stopover for the goods trains passing through it, another 'developmental' connection, which the British had provided through the railway track, just as they had built a rest house for the bureaucracy to come and enjoy the natural scenery.

The temporal and spatial contexts of the narrative are defined in the very first pages of the novel, "The summer of 1947 was not like other Indian summers". It was hotter and drier than other summers and the monsoon was late. The writer informs us, "The summer before, communal riots, precipitated by reports of the proposed division of the country into a Hindu India and a Muslim Pakistan, had broken out in Calcutta" (1). Within a few months the death toll had risen to several thousand and soon the riots spread to the other parts of India, "By the time monsoon broke, almost a million of them were dead" (2). Another ten million were displaced and in flight from one part of the country to the other Khushwant Singh graphically describes this colossal migration, "They travelled on foot, in bullock carts, crammed into lorries, clinging to the sides and roofs of trains" (1). Practically, the whole of the North Western part of India was in turmoil and people were living in constant fear and terror, "The only remaining oases of peace were a scatter of little villages lost in the remote reaches of the frontier. One of these villages was Mano Majra" (2).

This sleepy village soon assumes a strategic importance after the partition, a village with "only three brick buildings, one of which is the home of the moneylender Lala Ram Lal. The other two are the Sikh temple and the mosque" (2). These three buildings enclose a triangular common meeting place for the villagers, who sit under the large peepul tree in the centre. The rest of the village has mudhouses and low-walled courtyards. A number of narrow lanes radiating from the centre dwindle into footpaths and soon reach the surrounding fields. There are about seventy families of Sikhs and Muslims in the village and for generations both the communities have lived in peace and harmony.

Another major landmark of Mano Majra is the river Sutlej, which flows in all its majesty and grandeur about half a mile away from the village. Being the largest river in Punjab, after monsoon its waters rise and spread across a vast sandy bed to become more than half a mile in breadth. "About a mile north of Mano Majra the Sutlej is spanned by a railroad bridge. It is a magnificent bridge – its eighteen enormous spans sweep like waves from one pier to another, and at each end of it there is a stone embankment to buttress the railway line" (3). On the eastern side of the bridge is the railway station of Mano Majra.

In the novel, Khushwant Singh focuses all his attention on Mano Majra and its surroundings and makes it a symbol of the whole of rural India. The time frame of the narrative is also limited to what happened in the few months before and after the partition of the country in 1947. With sympathetic realism he portrays a few of the events that define significant changes in the life and perceptions of the innocent villagers.

The normal life of the village was regulated by the coming and going of the trains. Many of the express trains did not even stop at the small station. "Of the many slow passenger trains, only two, one from Delhi to Lahore in the morning and the other from Lahore to Delhi in the evenings, are scheduled to stop for a few minutes". When these trains approach the bridge, the drivers invariably blow two long blasts of the whistle. In the morning as soon as the whistle is heard "all Mano Majra comes awake" (4). The mullah of the mosque knows that it is time for the morning prayers and the priest of the Sikh temple also gets ready to intone his holy songs. Throughout the day the arrival and departure of trains seem to inform the villagers when to start work and when to rest. Finally the coming of the goods train in the late evening, gradually lulls them to sleep. Thus the simple villagers spent their simple idyllic lives till the summer of 1947. Things suddenly changed for the worse after this.

The writer has woven the whole plot of the novel around three major incidents. The first is the murder of the moneylender, Lala Ram Lal, and the second and the third are the coming of the two ghost trains from Pakistan. With the greatest economy of means the night of the dacoity and murder is described. We are told that when the shots were fired Juggut Singh or Jugga was with his sweetheart Nooran on the banks of the river. In this way we are informed that Jugga had no hand in the dacoity and the murder. Still the police arrested him as he was out on parole from the prison. In spite of being innocent he was suspected and put behind bars, as he was the son of a dacoit. Another important character of the novel to be disturbed by the firing of the shots was Hukum Chand, the magistrate and the deputy commissioner of the district, responsible for maintaining law and order. He was camping at Mano Majra for a few days and was busy with a teenaged dancing girl, Haseena. The gunfire reminded him of his duties.

The morning after the murder a young educated person Iqbal, alighted from the train at Mano Majra. He was a social worker and belonged to the communist party. Since he was an outsider the police promptly arrested him too, for the murder of the moneylender, though they knew very well that he was not in the village that night.

It is interesting to note how the writer has used the murder of Lala Ram Lal as a central event to introduce some of the key characters of the novel. With a few deft strokes he has drawn a vivid picture of their life and feelings. Especially the character of Jugga has been revealed in a few telling incidents. We know that he was the tallest and the strongest man in Mano Majra and though his father had been hanged for a murder, he himself was more a victim of social injustice than a born criminal. When Jugga and Iqbal were being escorted to the police headquarters in a tonga, they started talking to the policemen about the cruelties being perpetuated on the innocent Sikhs and Hindus in Pakistan by Baluch soldiers. Jugga's natural goodness came to the fore and he cried vehemently, "They cannot escape from God. No one can escape from God" (66). These words surprised both the policemen and Iqbal, as they never expected a habitual sinner to be so God-fearing. Moreover, when Jugga saw the tonga driver whipping the horse again and again he tried to restrain him. This showed his compassionate attitude towards the helpless dumb animal.

The second part of the novel has the significant title "Kalyug" or the age of sinners. We hear a lot about the atrocities and mindless violence of the partition. The peaceful life of Mano Majra was badly shaken when a ghost train from Pakistan reached the village. It created an unprecedented confusion in the minds of the people. Even Hukum Chand, the deputy commissioner, could not sleep that night because of nightmares. The sight of hundreds of dead bodies totally unnerved him.

Next morning, he made up his mind to send the Mano Majra Muslims to a refugee camp, apparently for their own safety. By this time a number of refugees had crossed over the river from Pakistan to seek shelter in the village. Hukum Chand did not want to encourage them, as it would add to his problems. But the subinspector informed him that the simple peasants of Mano Majra had no heart to refuse help to people in need. They firmly believed hospitality to be their sacred duty.

Khushwant Singh has given a graphic picture of the love and fellow feeling between the Sikhs and Muslims of Mano Majra. As the Sikhs started debating amongst themselves about the position of Muslims in their village, Imam Buksh, the mulla of the mosque came there with some other Muslims and asked them about their decision. A young Sikh said, "As long as we are here nobody will dare to touch you. We die first and then you can look after yourself" (125-126). These words touched the heart of Imam Buksh and wiping his tears he replied, "What have we to do with Pakistan? We were born here. So were our ancestors. We have lived amongst you as brothers" (126). Saying this, when he broke down, Meet Singh clasped him in his arms and began to sob. Several other villagers also started crying and wiping their tears. Finally, a sad day came, when on the practical advice of the Lambardar, the Muslims agreed to go to the refugee camp for a few days, not knowing that they would be soon be sent to Pakistan from there in a train that would have to cross the bridge near Mano Majra.

The last section of the novel shows how the feelings of revenge and retaliation finally reach the village. One day the people noticed hundreds of wounded corpses floating on the swollen waters of Sutlej. This shocked and angered them. And then another ghost train reached the station from Pakistan. There was no doubt in anyone's mind about what the train contained. That evening, the entire village turned up at the gurudwara, to find solace in prayer. At night, as they were dozing in the temple a jeep stopped there. Some young Sikhs in khaki uniforms and rifles on their shoulders entered the hall and exhorted them angrily to take up arms to protect themselves. They asked the villagers to join hands and retaliate as the only means of stopping the mindless massacres in Pakistan. Soon they hatched a diabolic conspiracy of attacking the train going to Pakistan, the next night. When the deputy commissioner heard of this he was totally at a loss to decide what to do to save the train. In desperation he could think of nothing better than to set Jugga and Iqbal free, in the faint hope of something being done. The writer shows that at a moment of crisis everyone seemed to have lost his power of effective action. The deputy commissioner, with all his authority, felt totally helpless and tried to console himself with tears and prayers.

Iqbal, with all his learning and foreign education, wanted others to do something to save the train. He tried to drown his concern for the Muslims in whisky. It was only Jugga, the illiterate villager of Mano Majra who decided to do everything he could, to save his brother Muslims and his ladylove Nooran from mindless slaughter.

The last pages of the novel are a tribute to the unselfish courage of Jugga. The literary skill of Khushwant Singh also reaches its height. In a dramatic climax we are told that as soon as Jugga learnt that the conspirators were planning to tie a rope, as tightly as steel over the first span of the bridge, a little above the funnel of the engine, so that the people sitting on the roof tops of the train should fall and be killed by the waiting avengers, he made up his mind.

At night, after visiting the gurudwara he reached the railway bridge and started climbing it. The train got closer and closer. The hidden conspirators warned him to desist, but he reached the rope and started hacking at it with his kirpan, unmindful of the unkind bullets of his fellow Sikhs. The leader of the conspirators fired at him and he lost a leg. Still he continued cutting the rope with his right hand. Gradually the rope started giving way and only a few shreds remained. Khushwant Singh tells us, "He went at it with his knife, and then with his teeth. The engine was almost on him. There was a volley of shots. The man shivered and collapsed. The rope snapped in the centre as he fell. The train went over him, and went on to Pakistan" (181).

The forces of power and politics are several – the outsider Iqbal, a communist, bearing a name which has its own secular appeal, the magistrate who represents an administration which has entered into the game of manipulation; the British who had ignited a train of events without any thought of its consequences, the army, which has unknowingly become a tool in the hands of religious separatism and finally the people who are being manipulated by these multiple forces. The narrative is constructed around them. It is possible to define three different space patterns of the village occurring at different stages of the narrative:

(i) The village community is at the centre, with its different compartments and the fields, form the outer circle. All else is outside the village. The first disruption comes through the dacoits and the second through Iqbal's entry.

(ii) The jail and the rest house become the centre with helpless victims lodged in the former and made to fight out group rivalries through the intentional intervention of the police. All this while the magistrate acts out the role of the string puller in his rest house and constitutes the second pole.

(iii) The third pattern emerges with the entry of the army and the forced evacuation of the Muslims, an evacuation which cuts across the village population, almost one-half of which is carried off. There is a shrinking of emotional and community space while geographical space remains the same, only to become a territory to be encroached upon by others.

These spatial patterns become even more clear in the film version when the fields as a site of a midnight romance; the cells as barriers controlling anger likely to burst out in other ways, and the sobering impact this has on Iqbal who begins to see his own ideological beliefs from the other end; the evacuation scene with the army trucks being loaded and the villagers being pushed away like wild beasts meant to be kept at bay – all these come out graphically.

As fear and violence stalk this land and age-old wisdom finds itself being ousted by new ideologies, the present moment is expanded through history, memory and modernity. Khushwant Singh has skilfully explored the memories of Hukum Chand and the modernity of Iqbal to give them a human face. On the first day of his visit to Mano Majra, Hukum Chand wanted some entertainment for the evening. Initially, he felt uneasy with the young dancing girl and did not have the nerve to take a good look at her. When she started singing a song he realized that he knew it well for, "he had heard his daughter humming it" (27). The memory of his daughter troubled him. "He took another whisky and dismissed his conscience. Life was too short for people to have consciences" (27). Another look at the girl convinced him that she was only a child and perhaps younger than his own daughter. He tried to drown his inner doubts with another whisky. "Life was like that. You took it as it came, shorn of silly conventions and values which deserved only lip worship" (28).

Later on in the novel, when Hukum Chand hears about the impending ambush of the train, he feels anxious and helpless and ashamed of his own behaviour with Haseena and thinks, "That was too ludicrous! He must be losing his grip on things. He was getting senile and stupid" (175). Such self-confessions reveal the inner personality of Hukum Chand and the reader feels that all human beings have their weaknesses. What could the magistrate do before mad mobs? He had no power when the fanatics took matters in their own hand. It was all the fault of the central government at Delhi. "What were the people in Delhi doing? Making fine speeches in the assembly?" (176). On the way the magistrate tried to console himself and yet his heart felt sorry for the Muslim passengers of the train and Haseena. He could only pray and weep for them in his helplessness.

Similarly, when the highly educated, modern, young Iqbal had comes to Mano Majra, he had wanted to do a lot for the villagers. He tells Meet Singh, "Now with the partition there is so much bloodshed going on, someone must do something to stop it. My party has sent me here, since this place is a vital point for refugee movements. Trouble here would be disastrous" (35).

His name Iqbal without any surname was ambiguous. He did not take his religion seriously and as the writer tells us his name by itself could not reveal his identity. "He could be a Muslim, Iqbal Mohammad. He could be Hindu, Iqbal Chand, or a Sikh, Iqbal Singh. It was one of the few names common to the three communities" (35). In Mano Majra, Iqbal Singh would have been better and Iqbal may not have to suffer so much. When he was put in the prison for the murder of Lala Ram Lal, the police conveniently called him Mohammad Iqbal and declared him to be a member of the Muslim league.

His idealism and theorizing were shattered by the rough handling of the police. He felt humiliated and insulted. Though, later on he realized that his stay in the prison would help him become a leader and a hero in his own party. Coming out of the prison, he learnt about the plot of attacking the train. He knew that he cannot do anything, being a stranger in the village. He had not appreciated the simplicity and hospitality of the villagers and had preferred his tinned food to the fresh milk and vegetables offered by the Lambardar and Meet Singh. Having lived in foreign countries for a long time, he could take a more critical look at the shortcomings of the villagers and found them unclean.

Meet Singh had felt disappointed, at all his theorizing at the crucial moment of action. Iqbal had no remedy to stop the mad killings going on everywhere. He told Meet Singh, "Bhaiji, when people go about with guns and spears you can only talk back with guns and spears. If you cannot do that, then it is best to keep out of their way" (169). Iqbal knew that a sacrifice might be worth making if there are people to applaud your action. Finally, it was left to the bravest man in the village, Jugga to save the train, at the cost of his own life.

Thus we find, that though the division of the country was made possible through evacuation and revenge, through political and antisocial forces, there was a fresh coming together of positive forces. The dancing girl Haseena, who is outside narrow religious definitions and Jugga who wants to save

Nooran so that his child's birth can take place, even if it is in another land, are rustic characters who rise up to sustain humanistic forces.

References

Iyengar, Srinivas K.R. *Indian Writing in English.* (1962). New Delhi: Sterling Publishers, 1984.

Singh, Khushwant. *Train to Pakistan.* (1956). New York: Grove Press, 1989.

16

Centres and Margins in *Chemmeen*

JESSY MANI

Villages, basically, are social units signified by the bonds between the inhabitants, their local deities and the land on which they live. The harmony between the people, the territorial space and the deity determine the social and cultural fabric of the village. The community centres its beliefs, myths and symbols around the deities thus creating a local cultural context which excludes those outside their own territorial boundaries. The geographical and cultural spaces become defining points and create borders that generate a "sense of belongingness and allegiance" (Madan 14). Within the community sects and sub-sects jostle for space that determines power structures and centres and margins.

Spaces, centres and margins are the tropes that get defined and redefined in the scheme of the narrative, *Chemmeen*, Shiva Shankar Pillai's award-winning novel published in 1957. The narrative is as much about social spaces as about emotional or territorial spaces. These spaces are continually rewritten and restructured. The subtext of spaces, centres and peripheries creates power structures where meanings and positions are battled. Within these structures frameworks are determined and identities of self and the other are created. The question of self also raises question about how the self is created and located, how it relates to the other, how the relational dynamics work, and also how and where genders are positioned within these frameworks.

In this article I will seek to problematize how the human space in the narrative *Chemmeen* is relational to the geographical space, the manner in which these spaces are contested and determined, structures of meanings are created. As in all rural communities space here too is a fluid entity and boundaries between public and private spaces blur. The fishing community exists as a moral force, a custodian of values that breaks into the individual space of all the characters.

Chemmeen is a traditional narrative, in fact a folk tragedy with the overwhelming presence of natural forces, community overlordship and suppression of individual desires. It is the story of a village of fisherfolk, their beliefs and traditions. Born into that community, Karuthamma is aware of the codes that bind her but cannot help falling in love with the Muslim trader, an outsider. Her father cashes on the affair and fulfils his ambitions of buying a boat. When Karuthamma marries another man the past keeps haunting her and the novel ends tragically for all the principal characters.

The narrative focuses on the codes and beliefs of the fisherfolk. Their lives revolve around the belief that their women have to be chaste as their goddess demands. She is a cosmic power and she protects her community, grants its well-being but when displeased her wrath brings ruin and destruction to the sea front. For the fisherman who confronts the sea everyday, the dictates of Kathalamma, the goddess, is central to his existence so the codes of morality are inviolable.

The imaginative geography of the narrative includes the seascape and the emotional and mythical terrains woven around it. The seascape is not merely a territorial location but an emotional space embedding an emotional solidarity. It determines the way in which the fishing community exists, the ways in which they relate to the sea and to each other, the patterns in which myths are created to codify their lives and how their individual lives are woven into the life of the community.

The sea goddess, Kathalamma, binds her people in code of values and beliefs that cannot be challenged. She is a stern goddess difficult to please, a goddess who expects her women to be pristine and virginal and her men to be moral and brave. If provoked she can throw monsters and reptiles on the shore and drag men through treacherous currents and boggling whirlpools. Her people must not violate her code and defile the front.

These set of values, encoded deeply in the cultural and imaginative spaces of the community, are transmitted through oral traditions of lore and songs which were highlighted in the film version (1965), that help to delineate the community. The women are taught to be chaste in thought and deed. They are the "inheritors of some old truths and of a way of life." The myth of the first fisherman who alone fought the waves, and the sharks and the whales 'on a piece of wood' exists to remind the women that they must conform:

> The waves rose high on the sea. The whales approached him (the fisherman) with their mouths gaping. The sharks charged the boats with their tails. The current dragged the boat into a terrible whirlpool. But he escaped from everything miraculously ..... how did all these things came to pass? Because, on the shore a chaste and pure woman was praying steadfastly for the safety of her husband at sea. (9)

It is interesting that the burden of conformation lies mainly with women thus morally foregrounding them. Karuthamma, the heroine of the novel, feels cloistered by "the walls of the fort" the taboos of the "children of the sea... a fort with no doors, no windows." However she has no choice but to conform. The fear of the wrath of the sea goddess compels every woman into submission. The myths then become a means to create gender constructs and to locate the gender on the margins if they do not conform. Karuthamma's liaison with the Muslim trader, Pareekutty, places her on the margins and, later when she marries, her husband is excluded from the community and thrown out of his job because of fear of doom. The sea goddess, the community fears, would never be bountiful to them and her anger would be manifested through disastrous waves and sea monsters thrown on the shore. The territorial, cultural and mythical lines run into each other creating structures of submission and texts of exclusion.

The subtext of centrality and marginality constructs the identities of both the community and the self. The centres are determined by traditions of conformation and the self is the frame, the reference that defines the 'other'. The self 'others' the other. As Lacan defines the 'I' that "situates the agency of the ego, before its social determination... projects the individual" into a scheme of definition so is the self projected through the otherness of the other (Lacan 1-7). This grants a certain kind of validity to the self that has an empowered identity. The 'other' then becomes the inarticulate, invisible presence located on the margins.

The centre spaces in the narrative create identities of self and through these identities definitions are forged and texts of belonging and alienation are sculpted. The fishing community is the self empowered by its moral and ethical legitimacy. The spaces within the community are well-defined in terms of social positioning. There are the boat owners, the working fishermen, and the lower men and hoisted over all are the headman, the chief arbiter, and the priest. The headman settles all matters. Nobody can own a boat or marry without his consent. He can question any decision. The community, thus, lives in an ordered and patterned framework codified by a community ethic. It has the right to intrude upon private spaces. When Chembankunju buys a boat, his act is perceived as a violation of community ethics because he had not yet got his daughter married. The boundaries between private and public space merge. The community is the empowered moral police. Again they become the voices of convention at the marriage ceremony of Karuthamma and raise questions about her purity. Even later these voices and presences intrude upon the personal spaces of Karuthamma's home. Her affair with Pareekutti becomes everybody's business and Karuthamma and her husband are never left alone to lead their lives. Indexes of morality authorize the community to assume a centrality and rewrite margins.

The spaces in the scheme of the community are closely guarded and those outside are not admitted. Pareekutti is an outsider in Karuthamma's world. He is a trader and had come to the front as a young boy and has grown up on the shore but he cannot be integrated into Karuthamma's world. His religion also alienates him and there are evidences in the text that people like him are seen with mistrust. Mothers advise their daughters to stay away from such outsiders who are not guided by the code that bind the insiders. Chakki, Karuthamma's mother, on her deathbed tries to integrate him into their familial framework by making him promise that he would perceive Karuthamma as his sister but it is a forced conversion and it never works.

For those who belong to the community positions are battled even as they are composed. Thus the positions are never a constant. It is a variant structured and restructured. Chembankunju, as the narrative opens, seeks to move to a socially and economically viable bracket. He becomes a boat-owner and by becoming one he others himself. He refuses to relate to his earlier contexts, his friends and neighbours have great hopes of attaining social prominence through their associations with him. But he moves beyond them. He wishes to recreate the world of Kandankoran, known for his wealth and grandeur. He aspires to live in similar luxury, and desires that his wife be like the beautiful Pappikunju who lived a regal life. After Chakki's death when he marries Pappikunju, they try to recreate that world but that world is lost to them. Chembankunju, thus, is posited in a very complexly constituted position. He is the self that becomes the other.

The gender has to contest for centrality and even as they battle for space new positions emerge. Conformation to gender roles and role expectations determine their legitimacy. As wives and mothers they must conform to established patterns and carry on with the traditions they have been conditioned to accept. The folklore locates as the centre the myth the first fisherwoman whose virtue brought her husband safely back home. The myth is another variation of the broader cultural references to Sita and Savitri, glorified for fulfilling role expectations. Counter to the myth of the virtuous wife run the references to the fallen woman. These stories act as warning signposts in the lives of women. "The low caste women coming from the inland" are among the ones that pollute the sea, its community. Those outside their own territorial bounds, the others are perceived as perverse and degraded. The boundaries of inclusion and exclusion are clearly drawn and ferociously guarded

Almost every tradition celebrates and validates maternal configurations. Chakki, Karuthamma's mother is valorized both by the narrative voice and by the characters in the narrative. The maternal artefact defines her vision and moorings. As a mother of young daughters she has to school her daughters and condition them to become virtuous wives and self-effacing mothers. Her womanly instincts can sense that Karuthamma and Pareekutti feel deeply for each other but as a mother she cannot allow her daughter to carry on with a man who she knows the daughter can never marry. She has to warn her daughter and alert her, "the shrubs on the seafront and the cover of the boats stacked on the shore – these are the places you should be wary of." She has the practicality to know that an alliance between the two lovers would never be possible so she wants her daughter to be married before things get troublesome. The issue of the daughter's marriage weighs over everything else and she has to compel her reluctant husband to confront the problem. She is the anxious mother when she sends her daughter away to her new home despite her fatal illness because she knows that the daughter's stay will provoke people to gossip more. She even makes Pareekutti promise that he would perceive Karuthamma as his sister, a more honourable configuration than the earlier context in which the two related to each other.

Chakki can only see herself in the roles of a mother or a wife. As a wife she has been dutifully virtuous and stood by her husband and shared the economic burdens of running the home. These are the relational contexts in which she can perceive herself and in which others perceive her. There is no other reference point to define her either in the community where she lives or in her perception of herself.

Pappikunju, the woman Chembankunju marries after his wife's death, is a counter reference to Chakki. For her centrality is a space that becomes variant and shifting. As the wife of Kandankoran known for her fabled wealth and beauty she is "visible" in ways that denominate her as a body. Her body glows like 'gold' and there are plenty of references in the text that support that she is objectified in the male gaze and that codifies her femininity. Chembankunju wants Chakki to become desirable like her. Her second marriage is seen as a deviant from the norm. Compelled to remarry for economic reasons the patriarchal perspectives do not approve her choice or her course. People from her own community feel that she has lowered herself marrying beneath her. The subtext is also that her position alters because she refused to remain the valorized widow figure that is part of our cultural ethics which prescribes a sexually inactive doting mother as the norm. Such a figure conforms to an asceticism, part again of a broader cultural framework, and also proves her constancy to the dead husband, the dominant reference point in relation to which a woman is always perceived.

Woman, thus, seen always in relational terms, is not simply a biological binary to a man. Her being and position are loaded with references and frameworks where man is the centre she has to relate to, the self through whom she has to define herself. Social and cultural structures have always grounded her in a subservient status. Of the available frames through which her being is perceived and through which she perceives herself, guilt is the dominant context. A woman is guilty for imagined and real offences. Hence she is always apologising for her 'being', her aspirations, her actions, her desires. A woman is always perceived to have a past and a woman with a past is necessarily a fallen one, and thus always a target for witch-hunting. From the Biblical Eve to the mythical Ahilya to Hester Prynne in *The Scarlet Letter*, our cultures are loaded with instances of the fallen woman.

Karuthamma, the heroine of the narrative, is a twice marginalized figure. Her guilty past marginalizes her. As the narrative opens her love for the Muslim trader, Pareekutty, is condemned by her community not merely because he is an outsider but also because being a fisherwoman she must be chaste and pure. She deviates from the accepted norm and her deviation alienates her from the frames of security available to other women. After she is married to Palani, she is constantly persecuted for her guilty past and she is persecuted not only by her husband but also by the invisible watchtowers that spread stories about her. Despite her avowals of her truthfulness and her constancy, the shadow of Pareekutty always stalks them.

It is not enough that she must be seen as guilty. It is also necessary that she should be made aware that she is guilty and should suffer the disgrace crime brings along with it. She too has an invisible scarlet letter to wear signifying her past. The community never lets her forget that she is the condemned. References to her affair keep cropping up either in the gossip of the women, in the accusations of her husband or in the altercations Palani has with his mates over the issue.

Thus Karuthamma is always justifying herself as a dutiful wife, proving her constancy. Guilt then becomes a strategic weapon which the husband wields over his wife. It allows him the license to question her, seek assurances of her constancy and determine the power equations between the two. So Karuthamma always has to answer, assure, promise:

> She would never behave or live in the way in which her husband would hate his homecoming. She would never cause the sea to rise into waves enough to engulf the houses. Poisonous sea snakes wouldn't crawl on the coast. Nameless sea monsters would not raise their heads and gape their mouths open in the storm. She would live like a good fisherwoman. (130)

She always has to prove that she is not straying anymore, that she will be faithful to him. The guilt is embedded in her psyche and even a casual memory of Pareekutti upsets her and she feels she is committing a crime. The tortures gradually increase and Palani becomes immune to her pleas, her tears. He feels he is the wronged one and that a bad woman was married off to him. When she goes to sell the fish in her advanced stage of pregnancy he has no sympathy for her and he gets quite used to her tearful face and her pleas. These become the norm and the pattern in which the two relate to each other.

She is othered being a woman and in contexts in which gender is marginalized. In the final sections of the novel she liberates herself very boldly and achieves a centrality in a feminist and individual way. She frees herself from the guilt context, acknowledges her feelings and desires, and asserts herself. When she realizes that her husband has known that she still cares for her lover, she acknowledges her feelings without any apology, admits the truth without fear. It gives her strength and courage to move out of familial, social and cultural constraints. She leaves everything behind to walk away with her lover and never to return. The men in her life pale to insignificance. She rejects the contexts that had so far defined her, the configurations and roles that she had to relate to. In a curious way she rises above her contexts, its codes and norms, vindicates herself as a woman. Though the narrative does not end happily, it validates her and she rises above role expectations and conventional morality to become a woman and assert herself.

Thus the patterns of centrality as they work in the narrative create a relational marginality by which the centres get firmly delineated. We also see that these spaces have a fluidity and that they merge into each other and create newer positions, more reference points and that spaces, positions are shifting and variable entities.

References

Lacan, Jacques. *Ecrits: A Selection*. Trans. Alan Sheridan. New York: W. W. Norton, 1977.

Madan, Vandana. *The Village in India*. New Delhi: Oxford University Press, 2004.

Pillai, Thakazhi S. *Chemmeen* (1957). Bombay: Jaico Publishing House, 2004.

17

The Living Space Between Mindscapes and Landscapes

Village in Rahi Masoom Reza's *Adha Gaon*

AVINASH JODHA

Villages have been mapped in multiple ways, through socio-political discourses, from religious and economic perspectives and imaginatively in works of art and literature. More often than not these mappings have been predeterministic where the villages are treated as mindscapes or landscapes with some differences nevertheless the same attributes. The urban imagination maps a village and villagers as physical objects bound to each with some simple agrarian logic where in Thomas Gray's terms *The ploughman homewards plods his weary way*, or *jocundly drives his team afield*, his *sober wishes never learn to go astray* and he along with the others *keeps the noiseless tenor of his way* (*Elegy*). The image is too invigorating-man in almost perfect utopian harmony with nature, his family, surroundings and society.

The redundant stereotyping of village and villagers as an image ignores the subtle nuances of the space of village as a social construct construed through acquisition of geographical space, its distribution and organization, power relations, as a product of struggles between impositions, acceptance and active and passive modes of resistance. Michel Foucault points out:

> We do not live in a kind of void inside which we could place individuals and things. We do not live in a void that could be colored with diverse shades of light, we live inside a set of relations that delineates sites which are irreducible to one another and absolutely not superimposable on one another. (Foucault 22)

Foucault refuses to look at space in purely physical or abstract terms, as a landscape or a mindscape. He looks at space as a site delineated by the set of social relations in which we have lived and continue to live, a site which *draws us out of ourselves, in which the erosion of our lives, our time and our history occurs, the space that claws and gnaws at us* (22 emphasis added), the space that is the product of the complex matrix of time, space and social being. The theories proposed by Foucault, John Berger and more recently Edward W. Soja have had a radical influence in the understanding of the urban spaces vis-à-vis the advancement of capitalism. These theories can have a meaningful application in the context of the rural sites i.e. in the understanding of the village as a socially produced space. The treatment of village in Rahi Masoom Reza's *Adha Gaon* can serve as a potential example as the text is a strong departure from the stereotypical representations of village and rural life. The problematizing of village as a socially produced space raises several fundamental questions – what are the specifics that are operational in village as a socially produced space, how do these specifics interact and intersect with each other, how does a village as a distinct site relate to other villages or the urban sites and nation states, how do these spaces influence each other and how village and the idea of village has evolved in contemporary times.

Adha Gaon foregrounds the village as a space that had been lived in, is lived in and the space that itself lives, a space that is alive to its history and has been an active participant in its making. Though Reza in the beginning of the novel claims it to be a story of time:

> *Yeh kahani na kuch logo ki hai na kuch pariwaron ki. Yeh us gaon ki kahani bhi nahi hai jisme is kahani ke bhale-bure patra apne-aap ko purn banane ka prayatn kar rahe hai. Yeh kahani na dharmic hai na rajnitic, kaunki samay na dharmic hota hai na rajnitic...aur yeh kahani hai samay hi ki.* (11)
> (This story is not of some individuals or some families. This is not even the story of the village, in which the good or bad characters of the story are trying to complete themselves. This story is neither religious nor political because time is neither religious nor political...and this is indeed a story of time.)

The story of time, however, cannot be spaceless. The dreams and aspirations, confusions, of people are rooted as much in space as in time, the ruins do not just tell the story of time but of space as well. The new constructions on the old ruins are not acts of abstract time but are the products of social relations in interaction with time and space. Though Reza has his primary focus on time but the images that he uses are spatial in nature:

> *Ghazipur ke purane kile main ab ek school hai....Yeh asambhav nahi ki ab bhi is kile ki purani diwar par koi aa bathe aur apni aankhe band kar le to us par ke gaon aur maidaan aur keth ghane junglon mai badal jai aur tapovan mai rishion ki kutiyan dekhai dene lage. Aur wah dekhe ki ayodhya ke do rajkumar kandhe se kaman latkaye tapovan ke pavitra sannate ki raksha kar rahe hain.* (9)
> (In the old fort of Ghazipur now there is a school....It is not impossible that if someone today comes and sits on the old walls of the fort and closes his eyes he would see the transformation of villages, fields and farms into dense forests and huts of old sages would appear in the Tapovan. And he would see that the two princes of Ayodhya with their bows are guarding the pious calm of the Tapovan.)

The immediate landscape from the walls of the old fort – the villages, fields and farms – has come a long way from a *Tapovan* of old sages and their huts, guarded by the Princes of Ayodhya to the present day villages and farms. The old fort itself was constructed for a specific purpose and now the same space has a school and serves an establishmentarian purpose. It is not just time that has done it all; it is the outcome of the way in which the space, with all its physical limitations and possibilities, has been used as a site of control and resistance. The social theorist Anthony Giddens points out:

> The phrase might seem bizarre, but human beings do make their own geography as much as they make their own history. That is to say, spatial configurations of social life are just as much a matter of basic importance to social theory as are the dimensions of temporality. (qtd. by Soja 154)

The concept of socially produced space is fundamentally associated with various structures within given geographical boundaries. There are several visible structures in novel, the demographic structure of the village, the power structure, the economic structure and the structures within communities and families. Each of these structures corresponds to a complex hierarchy.

At the centre of the novel is the village Gangauli, situated about ten miles from Ghazipur, it takes its name from its former king Gang. It was later won by one of the sons of a chieftain of Tuglaq. The Sayyeds of Gangauli are the descendants of this chieftain. When the novel opens, a few years before the independence of India, the Sayyeds are the landlords of the village. Reza carefully presents the physical dimensions of the village. In the north of the village is the grave of its founder Nurrudin Saheid and in the south of this grave is Karbala a space that symbolizes the place where Imam Hussain attained martyrdom. In the west there is pond and near it are a few mounds laden with fruit trees on which the Sayyeds of the village come on the tenth day of *Moharram* for *Namaz*. In the west of the pond is a deserted factory constructed by an English officer John Gilchrist and on the North and the South ends of the village live the families of the Sayyeds, ten in all. There are three gates to the village one in the North and two in the South. Between the Uttar Patti (North Strip) and the Dakhin Patti (South Strip) there are the houses of julahas or weavers and Rakis who are Muslims but are considered inferiors by the Sayyeds. On the periphery of the village are the houses of Hindus primarily the lower castes Chamars, Bhars and Ahirs (13-14). This is Reza's Gangauli in its geographic and demographic proportions. It was not always the same, with the transfer of power into the hands of the Sayyeds the Hindus were pushed to the periphery and even the Sayyeds are divided into Uttar Patti and the Dakhin Patti.

The physical dimensions of Gangauli, and the concentration of its population in specific locations reflect the power relations that exist in the village. On the surface level the composition of Gangauli is fairly simple; on two sides of the village are the Sayyeds who own the land and between them are the houses of the tillers of their land, and artisans or people who conduct menial jobs bound with their castes. However, within this simple composition of power relations and their reflection in the physical space of the village there are multiple hierarchies operational within the structures of the communities, family relationships and the spaces of the homes and worship. These hierarchies are strictly guarded in both the public and the private domains. The Sayyeds see to it that the Hindus or the inferior Muslims remain submissive. Within the Sayyeds themselves there is strictly maintained code of conduct whereby each has his assigned place in the *Imambara* (the place of worship for Shias) that cannot be alternated. Within their families there are their wives, the respected *Sayyddanis* and their mistresses the *Rakhinis* who can be from low caste Hindus or the inferior Muslims and within these women and their children there are multiple hierarchies (23). The *Rakhinis* have to be humble in their approach to the *Sayyddanis*, they have to sit on the floor and in some cases the husband will not eat the food cooked by them because as a true Shia he is not supposed to touch anything wet from the hands of a *kafir* (a non-believer) (41). The children from such alliances take the names from their fathers but are not treated as equals.

The hierarchies signify the stratification of the society in Gangauli primarily along communal lines and correspond to the historically sustained social hierarchies. They also indicate the gradual evolvement of the power structures in the society whereby multiple levels of exploitation are legitimized in the name of preserving ethical and traditional values and divisions. The lower classes are supposed to comply, treating the divisions of power and exploitation as a pre-condition. The lower classes, women and the illegitimate children of the Mir Sahibs are not completely unaware of the involved exploitation and the pain of subordination. Their discontentment finds an expression in occasional outbursts. Looking at splits that exist in Gangauli it appears not just an 'Adha Gaon' but a village splintered in innumerable parts and in innumerable ways. The question arises why do the subjugated abide by the exploitative structure of these hierarchies, why is it that Gangauli doesn't simply explode, what is it that holds it together even if too precariously. The reasons vary from the material to the metaphoric. The lower classes depend upon the Mir Sahibs for their livelihood; women's dependence on society and their social conditioning make them hold on to their husbands, as there are no other options. Through their compliance they get a favourable treatment and are able to salvage some pride. Reza brings out the simultaneous existence of the pain of subordination and exploitation and the notions that produce their passive acceptance:

> *Benam rehna shayad zamindaron aur unke hawaliyon-mawaliyon ki betiyon ke takdeer hai; isliye yeh benam ladkiyan kanduri ke farsh pe bethane aur biradari ke dusre mamlon mai shareek hone ya na hone ki hokar reh jati hain. Bas, yahi ek izzat hai jo kisi rakhini*

> *ko nahi milti, aur shayad isiliye yeh sharif ladkiyan apni benami ko jhel jati hain.* (23)
> (To remain nameless is perhaps the destiny of the daughters of the Zamindars and those of their servants; therefore the entity of these nameless girls is limited to sitting on the decorated floors and in participating or not participating in the other matters of the community. It is just this respect that is not given to a mistress and perhaps this is why these respectable girls bear the pain of anonymity.)

The daughters of the Zamindars lose their names as soon as they married and their names submerged into their new roles, 'Bahu', 'Dulhan', 'Dulhin'or even 'Aziz Dulhan' or 'Nafis Dulhan' depending upon the kind of dowry they bring with them (23). They do not take any offence even as their names are snatched from them and are replaced by titles that consistently remind them of the financial status of their fathers. Their acceptance of this anonymity and even a sense of pride in having these titles originate from their awareness of the disgrace in being called a *Rakhini.* Such is the nature of socio-cultural conditioning that there are no sudden outbursts and there is a considerable level of acquiescent acceptance of the prevailing conditions.

The intricate patterns and the multiple levels of respectability shield the inherent exploitation and play a crucial role in keeping the village together. While the wedded women hold on to their titles, the *Rakihinis* find solace in bearing the children of Mir Sahibs, and the lower classes attempt to ignore the pain of subjugation through their faithfulness to the Mir Sahibs and their subsequent favours. The economic and the power structures of the village play a significant role in keeping the village together and create an environment conducive to continual exploitation and its unquestioning acceptance. However, the greatest force that underlies the unity of the village is the faith of the villagers in the space of the village, the space they have inhibited through history, their sense of belonging, loyalty and responsibility and the values that have entered their psyches through personal and collective experiences.

The sustenance of Gangauli is primarily rooted in the ability of its inmates to rise above personal and societal rifts in crises that endanger the village. The boundaries of the village, in a way, are unsurpassable. They speak of a mutual bond of trust that cannot be broken by involving outside agencies whether it is the government or sectarian propaganda. The issues of the village have to be settled within the village. The villagers, regardless of their communities or social status, respect its consensual system of justice punishments, and impeachments that include monetary fines and even social ostracizing. When there is a violent clash between the Mir Sahibs of Uttar Patti and Dakhin Patti, the two groups appear absolutely implacable and there is every chance that they could go to any extremes to harm each other. But when the police arrive, the wounded are already removed from the site and everyone acts as if nothing has happened (77). Another platform that compels them to suspend their internal strife is that of the religious ceremonies. These ceremonies demand an active participation from everyone and the Mir Sahibs from both Uttar and Dakhin Patti within a few hours of the clash come together in the *Imambara* for the regular *Majlis* (a gathering for prayers). There is no visible chance of any reconciliation or of exchange of words between the two groups. Even the Maulvi is reluctant to begin, but as soon as he calls, "Hey Shubbu, Padho Bhai" there is an immediate response and the *Majlis* goes on in the usual way (85).

Gangauli is not simply a point on the map for its inmates; it embraces their entire being. Therefore even as the residents of Gangauli scale the outside world, they keep coming back to it, regardless of their positions in the social hierarchies of the village. Gangauli completes them; it provides them an anchorage, a stable sense of identity and belonging. When a Mir Sahib goes to town and sees a train for the first time, he begins to dream and fancies a train of his own parked outside his house in Gangauli but when he feels that the train would be a little too big for the place, he gives up the dream and settles for a car instead (68). Even the wildest of their dreams has Gangauli at its centre. None of their dreams are big enough to compromise their belonging to Gangauli:

> *In khavabo main Gangauli chhodne ki baat kabhi nahin aati thi....Uttar-Patti ka phatak itna bada tha ki usme Hakim Sayyed Ali Kabir ke sare khavab na sirf saama jate thay, balki kuch jagah bach hi rahti thi.* (68)
> (In these dreams there was never anything about leaving Gangauli....The gate of Uttar Patti was so big that it could home all the dreams of Hakim Syyed Ali Kabir and there would always be a little more space to spare.)

Their dreams and aspirations are inextricably bound with Gangauli. Even the Rakis who are successful in business and frequently travel into different parts of the country despite their subordinate status in the village come back to it. Their financial wellbeing does not sever their ties from the village and though they have to put up with the Mir Sahibs' condescending attitudes, they do not leave the village. Their resistance too is grounded in Gangauli and finds an expression in the form of their new houses and a mosque of their own. Similarly those who leave Gangauli in search of employment carry their village in their hearts and they find it difficult to relate themselves to the cities.

The residents of Gangauli are not simply Hindus or Muslims; their religiosity also bears the influence of the space of Gangauli and has a distinctive identity that cannot be reduced to any standard parameters of inter-communal relationships. The communal harmony in Gangauli is rooted in the evolvement of its society and though religion is an undeniable force it is tampered by the soil of the village. Imam Hussain does not simply belong to the Muslims of the village but even the Hindus attach a great reverential value to him alongside their own Gods. They also look at Imam Sahib as someone who is their own. When the Tazias are carried out, the Hindu women of the village bring their children for the blessings of Imam Sahib and the Muslims see no heresy in participating in the Diwali celebrations (80). Both the Hindus and the Muslims, without compromising their religiosity, are able to relate to each other because of their intrinsic faith in the village and their society. Their harmony, at the same time, is associated with certain values and beliefs that consolidate mutual respect. Chikuaria, the son of Gaya Ahir, is not ready to believe that Imam Sahib was a Muslim:

> *Master Sahib ne lakh lakh samjahaya ki Imam Sahib pakke musalman they, lakin wah jaanta tha ki Imam Sahib musalman nahi ho sakte. Musalman to Maulvi Bedar hai jo Hinduon ka chua nahi khate. Musalman to Hakim Ali Kabir hai jo bat bat par darwaje ke hoj main, apane ko pak rakhne ke liye nahate rahte hain.* (173)
> (The teacher tried to explain to him a million times that Imam Sahib was a staunch Muslim, but he knew that Imam Sahib could not be a Muslim. Maulvi Bedar was a Muslim because he did not eat anything touched by a Hindu. Hakim Ali Kabir was a Muslim who kept bathing in the pool outside his door to keep himself untainted.)

The sanctity of Imam Sahib is beyond Hindu or Muslim faiths for the illiterate Chikuria. He, like many others, is not ready to give it up for some rhetoric of Hindu-Muslim animosity. Similarly the Muslims do not consider themselves as outsiders because they hold on to their faith that Imam Hussain wanted to come to Hindustan:

> *"Husain ko manane wale kabhi Hindustan ka bura nahi chhah sakte. Aakhir Maula aur Aaka ne kuch soch kar hi to 'Kafiraun' ke is mulk ko chuna hoga....Hussain Hindustan nahi aa sake, hum aa gaye hain...to hum aab yaha se nahi jayenge..."* (58)
> ("Those who have faith in Hussain cannot be against Hindustan. After all, the Almighty and the Master must have had some reason to choose this country of the 'Kafirs'....Hussain could

> not come to Hindustan, we have made it here....now we are not going to leave from here....")

They are equally certain of the fact that Hindus cannot be their enemies because a Kashmiri Brahmin fought alongside Imam Hussain in Karbala and sacrificed his life for Imam Sahib (58-59). These little beliefs may or may not have a historical basis but they have been strengthened with generations of peaceful co-existence and have their roots in the living space of Gangauli.

The socially produced space, however, cannot remain static; it is continually transformed by newer impositions of order, both from within and outside, and the subsequent resistances. The hierarchies of social structures demand compliance at least at the surface level but within them they have so many contradictions and chinks, that from each originates a resistance that may remain passive for a while but comes out eventually challenging and transforming the established structures and order. The excesses of its own social structure gradually loosen up the space of Gangauli. The acts of private transgressions begin to influence the public domain and the protests acquire a regular character. The sexual exploits of the Mir Sahibs culminate into the development of an incestuous relationship between a half-brother and a half-sister Migdad and Safunia (214). Their tragic fate exposes the duality of the life led by the Sayyeds that comes to its full circle with the marriage. The marriage itself is a protest where Migdad refuses to run away from the village or to keep Safunia as his mistress. He insists on the impossible *Nikah* (marriage) of a Sayyed with a low caste and succeeds with his raw power and with the help of Maulvi Bedar who bears a grudge against the Uttar Patti. He is pushed out of the village and lives an isolated life but his isolation cannot continue for long as he is a successful farmer and plays a specific role in the village economy. With the death of Safunia he is reunited with the Sayyeds. This relationship transforms the order of the village in multiple ways whereby the unthinkable becomes possible in terms of *nikah* between a Sayyed and a Kafir or inferior Muslim, challenging the very need of keeping mistresses and depriving them of respect. At the same time the daughter of the couple stares the community in the face and jolts the complacence of the Mir Sahibs.

The sons and daughters of the mistresses prove a little better than the pure Sayyeds. The Hakim Sahib has to put up with the popularity of the new doctor Kamalludin (261). The Rakis of the village grow richer through their business transactions and live in 'pukka' houses with a shining mosque of their own while the Imambara of the Zamindars loses its colour (293). The Hindu lower caste Parsuram joins the Congress and realizes the very likely possibility of acquisition of power with the end of Zamindari. The children of the village transgress the hierarchies and interact with each other in the schools and colleges of the cities. The space of Gangauli rapidly changes with the widening of the inherent splits and the need for the emergence of a new social order.

The elements of change are inherent in any given structure. Imposition of any order almost simultaneously opens up the dynamics of multiple resistances. However, within the interstices of a given structure the transformation of the social order takes its own time but village as a social space is open to outside influences as it has a specific location in terms of its geo-political and socio-cultural position within a nation state. The ideology and governance of a nation state, howsoever gradually, bears its influence on a village. The transformations that are the outgrowth of the internal space of the village and those that are imposed from outside elicit different responses. While the former do not split the village and have a regenerative nature the latter may force a change that has no ground in the village and thus may impair the living space of the village irrevocably.

The debate over the formation of Pakistan exercises its influence over Gangauli and from a fanciful notion for the villagers it becomes a reality that has to be contended with, as it forces a choice upon them. The village only gradually awakens to the reality of partition and Pakistan as outsiders creep into the village bringing in their notions of the Islamic land and the endangered position of the Muslims in independent India. The village offers a rigorous resistance to the idea of Pakistan as the people feel themselves tied to their land and to each other. At first they are not even sure about the nature of Pakistan, the idea of their village traveling to Pakistan is too unreal to be credible to them. They cannot believe that the Hindus, with whom they have led their lives, have shared their pains and pleasures for generations would suddenly turn hostile and kill them for some historical logic. The questions that the villagers ask to the advocates of partition might appear simplistic but they challenge the ethics of political decisions taken on their behalf by a selected few. Reza in the novel says:

> *Yeh naam hai bade dilchasp. Arabi ka 'Fateh' Hindi ke 'Garh' mai ghulkar ek ekai ban jata hai. Isliye to Pakistan ban jane ke baad bhi Pakistan ki haqiqat mere samajh main nahi aati. Agar 'Ali' ko 'Garh' se, 'Gazi' ko 'Pur' se aur 'Dildar' ko 'Nagar' se alag kar diya jayega to bastiyan viraan ho jayeengi aur agar Imam ko Bare se nikal diya gaya to Moharram kaise hoga.* (12)
> (These names are very interesting. The 'Fateh' of Arabic mingles into 'Garh' of Hindi and becomes a unit. Therefore even after the formation of Pakistan I cannot understand the reality of Pakistan. If 'Ali' from 'Garh', 'Ghazi' from 'Pur' and 'Dildar' from 'Nagar' were separated the localities would be deserted and nameless and if 'Imam' from 'Bara' were removed how would 'Moharram' take place.)

Reza brings out the precise folly in the idea of Pakistan. It was an act of political will as it did not have its roots in the shared history and culture of India that inextricably bound names and people with each other who could not be divorced overnight with *the stroke of midnight* in any *tryst with destiny*.

The advocates of partition concentrated on the geographic and demographic division of the country. They could not envision the thousands of living spaces like Gangauli that had come into being through a shared history, a culture that evolved through centuries of co-existence. The cultural character of the country was indivisible along any communal lines and when that was done it left two impaired and half nations and numerous half villages like Gangauli. The wounds that still remain open and even now, for those in power, they serve a political purpose. In a recent book published by Rajkamal, *Jinnah: Ek Punurdrishti* (1995), Jinnah is reported to have said that *Pakistan was the biggest mistake of his life* but the realization, if there was, was a bit too late, the harm was done.

Though Gangauli does not go into Pakistan geographically but many of its inmates choose Pakistan. The choice of Pakistan is made not because they have any intrinsic faith in the ideology of a separate Muslim state but for many of them the reasons of immigration are personal in nature. Tannu Bhai who is against the idea of Pakistan lands up there because he could not get the love of his life and escapes the family imposed on him by his society (291). Many of the young are in search of newer possibilities and some others choose Pakistan as they are sick of their subordinate status in Gangauli (315). Those who remain in Gangauli consider Pakistan an abstraction; they are more comfortable within the space of Gangauli even as the centres of power are rapidly shifting. Parsuram becomes an MLA and the Mir Sahibs seek his favours (292). One Mir Sahib opens a shoe store (324) and others seek to devise new strategies to survive in the changed socio-political scenario, and to come to terms with the reality of the loss of Zamindari and possibilities offered by democracy.

Fredric Jameson has remarked, "We cannot return to aesthetic practices elaborated on the basis of historical situations and dilemmas that are no longer ours....the conception of space suggests that a model of political culture appropriate to our situation will necessarily have to raise spatial issues as its fundamental organizing concern" (qtd. in Soja 62). The focus has to be kept on the here and now. Even today when a Babri Masjid is demolished, and cities and places are renamed the same folly is repeated in a different form. The truth is that demolition of a Babri Masjid does not wipe out the Muslim character imbibed in our culture and our individual selves. Renaming Bombay as Mumbai or Madras as Chennai does not rule out the colonial past, what has been imposed, exchanged and resisted. Reverting to a historical time, or a state of being is being led by an abstraction a denial of socially produced space.

Any discussion on villages has to focus upon the matrix of space, time and social being and has to bring into consideration the multiple facets that have interplayed in their evolvement into present forms. The understanding of village-spaces in the present necessitates a serious consideration of the people who migrate to urban centres every year in search of employment and livelihood, villages that have been swallowed by the ever expanding cityscapes, villages that are scattered in the slums of metropolis and the immensely popular prototypes of villages like 'Chokhi Dhani' or 'Aapno Gaon' (located in Rajasthan and Gujarat such resorts attempt to recreate the environment of villages through their architecture and the ethnic wear of the attendants). These prototypes warp the urban imagination; they present villages, as we want them to be, as recreational spots with a difference. They create an illusion of a village as a cluster of huts and colours, a space that offers ceaseless entertainment and merriment, without a single hint of the struggle for survival. They enforce further the mapping of villages as mindscapes and landscapes, shifting from the complexity of the real *living spaces* to the convenience of the *make-believe*, while the space of the real villages is still alive and evolving as there newer impositions and newer resistances.

References

Baranwal, Virendra K. *Jinnah: Ek Punardrishti.* New Delhi: Rajkamal Publications, 2005.

Foucault, Michel. "Texts/Contexts: Of Other Spaces", *Diacritics*, Spring, 1986.

Reza, Rahi M. *Adha Gaon* (1966). New Delhi: Rajkamal Publications, 1990.

Soja, Edward W. *Postmodern Geographies: The Reassertion of Space in Critical Theory.* Jaipur: Rawat Publications, 1997.

18

Village as Nation

Reza's *A Village Divided*

URMIL TALWAR

A Village Divided[1] is the story of a village and a community divided – of division within the Muslim world, divided families and loyalties, and a nation torn into two.[2] The narrator brings out different manifestations of this divide at several points in the life of an individual, a society and a nation. Using the metaphor of a village the narrator raises several questions related to nation as a homeland with specific reference to the identity of the Indian Muslims. Through this novel Reza reveals the effects of the partition of India and the abolition of the zamindari system on the Indian Muslims. Like Jane Austen, he works on a two-inch piece of ivory and through focusing on a few respectable middle-class families that have some landed property, he portrays the minute details of a social set-up. He describes the gender relations, the family structure, the class and caste system and the rules of purity and pollution that divide the society from within. Education is divided along political ideologies. The novel also looks critically at history, the concept of a nation,[3] the politics and of the division and individual identity. In this paper I propose to look at the bearings of religion[4] and politics on the individual and the community to which the individual belongs.

The village is populated by Muslim zamindars, weavers, traders, and *nais* (barbers), the Hindu zamindars, brahmins, *ahirs, bhars*, labourers and untouchable leather workers people representative of the various classes and castes that go on to constitute the village. He gives a detailed description of the village Gangauli, and goes into the history of its name, its social stratification and class hierarchy. The novel depicts not only the division of society into Hindus and Muslims but also the intra-religious differences between the Shia and the Sunni Muslims, and the division into *Dakkhin Patti* and *Uttar Patti*. He reveals their petty mindedness in bribing the police to prove the supremacy of their faith. The narrator offers an insight not only into the experience of an individual but gives voice to the community as a whole. He explores the psyche of the people of Uttar Pradesh during the transitional period of transference of power to India, dominantly becoming 'Hindu', and Muslim Pakistan. The chronicle of the nation – the partition of India and the formation of Pakistan – is so densely intertwined with the fictional narrative that it is impossible to say where the fictional narrative ends and the political chronicle begins. The writer in fact has delved deep into his personal and social history and has succeeded in codifying the social reality of the period other than the elitist vision of historicity. Those who speak in this novel belong to the low-middle class of the Muslim community; they do not occupy the centre in the national or provincial arena of formal and institutional politics, yet they must be heard. Their views and impressions need to be taken into consideration. They articulate the mood and the sensitivities of the large number of aggrieved and tormented people who had 'no say' in the transfer of power to the two sovereign nations.

The ten chapters of the novel unfold a period of thirty years or so covering the II World War, Quit India movement and bringing it to independence, the formation of Pakistan and the aftermath right upto the abolition of the zamindari system. These ten chapters run parallel to the ten days of mourning during Moharram when the family and the village community gather in *majjalis* in *imambaras*. The memory of the sufferings of Hussain and his companions at Karbala gives them the strength to bear their own sufferings. The Moharram works as a metaphor for a mourning which embraces the agency of the partition as well as the narrative structure of the novel with the ten days expanding into ten chapters and three decades.

Right in the middle of the novel, there is a dividing line caused by the "Introduction", a strategic displacement to signify the break in history. This actually is the time of partition of India and formation of Pakistan and the "Introduction" divides the novel into pre and post independent phases. In the pre partition times, it has been pointed out that the Hindu and Muslim communities lived together for centuries in peace and amity. In fact, their points of contact and association were based on enduring inter-social connections, cross-cultural exchanges and shared material interests. Neither the followers of Islam nor of Hinduism were unified or cohesive in themselves. Their histories, along with social, cultural and occupational patterns, varied from class to class, and region to region. Most Hindus and Muslims living in harmony and goodwill could not come to terms with the ill will and hostility that was conveyed through speeches and pamphlets distributed by the activists of Muslim League. There were many places in India where the message of the Muslim League failed to impress. In this novel too the activists from Aligarh visit Gangauli and try to provoke the Muslims, appeal to their feelings of religious solidarity and appeal to their reason. They cleverly employ the various constructs of national identity such as religion, language, memory and territory yet they failed to persuade the older generation of Muslims to leave their land and migrate to Pakistan. Phunnan Miyan questions these propagators and activists, whether Gangauli would go to Pakistan or stay in Hindustan. When the reply is that it will be in Hindustan, Phunnan Miyan becomes indifferent to the whole issue of partition and replies, "Eh, bhai! Our forefathers' graves are here, our Tazia platforms are here, our *fields and homes* are here. I'm not an idiot to be taken in by your 'Long Live Pakistan!' " (emphasis mine 141). The bond of the land and fields is stronger than that of religion. There are others like Ali Kabircha who also are not in favour of Pakistan. He stresses the fact of rootedness, there is no way that homelands can be shifted. The political short-sightedness is shocking. "Our forefathers lived here...our *tazia* platforms and imambaras are here...*our honour and self-respect* is here! Gangauli means something to us! If we don't care about it, then are some traders going to?" (emphasis mine 40).

The real and the imagined collide in his mind. He does not even accept the fact that the British are about to leave India or that zamindari would be abolished. But for others the formation of Pakistan began to take shape as an 'imagined community' aligning themselves not with the political ideology but with the Muslim cultural system. After fighting in the II World War, Tannu is happy to return to Gangauli, a place where he has grown up and thinks to himself:

> There must surely be some relationship between man and the land. Otherwise how could anyone take joy in returning to the mud houses of Gangauli and its people, sweet smelling like black earth, after beholding the great ruins of Rome and Pyramids of Egypt. (207)

When Tannu asks Mighdad if he intended going to Pakistan, Mighdad replies, "I'm a farmer, Tannu bhai! Wherever my crops are, my land is – that's where I am!" (202). He wishes to send his father there because he has become a staunch religious follower, wearing *sherwani* coats, and speaking Persian. Tannu is insistent that he belongs here: "I myself am this village. When death came very near I certainly remembered Allah, but instead of Mecca or Karbala, I remembered Gangauli.... Gangauli is my village. Mecca is not my city. This is my home and Karbala is Allah Miyan's.... we too love our home as much as He loves His?" (234).

The idea of Pakistan is strange and unacceptable, a game. He begins to wonder:

> Did Indian Muslims really belong to this land? Surely the Rajput Muslims of Dildarnagar and Gahmar were formed of this earth. So why they are going to vote for Muslim League? Why did they feel a *need for a homeland*? Did they really want to create Pakistan? Did all of them, who were going to vote for Muslim League, know what Pakistan would be, and what it would be like?" (emphasis mine 236)

Most people were indifferent to the newly created geographical entities, and were committed neither to a Hindu homeland, nor to an imaginary world of Islam. They were unclear whether Gangauli or Aligarh, Lahore or Gurdaspur, Delhi or Dacca would remain in Gandhi's India or Jinnah's Pakistan. Religion functions as a dominant determinative force for the formation of Pakistan and the people were caught up in the crossfire of religious hatred. For the earlier writers like Manto, Bhisham Sahni, Krishna Chander, Khushwant Singh, partition was a lived reality and through nostalgia they sought to recover and explore the carnage and the human depravity as in *Tamas* and *Train to Pakistan.* Reza's novel only reports of the carnage happening elsewhere – Lucknow, Calcutta, Amritsar, Lahore, etc. The Hindu activists too came to Gangauli but the Thakur of the village stood up against the Hindus and did not let the carnage take place here and told them:

> The best thing for you people is to go back! Did Bafatiya, and Dildarva and Kalu rape the Hindu women of Noakhali? If you people are so brave and so worried about the honour of the Hindus you should go to Calcutta and Lahore! What is there that you attack these people? (259)

Hearing this and seeing the *lathis* raised the crowd split and tore apart. The Hindu crowd could not comprehend why Thakur Sahib wanted to save the Muslims. And it is to this Hindu-Muslim unity that this novel is dedicated. This dedication was initially left out from the first translation and insignificantly added in the second translation as Jasbir Jain has pointed out in her yet unpublished paper "The Text in Conversation":

> Yeh adha gaon apne dost
> Kunwar Pal Singh ko
> Bhent karta hu
> Kayuki agar unka saath na hota
> To shaayad mein yeh kahani likh he na paata. (5)

In this dedication the writer explicitly makes a statement about the benign role of the Hindus who prevented the carnage. Again the references to the mutiny of 1857 and the Muslim participation in it against the British do not feature in the translated text thus distorting the history of Hindu-Muslim relations and their united efforts at nation building.

Indeed, most Muslims neither understood nor approved of Pakistan, except as a remote place where they would go, as on a pilgrimage. Some left, hoping to secure rapid promotion, but not to set up permanent homes there. Hakim Sahib questions Tannu about the formation of Pakistan, "What is to be done when it is made?" Tannu replies, "Perhaps, even Jinnah Sahib doesn't know the answer to that"(207), but they are all certain that they will vote for the Muslim League. A part of the community departs for Pakistan with utopian vision of a 'Promised Land' leaving behind a vacuum. Abbas believed, "Once Pakistan is created Muslims will have a great time...absolutely great!"(47). In the visions of such men secular leaders and nationalist Muslims had no legitimacy.

In fact it is ironical that Tannu who calls Gangauli his mother, his village and his home, leaves for Pakistan. Along with him Abul Qasim, Baddan bhai, Tassan Qaisar, Akthar and Gigge leave India never to return. Saddan goes to Pakistan leaving his father Hakim Sahib, his wife and his daughters behind without any means of subsistence. Tannu, who had married Sallo much against his own wish, does not bother to take her and his daughter to Pakistan. But the new country is an alien land and leads to unhappiness. Both Saddan and Tannu are looked upon as outsiders or refugees in the country, which they have accepted as their own. When Saddan comes to India, he seeks permission to come home. Despite their fiery idealism they feel terribly lonely and home sick and can hardly earn enough for their needs. Return is equally difficult as the past cannot be undone. They are prisoners of their choice. Saddan returns to Pakistan saying that he would send some money for his father well knowing that it would not be possible Hakim Sahib too refuse to go with his son, "How can I take my fields to Pakistan? I'll not desert the graves of my family. I'm staying here to die" (257). The whole idea of Pakistan is foreign to the villager who is bewildered by the illogical claims and repeatedly the issues of rootedness in the land of ancestral rights and history surface in their minds. The contradiction in the proposition of leaving a homeland to inhabit another bewilders them. But yet pushed by environmental pressures they support the Muslim League. Kulsum Dadi and Hakim Sahib have their own personal reasons for supporting the Muslim League. And a large section of traders and weavers decide that they should vote for the League as their religious duty (227).

It is in fact ironical that the Muslim League won its demand for Pakistan without having launched any extensive mass movement. In 1940 the demand for a separate Muslim state was put forward in the Lahore Resolution and in 1946 the electoral success of Muslim League led to the formation of Pakistan. Reza deploys irony to demonstrate the suddenness with which the formation of Pakistan took place that involved the question of nation and nationality, of loyalty and the fate of the Muslims who chose to stay back. Several other writers like Manto and Qurratulain Hyder too grappled with this immediate and pressing issue of belongingness and loyalty. To which country do they belong? What are their links with their erstwhile homeland! Saadat Hasan Manto, the famous Urdu writer, left this question unresolved in "Toba Tek Singh" and

"The Dog of Tetwal". In 'Toba Tek Singh' one of his finest stories, he captures the mood:

> As to where Pakistan was located, the inmates knew nothing... the mad and the partially mad were unable to decide whether they were now in India or Pakistan. If they were in India where on earth was Pakistan?...(65)

Pakistan, a prized trophy for many Muslims, was won, but people on both sides of the fence were tormented by gruesome killings, by the irreparable loss of lives, and by the scale and magnitude of an epic tragedy. Mostly the partition stories took up the issue of Hindu or Sikh or Bengali families that migrated from Pakistan to India. Unlike these writers, Reza emphasizes that communal violence is not the country's core ethos. The choice had to be made and then fought for. One of the Muslims says, "Haven't my ancestors and your ancestors always gone together with the ancestors of Thakur Sahib to attack Salimpur? So why isn't anyone asking us to come with them to attack the fort?" (257)

Reza here envisions a coexistence of the two communities as a reservoir of potentialities that can be aped as an alternative mode of being outside the sectarian and exclusionist framework imposed by the partition. Both Hindu and Muslim families pray at the mosque and offer sweets at the hermitage of Hindu holy men. The Muslims give donation for Dusshera celebrations and Zaheer Miyan had given five *bighas* of revenue-free land to the monastery of a Hindu holy man. The novel is a powerful record of the composite cultural traditions of Hindus and Muslims that bind Indian society even today. Reza believes that the common man's politics is not divisionary and does not intrude on religious faith. Religion proves to be too flimsy a ground for the creation and sustenance of Pakistan and the novelist raises some fundamental questions about religion and politics and their bearing on individual lives.

The abolition of the zamindari (landholding) system in 1951 stripped the large landlords of the bulk of their estates and awarded the land to the cultivators. The rural influence of the former Muslim landlords was reduced, even more than that of their Hindu counterparts. The Muslim zamindars with larger landholdings suffered more because of the division of families, with one branch, especially the young, educated professional men migrating to Pakistan and other consisting of the older generation pushed into anonymity in their villages. Those who stayed found the going hard. All of a sudden the economy changed. For the zamindars their universe had suddenly collapsed: they had no "land left equivalent even to the hub of the great wheels which was once their zamindari". In just a few moments they collapsed like the tomb of Nuruddin the Martyr, a familiar landmark in Gangauli village. In their prayers they cursed the Congress Party. Hakim Sahib who was dreaming of buying a train when his son would become a collector, now has nine mouths to feed with no means of subsistence. His son – his hope for the future – has left for Pakistan, his land has gone to the tillers and his patients now go to Dr. Kamaluddin who treats them with homeopathy. When Hakim Sahib's foot slips and he falls to the ground and in this delirious state he is heard muttering:

> ...whether zamindari's gone or not,... I'm not about to go and leave you....I'm not Saddan (his son). Father you know those lands you left, they're not ours any more. Gandhi said that they belong to the chamars and bhars. I kept on saying that I'd inherited them from my father. But no one listened.....I couldn't desert the Lord (prayers offered to the Lord in *imambara*) and go to Pakistan....Eh, Baba, You bear witness, I forgive Gandhi....(326-327)

And then this is an end not of an individual but of an era. Attia Hosain's novel, *Sunlight on the Broken Column,* also describes the faded fortunes of the landed aristocracy and captures the sense of an era having passed once and for all.

A Village Divided is also a counter discourse where the traditional zamindar archetypal constructs are interrogated and challenged. The zamindar's courtyard, the hub of all social and political activity and a centre of power, becomes desolate after the partition, more so after the abolition of zamindari system. The power relations of the zamindars dwindle with the implementation of land ceiling. After the partition the exploited, the oppressed and the discriminated low caste Hindus obtained power as they had joined the Congress. The low caste untouchable Parsuram gains power. And he is depicted behaving in the same manner as the zamindars of the pre independence era. The only difference is that he has no land and wields political power as he is an MLA and member of a Congress Committee.

Reza deploys irony to demonstrate the suddenness with which the formation of Pakistan took place that involved the question of nation and nationality, the question of loyalty and the question of belongingness of the Muslims who chose to stay in India. These Muslims were nationalistic, they opposed the partition and chose to stay in India of their own accord, yet they were treated as suspects and had to deal with the new power equations that emerged in post independent India. These Muslims felt overwhelmed by the climate of hostility, suspicion and distrust; they had a litany of complaints. Social discrimination and political marginalization created ion them a sense of insecurity.

Hammad Miyan is wrongly accused of patronizing criminals by Parsuram the local Congress MLA. He tells the President of District Congress Committee that Hammad Miyan's house 'is a den of Pakistanis' (321), and he is stirring up Muslims for communal riots. In this quarrel the whole village gets divided. The upper castes and Thakurs of Barikhpur side with Hammad Miyan, the low castes and the Muslim traders join hands with Parsuram. There are fights and several fields are looted. Hammad Miyan had a shopkeeper file a false case of non-payment of debt and fraud against Parsuram. He makes a loose woman Devkathiya file a case of assault and rape against Parsuram. And Hammad Miyan himself presents a petition that his life was in danger from Parsuram requesting the court that he should be placed under a personal bond. Although in this case Parsuram is convicted but he sends a message to Hammad Miyan "Go and tell the Miyan to get himself to Pakistan!" (322). The umbilical cord of Pakistan was now cut but it had surrounded like a noose that stifled the Indian Muslims.

Reza here obliquely questions the identity of the Indian Muslims and also their loyalty. An individual identity is normally thought of in terms of incompatibility between the Indian and the Muslim. He overtly takes up this aspect in his novel *Topi Shukla.* The novel is set in 1960s in Aligarh and narrates the story of friendship between two friends - one Hindu, Balbhadra Narayan Shukla and the other Muslim, Iffran. The novel looks at the lives of ordinary people who are united against the common enemy - social prejudice, that defy friendship between these two communities. It also explores the culture and psyche of people who have nicknamed him 'Topi Shukla' making a sarcastic reference to the skullcap worn by Muslims. Topi Shukla belongs neither to the Muslims nor to the Hindus. His death consummates a rejection of all binaries.

The harmony and the goodwill between the Hindus and the Muslims is now replaced by fear and deep suspicion. The Saiyids, who for centuries had made Gangauli their home, now realize that they no longer have any links with the village they call their own. Whether Pakistan was created or not had no meaning to them, but the abolition of zamindari shook them to the core. Now they realize, it was all the same whether they lived in Ghazipur or in Karachi. Phunnan Miyan who was always friendly with the Thakurs, had Chikuriya as his close associate. This symbol of the Hindu-Muslim unity was destroyed as both were killed after Parsuram was convicted.

The novel is not merely a documentation of the political happenings but a tale of human suffering. The conflict is due to the urge to change and the desire to remain the same. The entire human drama of this novel stems from this dichotomy. Reza's description of the changing patterns of behaviour and nature of human relationships carries within it an element of sadness. In the pre independent India the caste hierarchy, the social taboos regarding food and marriage relationships are observed but after partition and land reforms these loose their grip on the society. In post independence times these were put aside. Fussu Miyan, a small landholder was struggling to eke out a living. He not only had to open a shop to meet his needs but he also could not find suitable husbands for his daughters. This social dislocation made him, in the beginning, a laughing stock but later he was the only one who could afford to lend the others some money. There were some who had limited resources to live on; some others relied on inherited charitable endowments or even pawned their family jewellery to maintain the facade of high living. The jingle of the bunch of keys keep the Saiyid ladies alive although their trunks and chests are empty yet these are the monuments of their past glory.

The author tries to establish a contrast between the composite culture of the past and the breakdown of trust in the present. The old traditional dogmas are shaken off by new knowledge. The Hakim and Kammo form the binaries. Hakim turns his back on the learning in this new world and retreats into an inner world privileging divine mandate, as the community prefers the western educated doctor. Sayida is sent to Aligarh Muslim University to study but her family and the society both criticize her and circulate stories about her loose character. Later when she takes a job and starts supporting her family she is appreciated and other girls look up to her. With her come the latest fashions and dresses to Gangauli and young girls and ladies look forward to her arrival on Moharram. The other girls wish that their parents too send them to study.

Reza believes that the common man is without any politics. Religion proves to be too flimsy a ground for creation and sustenance of Pakistan and the novelist raises some fundamental questions about religion and politics and their bearing on individual and community to which the individual owes allegiance. An individual is a social construct wherein the identity of an individual addresses issues of language, culture, nation and religion. These four are cohered and coalesced inextricably and the narrator raises questions about the use of Urdu language that is a mixed product of Persian and Hindi language. Urdu is the language of the elite or of the educated Muslims, the common-man uses Bhojpuri.

Reza offers an analysis of the economic and political motivations that underpin historical and social change. The novel *A Village Divided* at one level is also a subversion of history. It is a novel about the politics of attrition, hatred and vilification that has been going on in both the countries. Partition, the event, the memory and the metaphor remain central to this novel and it transcends its situation and raises vital questions of religion and politics, religion and nation state, intervention of the periphery in the elitist vision of history. The village is a metaphor, the region ceases to be isolated, insulated or parochial entity. It becomes a part of the wider world.

Notes

1. *Adha Gaon* was published in 1966 by Akshar Publications and was translated by Gillian Wright in 1994 as *The Feuding Families of Village Gangauli*, later in 2003 a fresh edition came out with the title *A Village Divided*. All quotations are from *A Village Divided*.
2. Jinnah and Iqbal were Western-style nationalists – their views of nations and what constituted nationhood was informed by nineteenth century European thought on the subject. Thus, a common religion and language were among the "signs" of nationhood, wholly independent of the question of one's own religiosity. More significantly, "nationhood" could only be fully realized in the context of a territorially defined nation-state; for Jinnah, therefore, Muslim nationhood could only be acknowledged or realized within the context of a separate nation-state. This sort of conception is not unique to Jinnah but to an entire generation of "modernist" nationalists, all of whom held similar views.

3. Benedict Anderson argues in the first chapter of his book *Imagined Communities*, that pre-national culture was a religious culture and he laid great emphasis on the role of constructed nature of culture in the development of nation. He defines nation as an "imagined political community" (12).
4. Religious exclusivism was the sole basis to the concept of Muslims as a separate nation, and this led to the division of the Indian sub-continent. But the question of separate identity of Muslims in post partition India is still an unresolved issue.

References

Anderson, Benedict. *Imagined Communities: Reflections on the Origin and Spread of Nationalism.* London and New York: Verso, 1991.

Jain, Jasbir. "The Text in Conversation: Translation as Dialogue". Unpublished paper presented at Jamia Millia Islamia in 2004.

Manto, Sa'adat Hasan. "The Dog of Tatewal" and "Toba Tek Singh". Translated in *Translating Partition.* Eds. Ravikant and Tarun K. Saint. New Delhi: Katha, 2001.

Reza, Rahi Masoom. *A Village Divided* (1966). Trans. Gillian Wright. New Delhi: Penguin Books, 2003.

Reza, Rahi Masoom. *Topi Shukla* (1977). Trans. Meenakshi Shivram. New Delhi: Penguin Books, 2005.

Singh, Khushwant. *Train to Pakistan* (1956). New Delhi: Ravi Dayal, 1986.

19

Self-Realization and Altruism in Shukla's *Gaon Ka Aadmi*

SONU SHIVA

As one cannot see a memory, thought or a feeling, so an altruistic intention cannot be directly observed. The terms like 'self realization' and 'altruism' are wholly abstract; they cannot be touched, sensed or interpreted in a way an object might be. In every successive generation one finds selfish individuals in increasing numbers. The selfishness is so much encouraged that ideals and altruism are driven to extinction. From the common experience of life it is generally observed that individuals put their self-interest before benefit to others. These individuals might belong to the educated civilized world, which is supposed to have the knowledge of the values of life and social co-operation. The presence of such individuals makes us wonder as to what has gone wrong with our reasoning and understanding of our social system. The purpose of this paper is to study the social interaction of an individual as well as the internal subjective processes involved in the forming of social relationships. The present paper is an initial exploration of a larger project and is thus tentative in its propositions.

The present-day system appears to be based on calculating costs and benefits of a self-sacrificing act if performed. The instinct of deriving immediate pleasure out of life has become a dominant feature and the real pleasure of living a purposeful life is consciously postponed for later years by giving infinite rationalizations in terms of shortage of time, money, competency, liking etc. Therefore self-interest serves one's selfishness and makes one to enjoy the immediate momentary pleasures out of one's life. This importance to self cannot be studied as a monolith but depends mainly on social exchanges and interactions. Social behaviour and one's involvement in social interaction process depends upon one's individuals needs, abilities, similarities or differences in inculcated values, situational contexts and one's proximity to a certain area or person. In Upamanyu Chatterjee's *English, August* the character Agastya Sen who is an urbanized young civil servant, is unable to relate himself to the world of the small village Madna. We find in him an introversion from people and things of this place. It is generally observed that a person who holds close proximity to a place yields long lasting positive outcome in comparison to a person who is spatially an outsider. There is a 'comparison level' found in individuals that is the standard by which an individual evaluates the attractiveness of the place or work allotted to him. As life at Madna falls below the comparative level of his urban life experience, the place and work related to it appear to him unattractive. Whereas Ganesh, the character of Bhupendra Nath Shukla's novel who is also an IAS returns to his village to work for the welfare of the rural society. As he belongs to this place he easily adjusts himself without any self-conscious effort. He follows and understands all those complexities of rural life that he has never really understood at the conscious level but has always obeyed. For an outsider it requires a conscious effort and attention to involve himself in a place and environment where he has been placed. The above situation shows that the same impressions, experiences, impulses and desires that one man indulges in can be rejected with utmost indignation by another depending upon his past experiences and the circumstances that have given rise to it. We can say about of these two characters Ganesh is the one who has set up an ideal in himself by which he measures his acts but Agastya has no such ideal. In Ganesh's learning of the 'self' and 'altruism' the presence and participation of his father and his affinity with rural India are the determinable factors to define his social performance. He has an accurate conception of his own capabilities and potential that helps him accomplish positive outcomes from his life. This character of Shukla is an answer to those individuals who blindfold themselves to external actualities of rural India and feel like a 'fallen Adam' if posted there, as it happened with Agastya or those individuals who as soon as they become an IAS think of themselves as belonging to a 'special class'. Such an individuals behaves like a 'king' of ancient India treating others as his 'subjects' as is the character Srivastav, collector of Madna in Chatterjee's novel. *English, August* highlights the lack of commitment in bureaucrats particularly IAS officers in rural development. The question whether by being an IAS officer one is sufficiently equipped and motivated to work for rural reform is addressed in Shukla's novel. Both commitment and consistency are visible in the two roles he performs – the first is an IAS officer, and the second, when he responds to the voice of his conscience to work for the villagers. Both roles display similar character qualities and values. The importance he gives to local requirements is noteworthy. His successful working is due to the perfect combination of power and development. One may think that with the present trends of liberalization, globalization and technology transfer how far one can translate one's ideas about development at the local level into reality. Vipin Kumar in his "Identity and Totality: A Synthetic Definition" observes:

> Derrida identifies the acute presence and persistence of violence, inequality, exclusion, famine and thus economic oppression

> affecting the human beings. Every struggling site is therefore obviously molecular. He doesn't see any urgency to lend many such sites some uniform characteristics. For Derrida there need not be any co-ordinating organization, which may stand for a totalitarian institution. (54)

As it is near impossible and practically difficult to grasp the social whole and the idea of having a world identity is a myth, therefore working for the local turns out to be something that is visible, certain and immediate. In Ganesh one finds an expansion of his 'self'. He inspires innumerable others and shows them a path of purposeful life. He is able to transform his individual consciousness to a collective one. In his relationship with the rural community there is an absence of solipsism and he shares his world with them. Merleau Ponty, in his answer to the question: How can the 'self' relate to the 'other' or 'others' without appropriating them or else surrendering to them as their victim? has elaborated upon this issue:

> Myself and the other are like two nearly concentric circles, which can be distinguished only by a slight and mysterious slippage. What is presupposed here is the abandonment of solipsism; the aspect that self and other are no longer unilaterally constructed or manufactured but are seen as emerging in an open space or a 'shared world'. Although this world may be inhabited in very different ways. It is by virtue of this shared 'being in the world' that self and other perception and understanding are possible. (Dallmayr 26)

Ganesh is in favour of distributive justice, because presence of injustice in society leads to violent conflicts. He serves humanity and works to remove disparities that are necessary for 'a livable common future'. Through his own personal experience has an in-depth understanding of the essence of rural life and the values that lie in living in a 'shared world'. He thinks that if people of the village are properly educated about their responsibility towards the nation, progress could be increased manifold. He is against the unilateral construction of social system, where political, economic and social powers rest in the hands of a few while all others are sidelined. This is perhaps the reason why as an IAS he directs his attention towards the problems of rural society, later gives his resignation and returns to his own village to look after his aged father and after his father's death continues those works that were dear to him. His father is his role model. Bandura in his theory of social learning and imitation suggests that behaviours are socially transmitted by models. These modelled components are incorporated by the observer as rules and norms to be used in future contexts (Shaw and Costanzo 67).

Ganesh's father Parmatma Bhaiya was a progress-oriented farmer. He spent much of his time in introducing the poor peasants of the village to the new ways of agriculture as well as government plannings and provisions available for the development of village. He was in favour of economic independence, which is no less important compared to political liberation. Ganesh is much inspired by these words of his father. The seed was sown long before in his mind before it flowered to its full in the years to come. The field of social psychology helps one to have a clearer insight as to how the thoughts, feelings and actions of individuals are influenced by the perceived, imagined or implied thoughts, feelings and actions of others, the way in which individuals are affected by social situations, develop altruism and a helpful attitude.

Altruism at one level can be understood as an act that promotes success of the other at the cost of one's own. There is a possibility that altruism may encourage selfishness in the recipients as there are enough people who try to derive benefit without paying the price and make an altruist pay for their success. Badcock in his new synthesis of Darwin and Freud tries to analyse such self-centred behaviour of individuals through the theory 'Diner's dilemma'. He believes that at the level of co-operation, the individual with a selfish gene thinks that free lunch is always best – you get a benefit without a cost. This is better than a lunch with a shared cost. But this in turn is better than no lunch at all, which although imposes no cost also carries no benefit whatsoever. The worst out come is having to pay for someone else's lunch – a cost without a benefit. Translating this example Badcock says:

> We can see that selfishness (a free lunch) is better than reciprocity (both eating, both paying), but that is in turn worth more than spite (neither pays, neither eats) and that the worst outcome is having to perform an act of altruism (you pay and the other eats at your expense). (Badcock 49)

In the above-mentioned example lies the problem of altruism. It is noticeable that quite early in his life Ganesh had decided his future course of action or as one may say had the gene for altruism that he had received from his father. He is basically a reformist and considers that the human brain is full of new ideas that are indispensable for its development. He favours values because only a person with great values and thoughts is capable of performing great works and thus help in framing an ideal state. Though it is generally observed that due to the presence of non-altruists i.e. if there is no one to repay the energy of an altruist, it becomes weak and is unable to reproduce. But altruism does prosper under certain circumstances like patriotism or love for the land. Bunker Roy the founder of Barefoot College at Tilonia and his wife Aruna Roy who resigned as an IAS to engage in the process of social change are real life examples. Thirty years ago, Bunker Roy left the world of urban comfort, headed for Tilonia and settled for the daily rural struggle. His Doon school and Delhi's St. Stephen's degree had no value in the world he had chosen for himself. Aruna and Bunker Roy work to alleviate the suffering of the rural poor, the marginalized and the exploited and imbue them with self-respect and dignity.

Shukla's characters Ganesh and his wife Yamini (who is also an IAS) pour their lifetime for the betterment of rural society. The success of Ganesh's altruism lies in his 'group selection' because if there is an absence of a selfish organism in the population of altruists, by benefiting each other the group will continue to flourish. Ganesh deeds inspired many others and thus the torch of realization of responsibility was handed further. But why people behave in such self-serving ways is quite controversial. According to Schlenker:

> The most common answer is to maintain and enhance their self-esteem. He does not rule out the possibility that the need for self esteem is innate, but he proposed that self serving actions and perceptions might have their basis in the social interaction process. The most relevant aspects of social interaction process are identified as controlling identities, public description of attributes, management of the self-image and claiming images. These processes are obviously not independent but are interrelated events that contribute to the maintenance and/or enhancement of the self. (Shaw and Costanzo 330-31)

Ganesh decides to work at the grassroot level of rural India and develops solutions to improve the environment and quality life of the rural poor. The altruism that he practises is of a different kind compared to the aspect discussed earlier in the paper. He is competent enough to punish the defectors and protect his acts from the exploitation of selfish players who capitalize on the co-operation of others. The rule of Ganesh altruism is "co-operate with co-operation but defect against defection" (Badcock 57). One finds that this type of altruism can evolve between totally unrelated individuals. All that matters in such form of altruism is that co-operation of one should be reciprocated and returned by the other. Its name therefore is *reciprocal altruism*. Ganesh's father dies, Ganesh dies, but the act of altruism continues. This shows that an individual is mortal but the gene of altruism that is present in the identical copies of itself or near relatives or in its reproductive success is potentially immortal.

References

Badcock, Christopher. *Psycho Darwinism.* London: Harper Collins Publishers, 1995.

Chatterjee, Upamanyu. *English, August.* London: Faber and Faber Ltd., 1988.

Dallmayr, Fred. "Social Identity and Creative Praxis", *Identities Local and Global.* Eds. Kailash C. Baral and Prafulla C. Kar. Delhi: Pencraft International, 2003.

Kumar, Vipin. "Identity and Totality: A Synthetic Definition", *Identities Local and Global.* Eds. Kailash C. Baral and Prafulla C. Kar. Delhi: Pencraft International, 2003.

Shaw, Marvin E. and Philip, R. Costanzo. *Theories of Social Psychology.* Tokyo: McGraw Hill International, 1982.

Shukla, Bhupendra Nath. *Gaon Ka Aadmi.* Delhi: Ankur Prakashan, 1988.

20

The Legends of Khasak

Place and Paradox

PRERANNA BISHNOI

To establish the context for a study of the spatial and temporal metaphors in regard to the quest for identity of the characters in O.V. Vijayan's *The Legends of Khasak*, perhaps the best opening would be a line from the book itself:

> It was a journey of things unmoving and inert, a journey through time. (157)

Everyday reality in Khasak is full of the most extraordinary things. This reality is presented through a secret code, a kind of conundrum about the world. The myths, the legends and the beliefs of the people are in a very natural way a part of their everyday life. Vijayan does not invent anything at all but simply undertakes a journey to capture and recount a world of omens, premonitions, cures and superstitions which, with the passage of time, achieve the status of legends.

Vijayan's most important problem was to destroy the line of demarcation that separates what seems real from the fantastic because in the world that he tries to evoke this barrier does not exist. In watching his own art unfold, Vijayan, in the persona of his omniscient narrator, is more like the villagers in his novel, surrendering to what he observes. Vijayan gives credibility to these beliefs and fantasies by calling them legends, thereby, implying that they are set in a less remote period than myths, and have some historical basis. Apart from legends we also have accounts of peculiarities of certain characters, and of their anecdotes that would become legends in the near future. These legends and stories of Khasak, narrated by the omniscient narrator and also by various characters, thus, give us an insight into the history of Khasak, the storytellers' perception of the world, their attitudes and values.

The legends of Khasak unfold within a spatial and temporal framework. French sociologist Maurice Halbwach argues that collective memories usually contain a strong spatial dimension and are linked to certain places in the landscape. We can understand how legends recapture the past only by understanding how it is preserved by the physical surroundings. The perception and meaning of this unified natural-cultural landscape, in turn, shapes people's experience of both time and space.

Only by investigating both time and space can we fully articulate what it means to be situated human beings. As W.J.T. Mitchell points out, "we cannot experience a spatial form except in time; we cannot talk about our temporal experience without involving spatial measures" (544). The first definition of "time" in the Oxford English Dictionary is "a space or extent of time" and the first definition of "space" is "denoting time or duration." These circular definitions demonstrate the congruity between time and space as concepts. As Foucault points out, spaces themselves have histories and "it is not possible to disregard the fatal intersection of time and space" (22).

Surrounded by hills and very far from the nearest town, the remoteness of Khasak is indicative of its insularity. It is like a cell – "an entity, a planet of the microcosm, it has its own aeons of time" (170). This disconnection in space generates independence in time. Khasak is a complete universe with a temporality of its own. Time here is like a pendulum oscillating between the past and the present. Instead of moving forwards into the future, the natives of Khasak, like the Greeks, see the past, unbroken and relentless, receding before their eyes and the future coming up from behind.

Time lay bound within the crystal waters of the Araby tank, in the rocks and creeks of Chetali, in the massive beehives that hung underneath the rocks, in the marshes and the graveyards, and in the deep wells. Around these structures stood thirteen mosques in ruin, forming a desolate ring around the village. Vijayan gives a detailed description of the village and the surrounding landscape as in Gert Jonke's *Geometric Regional Novel* in which the village lies in a valley surrounded by mountains, which again are laid out with geometric precision. On the east was the only pass that led into the valley of Khasak. On one side was the indomitable mountain, Chetali, opposite to it was a small river. Across the mountain pass ran a train that neither brought anyone in nor took anyone out. On the periphery of the village the mosques stood guards and in the centre was the village square in the middle of which stood a banyan tree.

The geometry of these structures allows the narrator to demonstrate a system which controls the occupants, a system of traditions and expectations that have been internalized by its inhabitants. These structures of time and space lead to binaries like – the past and the present; the inside and the outside; the inclusion and the exclusion. To negotiate this intricate lattice of time and space each inhabitant has his or her own story – stories to live in – a secret map of the world of which only they have the keys.

The natives traced their descent to the one thousand horsemen of Sayed Mian Sheikh who "long, long ago, in times now unknown to man" (10) pitched their camp in the palm grove. This "now unknown" and "lost time" (103) of Khasak forms a part of what Bergson calls "memoire reelle." As distinguished from normal memory – a faculty purely instrumental in the act of remembrance, "memoire reelle" is a form of unconscious memory where past events are preserved in their original intensity. From this spiritual reservoir such events can suddenly emerge into the present and fuse with it, acquiring new and deeper significance. As "duree," time ceases to be an irredeemable destructive force and becomes a preserving element, a form of continuity out of which, through "memoire reelle", the past can be called to a new life. It is possible, therefore, to achieve in "duree" a form of permanence that can redeem individual existence from ephemerality.

This is precisely what the legends do by changing historical time into nature, contingent into eternal. They generate centripetal forces from within the village that fight the forces from without. In Khasak these centripetal forces are exerted partly by the thirteen mosques that stood in a ring around the village. They form an "all-seeing" structure similar to an inverted panopticon. In them "lay stagnant the infinite time of Khasak" (18). According to a legend a curse lay on the mosques that no human could rebuild them. The mosques thus become a power structure that none could tamper with. Only the Sheikh's anointed Khazi, Nizam Ali, who had the power to cast spells and curses, could enter them.

The legend of the goddess of the tamarind tree reveals a similar kind of patriarchal power structure. The enormous tree, despite its great age bore fruit in abundance. On its branches lived the guardian angle of the chaste. It was believed that for a climber with a chaste wife the Devi would make footholds in the slippery lichen covered trunk. The fruit was eaten by bats as none wanted to be brought to test. Lured by the fortune, Chand Umma's husband was tempted to climb and fell dead into the marsh underneath. Since then Chand Umma lived in unbearable seclusion and waited for her son to grow up. She pinned her hopes in another time and place. Whenever her daughter asked when a certain thing would come about, relying on her magic calendar of moons, Chand would say it would happen "when we see the next Eid moon" (99).

Like Chand Umma, for Chukuru the "Diving Fowl" too, identity is not centred on present space but on time – past and future. Having drowned his wife in a well, guilt ridden Chukuru wandered from well to well retrieving fallen things and often when there was nothing to retrieve he would still dive in. Having come to a point of no return he takes a leap into the waters of eternity. He jumps into an ancient well and goes deeper and deeper into the well inside the well – "past the crystal doors and silken curtain of water into the mystery that had always lured him" (70).

According to Benedict Anderson, as opposed to a nation or region, place is a site of meaningful identity and immediate agency. Place becomes the geographical expression of the interactions between individual action and abstract historical process. De Creteau in *The Practice of Everyday Life* says:

> [...] the opposition between "place" and "space" will rather refer to two sorts of determination in stories ; the first, a determination through objects that are ultimately reducible to the being-there, of something dead [...] the second, a determination through operations which, when they are attributed to a stone, tree or human being, specify "spaces" by the action of historical subjects (a movement always seems to condition the production of a space and to associate it with a history). (118)

In Khasak everything had a place. Even the winds belonged – they were either the palm winds or the tamarind winds; the lizard was the hedge lizard, the goddess belonged to the tamarind tree, and the Khabandas were of the Araby tank. These multiple dimension of geographical place can be collapsed into a single dimension of social space. Some of Khasak's living legends depict the characters' attempt to carve niches and spaces for themselves.

Attar seeks out what Foucault calls "utopian spaces." Utopias are unreal spaces that present society in a perfect form, "they are sites that have a general relation of direct or inverted analogy with the real space of society" (Foucault 24). To establish his business, Attar, a biri maker, gets himself photographed in a hired fez, coat and tie. Obsessed with his picture and overcome with self love he would often go behind bushes and "in the privacy commune with his own printed face [...] captured with such fidelity in black and violet printers ink" (26). In enabling him to see himself there where he is not Attar's photograph becomes like the mirror image Foucault talks of "I come back toward myself; I begin again to direct my eyes towards myself and to reconstitute myself there where I am" (24). It helps him in escaping his reality and at the same time conferring with it. It can also be said that, like the Buendia family in Garcia Marquez's *One Hundred Years of Solitude*, Attar also attempts to capture time and to eternalize his place in it. To outdo his rivals Attar puts his printed photograph on his biri packets and brands them – "God bless M. Attar Photo biri" (26). In this battle of space with Attar, Nizam Ali advertises his brand of biri on little culverts and across quarried rocks, and scatters hundreds of his biri wrappers along the footpaths.

Appu-killi or Appu the Parrot occupies "place-less places." He is a cretin suspended in time and space. He has the lisp of a child and the gutturals of a man. His arms and legs stayed in their grotesque childhood, while the head and torso grew and across the pendulous lips settled a timeless smile. After his mother's death Appu seeks shelter in Foucault's "the other city" – the burial grounds and sleeps beside his mother's grave. Later the village tailor finds Appu a "crisis heterotopia" – "privileged or sacred or forbidden places" (Foucault 25) for those in distress – a hung space in a cradle made from an old bed cover hung from a tamarind branch. When the cradle gives way the tailor finds a "perch" for him in the corridor of the school run by Ravi. In an attempt to make himself a place in the crystal eyes of the dragonflies Appu catches them, slips a lasso around the tail and keeps them fluttering at the end of the string. Denied of space, he makes the dragonfly an extrapolation of his identity in time. As Appu stood in the "twilight of births and deaths" (85) the dragonfly becomes a death wish, a wish to conquer all times and all spaces in the eternity of death.

For it was believed in Khasak that dragonflies carry memories in their eyes, but only of the dead.

Space in Khasak can also be read as an expression of modernity's paradox – the tension between progress and loss – a creative yet ambivalent space carved out somewhere between the oppressiveness of the new order and the imprisonments of tradition, between modern alienation and cohesive organic community. Kuppu Acchan, a toddy tapper, in his attempt to negotiate the harshness of the temperance laws wears his chest armour and the tappers knife and climbs his most favoured palm and refuses to come down. Having lost his vocation he takes his place as a gossip monger in front of Aliyar's tea shop. In a bid to recapture his lost space Kuppu works himself to an insane despondency in which he could see things the way he wanted. He would get into knee-deep water in the brook and watch the sky reflected in the water and would be "a rider of the sky again, and now what slid past his shins would not be fish but shoals of little clouds" (114).

Even for the young children, in Ravi's school, space becomes an important determinant of identity. During the roll call a newcomer, Karuvu, answers to the name of Hyder Hazart. Looking up at the unfamiliar voice Ravi says:

"You aren't Hyder Hazrat."

"No, Saar."

"Then?"

"He lent me his slate and pencil, Saar." (49)

In Khasak there are certain communities that define their identity by continuously annihilating it. In a post-modernist reaction the basket-weavers withdraw their children from Ravi's school. We learn that it is their clan's secret that their language should have no script, as only a "scriptless language could help them penetrate the forest depths" (51). In oral tradition facts become detached from their roots in space and time and shift into legends, and legends into myths. According to the basket-weavers past is better preserved in myths than through any written history, for they believe in the plurality of vision, and in permanence rather than in the incidental.

Ravi, the chief prostagonist, also lives at two levels – "a mundane instinctive level of lust and longing, and a meditative level of detachment and spiritual quest" (Satchidanandan 20). Haunted by his sense of guilt he escapes into the nameless universe of trains. This notion of space allowes him to navigate across the unknown seas of time. Ravi would fantasize his room to be a train compartment, through the windows he would see the past being left behind, and the present fleeting as the train raced intò the future. Little does he realize that the escaping from time is impossible. As Gilles Deleuze in his essay "Memory as Virtual Coexistence" says:

> The past and the present do not denote two successive moments, but two elements which coexist: One is the present which does not cease to pass, and the other is the past which does not cease to be but through which all presents pass". (59)

Ravi is never really able to understand Khasak. The villagers use myths to read the present; Ravi tries, in vain, to use the present to reinterpret the myths. He does not realize the impossibility of the door lock ever becoming the key. There is a marked parallax between the way the natives look at Khasak and the way Ravi, an outsider, reads the village. This applies as much to geographical landscape as to social space and culture. As John Barrell in *The Idea of Landscape and the Sense of Place* says:

> A parish could be said to have a different geography according to who was looking at it. Thus, for those of its inhabitants who rarely went beyond the parish boundary, the parish itself was so to speak at the centre of the landscape [...]. For those inhabitants accustomed to moving outside it, and for travellers who passed through it, the parish was defined not by some circular system of geography but a linear one. (2)

This accounts for Ravi's surprise when he suddenly comes upon a picturesque village on the other side of the rail tracks:

"What place is this, Madhavan Nair?"

"Never suspected it was there, did you Maash?" (141)

Ravi's predicament can be evaluated more explicitly by what Foucault in "Of Other Spaces" says:

> I am thinking [...] of the famous bedrooms that existed on the great farms of Brazil and elsewhere in South America. The entry door did not lead into the central room where the family lived, and every individual or traveler who cannot by had the right to open this door, to enter into the bedroom and to sleep there for a night. Now these bedrooms were such that the individual who went into them never had access to the family's quarters; the visitor was absolutely the guest in transit, was not really the invited guest. (26)

Ravi's school that was "on the outskirts" of the village was for him only a "transit residency," a "Sarai" (7). The self-imposed alienation and the detached philosophical attitude with which Ravi views Khasak never really allow him any true access to Khasak. Ravi looks at Khasak the way he did in his astrophysics lab through "lenses that sought to look out far, very far, and space which looked in through every aperture, to strike the dark of the abyss" (89).

Appu-Killi writes all over the school wall, the one letter he had been able to learn in ten years – an "O." It is not the circularity of his lenses, but of this all inclusive "O" that makes Ravi realize the futility of modern learning, of "looking at the galactic desert outside," and he turns "the spectroscope inward [...] to be the sand of the desert, each grain of sand; [...] to be the lake, each minute droplet; [...] the laya, the dissolution" (193). Nevertheless, Khasak had already adopted Ravi much before he realizes his affinity to it. In the chapter "The Conversion" it is not the conversion of Appu-Killi that is important but of Ravi .

In going to Kuttadan the Oracle Ravi symbolically surrenders to Khasak and submits to its "rites and purifications" (Foucault 26), and then "out of the infinities a drizzle of mercy fell on his sleep and baptized him" (165).

Khasak reads its future in the fish with a silver crest and red spots that was a messenger of the Sheikh and swam down the crevices of Chetali only in the "times of elemental catastrophies" which was to be the death of her beloved son. Leaving his "nest of rebirth" (202) Ravi experiences a dilemma similar to that of Ursula in *One Hundred Year of Solitude*:

> "We will not leave" she says, "We will stay here, because we have had a son here"
>
> "We have still not had a death" counters Arcadio Buendia, "A person does not belong to place until there is someone dead under the ground." (14)

Ravi achieves in death what he could not achieve during his lifetime and as "The waters of the Timeless Rain touched him. Grass sprouted through the pores of his body" (203) he becomes yet another legend of Khasak.

The inhabitants of Khasak author their own private narratives to elude the village's spatial controls. As Reynolds and Fitzpatrick observe:

> These spatial stories and 'local legends' are written in the memory instead of the 'text' of [Khasak]. They Shatter the panoptic perspective because of their ability to render space familiar and livable. (80)

Each legend of Khasak is a tessera that takes a place off the social map and rituales it in another time and space, altering its social cartography and mapping it in a different way in the individual and collective psyche to transgress the restraints of spatial control.

References

Anderson, Benedict. *Imagined Communities* London: Verso, 1992.

Barrell, John. *The Idea of Landscape and the Sense of Place 1730-1840: An Approach to the Poetry of John Clare*. London: CUP, 1972.

Bentham, Jeremy. *Panopticon Letters.* London: Verso, 1995.

Bergson, Henri. *Matter and Memory.* Trans. Nancy Margaret Paul and W.Scott Palmer. London: Zone Books, 1990.

Campbell, J.F. "Poetics of Structure: Establishment, Movement, and Time in Gert Jonke's *Geometric Regional Novel.*" <www.centerforbookculture.org>

De Certeau, M. *The Practice of Everyday Life.* Berkeley: University of California Press, 1988.

Deleuze, Gilles. "Memory as Virtual Coexistence." *Bergsonism*. Trans. Hugh Tomlinson and Barbara Marbberjam. London: Zone Books, 1990.

Foucault, Michel. "Texts/Contexts: Of Other Spaces" *Diacritics,* Spring 1986.

Halbwachs Maurice. *On Collective Memory*. University of Chicago Press, 1992.

Marquez, Gabriel Garcia. *One Hundred Years of Solitude*. New Delhi: Penguin, 1996.

Mitchell, W.J.T. "Spatial Form in Literature: Towards a General Theory", *Critical Inquiry* 6.3 (1980).

Reynolds, Bryan, and Joseph Fitzpatrick. "The Transversality of Michelde Certeau: Foucault's Panoptic Discourse and the Cartographic Impulse," *Diacritics*. 29.03.1999: 63-80.

Satchidanandan, K. "A Sage and an Iconoclast". *Frontline* 22.8 (2005).

Vijayan, O.V. *The Legends of Khasak*. New Delhi: Penguin, 1994.

21

Displacements and Relocations

Ashis Gupta's *Dying Traditions*

SUPRIYA AGARWAL

Intellectuals over the years have talked about displacement caused by exile, immigration, colonial pressures and social and political reasons. On a reading of Ashis Gupta's *Dying Traditions* one is immediately touched by several kinds of displacements – both temporal and spatial in nature. Set in post partition era of India it is a story of a family, a story concerning the ups and downs of three generations – Sambhu Narain, his children and his granddaughter. It is also the story of the nation torn apart by violence and a comment on cross-cultural encounters. In this article I have focused on the displacement from the villages of individuals like Sambhu Narain and his family and the role the village plays in carrying forth traditions and socio-cultural values.

Dislocations in the novel taken for study are of diverse kinds and every individual's response to it is different. As pointed out by Jasbir Jain in *Dislocations and Multiculturalisms*, "Individuals respond in various way – through withdrawal and involvement, through submission/assimilation or through difference; through short-circuiting memory or through a hardening of identity constructs" (Introduction xii). History reflects that dislocations are inevitable, perhaps necessary for the journey towards maturity, self-knowledge and recognition, giving rise to new aesthetics. At the same time change has several social and psychological dimensions and contain within them opposites like desire and fear, adventure and disaster, trauma and hope. It is an unending journey which brings with it excitement and uncertainty, raising several issues for introspection. Going away from a village for settling elsewhere is a voluntary escape from the society of birth and therefore quite different from that of a refugee or a migrant. Such displaced persons are the ones who move out to the metropolis, the big city, because they find the cribbed and confined environs of their small close-knit communities limiting and inhibiting and want to take advantage of the freedom and openness of their new location. It does not lead to permanent severance from where a person belongs and keeps open the possibility of going back to it. As there are different kinds of exile, there are different kinds of narratives, which differ in their nature, range and density.

The story in *Dying Traditions* is narrated by an omniscient author who is also an eyewitness to every event that occurs. Focusing on the change of government in Bengal in March 1968, the unrest in 1971, the story moves back and forth in time. Sambhu Narain migrates to the city during the pre-independence period, visits London in 1939, works as a political journalist for years in Calcutta but after the death of his father moves back to Bishnupur, his ancestral village – a pastoral remnant two hundred miles north of the city – in the year 1959. During that period the Nehru government had passed legislation forcing the princely zamindars to give up large parts of their estates but Sambhu Narain was still the richest landowner who stayed in a brickhouse separated from the modest huts. His two sons and a daughter were educated in boarding schools in the Himalayas. Although his little empire had no legal authority over his tenants, there were hundreds of ways in which he could still exercise influence as serious and potent as anything the law courts could devise. It was the time when nothing lay beyond the reach of his authority, "every birth, every death, every marriage, every transgression, every punishment touched him in some way" (*Dying Traditions* 8).

Being educated and having the necessary exposure and knowledge, he brings back a new taste and culture for his fellowmen in the village. He staged plays every year at his own expense and sometimes even scripted them himself. Gradually, he overcame the skepticism of the villagers, until a few years later the event turned into something of a festival, attracting audiences from miles around, as it provided the peasants the opportunity to sell their wares and weavings and their produce, "there was nothing to stop the jugglers, fire-eaters, stunt cyclists and dancing girls with long, braided, perfumed hair to transform the humble village playhouse to a brief but spectacular carnival" (11). All this did not bother Sambhu Narain at all for there always remained a hard core of the faithful who drew their excitement not from the Ferris wheels or the whirling skirts but from the fire and passion of his plays, their lofty themes drawn from the Ramayana and Mahabharata. Sambhu Narain always reserved a major role for himself, not those of the classic hero but roles evoking the maverick, the outsider. His many tumultuous deaths always moved the audience to tears, especially his young children who were among his most ardent admirers. But what is noticeable is the change that comes over the years, in the response of Sambhu Narain's own children. The oldest Sanjit, began to scoff at the epics for their coarse simplicity. Rahul upon turning twenty says he can no longer stand the social hypocrisy of his father performing for the peasants, pretending to entertain while preserving an outdated code of morality and control. But Krishna the daughter remains steadfast in her loyalty from the day she could sit by herself on the rug spread in front of the stage to the day she went away to her in-laws and talked them into letting her return to the village for a few days in October each year, "so that she could laugh and clap as her father roared across the stage and then cry over his shoulder afterwards when the play was over and everyone had gone home" (11).

New technology and ideology displace old traditions opening society to development and exploitation at the same time. There comes Chanchal, the youth congress leader, who wants the annual district convention in Bishnupur during the October fair, bringing with him the seeds of deception, distrust and corruption. The narrative brings to focus the role of the priest, postmaster, police and politician in displacement of the old with the new. We perceive that religion, politics and economics together converge on the village community to use it for their own ends. What is noticeable in reality as well as in the narrative of the fiction is that in most cases, the sufferings descend more on women than on men. It is Chottki, the woman worker in the tea gardens who is exploited by the British officer and during the riots it is Alice, Krishna, Saira and several others of their kind who bear the brunt. They occupy a large portion of the narrative; they suffer but exhibit a lot of strength in the critical junctures of life. Janaki Devi, Sambhu Narain's wife, though not actively involved in the activities of the village, keeps an eye on everything going on around the house and when her husband dies, she watches the men carry away the bier without a drop of tear in her eyes and soon she recedes even deeper into the tomb-like serenity of her prayer room. She combats the oncoming change and disturbance by lapsing into prayers and silence.

The story takes into account the personal displacements of individuals, of tradition, culture and even relationships. The narrative as it proceeds does not follow the linear time sequence and this displacement results in the coexistence of all time. The book begins with the ascetic Sambhu Narain's return to have a glimpse of his house and a second disappearance. Even the title *Dying Traditions* itself is a pointer to displacement. Traditions rooted in the past, inherited and passed by generations are displaced for new notions, giving dynamic thematic energies and diverse plural forms to the narrative. It takes some time for the dislocated to form new identities, get relocated and complete the circle. Rahul, Sambhu Narain's son leaves village for the purposes of study and also goes to America on a scholarship, comes back to India, joins the political movement, gets involved in a jail-break and escape to America, returning this time to join Mukti Vahini movement which was fighting for Bangladesh's independence. For Rahul, life is an endless quest to break out of one cage after another – the cage of traditions, the cage of human frailty, the cage of decaying political institutions but in the end he finds solace in the village alone, coming back full circle to his native place like a migratory bird.

The author has chosen nature as the backdrop of all human activity and in symbolic terms. There is a wind blowing across the land, touching lives, reshaping lives, destroying lives. Sambhu Narain the aging landowner stands quietly defiant against the winds of change. To him, it is the 'script' that matters; it is the stage that vindicates life. The wind becomes a storm and deals a final blow to the crude wooden stage in the pastoral village of Bishnupur, set in the plains of Northern Bengal. The wind whips up hatred that sucks into itself the guileless Krishna, Sambhu Narain's daughter, her happy family and even the stranger Alice. The wind whips up religious madness and sets the seeds for a cruel war in Bangladesh. The village becomes the centre of all social and political activity; the urban world represents materialism, and consumerism while the village becomes the symbol of stability. Simpletons from the villages are unable to comprehend the changing ways of the world. After his son and daughter had met with the senseless end, Sambhu Narain is a broken man. He thinks, "something had gone wrong with the lives of men, Darkness had claimed their souls, and injustice had become a way of life" (1). Sambhu Narain's asceticism is also a withdrawal from life, change and pain. He did not return home after the funeral of his son and rumour had it that early in the morning he boarded a train gong north out of Sealdah station, perhaps buying a ticket to

Darjeeling, perhaps not knowing where he wanted to go, certain only that he was not prepared to go home.

Relocations are possible through faith in beliefs and traditions. In the novel there are instances and references which by contrast or similarity bring out the difference between the profane and the profound, the sacrilegious and the sacrosanct, mortal and immortal, time and timelessness. Sambhu Narain like the timeless Shiva lives the life of an austere ascetic. He like Shiva is the destroyer of evil like Hargovind and the saviour of Krishna and Rahul. Sambhu Narain, concerned with humanity teaches men by his own example that power can be obtained by penance, the great virtue of abstract meditation, leading to spiritual knowledge and ultimately to union or actual identification with the great spirit of the universe. As the author explains the mysterious change felt, man becomes helpless in the situation of life and seeks solace in the higher powers of life:

> All one could do was to remain patient, to wait one's turn for deliverance, wait for the muddy waters to cleanse their cold bodies, their inert bodies past the reach of contempt and abuse. For was it not in front of their eyes that the holiest river met, where all pilgrimages converged, where there was neither any beginning nor end. Till the beginning met the end and closed the circle, pain would return, horrors recur, and the minstrel's songs and the mother's lullabies swell and smother in the wind. (59)

Complex ideas of time and displacement are linked and evoked with great sensitivity, linking the past, present and the future, in which memory plays a major role. As pointed out by Gilles Deleuze in his essay, "Memory as Virtual Coexistence", "the present distinctly contains the ever growing image of the past" (51). At times when Rahul feels depressed and disgusted with the journey of life, one image haunts him – that of his father, holding his hand, towering over him, walking with big strides. Even when in States, hearing tinkling cymbals and people singing, he is reminded of minstrels who came to sing at the fair in Bishnupur and left behind forgotten legends of lost love. Even Vikram, Krishna's husband, after the funeral of his wife, while looking at dying fire and ashes moves back in memory as the image of childhood keeps returning to him, when he used to peer in darkness in search of bugs and other forms of crawling life.

Covering spatial and temporal dimensions, the protagonists of Ashis Gupta through their day to day encounters unfold the disjointed, fragmented and even discontinuous life one is forced to live, opening before us a paradoxical world which has elements both of orthodoxy and revolution. Vikram and others are in a state of trauma because of painful experience both at home and in their place of migration, heightening the sense of mourning. The fighting of the youth for a new state and the social collectivities can be considered as leading to retreat into essentialist diasporic instrumentalists as has been pointed out by Vijay Mishra in his essay, "Diasporas and the Art of Impossible Mourning". The experiences of Kerry Ahluwalia and Malini in States also reflect similar kind of feeling and pain, felt by the dislocated South Asians. For these characters the past is materially present and memory an essential backdrop of the inner discourse. Without memory, without a sense of loss to mythologize, life for many displaced people can become intolerable.

The writer has subtly opened before us, the pangs of dislocation felt by individuals within the nation and outside. Vikram had drifted to Montclair in pursuit of a job with a food brokerage company importing large quantities of Indian tea and there met Kripal Singh, whose original name was corrupted to Kerry, almost against his will. The name Malini had shrunk to Molly in a matter of weeks and Kerry was shot cold bloodedly by an indignant driver as he was giving driving lessons to his daughter Sonya:

> It was Sunday, and Sonya was doing just fine. But she was slow making a left turn on a busy intersection. The inpatient driver in

> a van behind her persisted in blowing his horn, adding to her confusion and nervousness. Finally, Kerry rolled down the window beside him and showed the man a glistening, unambiguous middle finger. The van followed Kerry and Sonya right back to their house. 'You fuckin cabbagehead. Cocksucking Paki,' yelled the man as he blew away Kerry's side with a single shotgun blast. (29)

Vikram after the funeral wept in silence both for his friend Kerry and for his daughter Malini who was in hospital bed and had fallen a victim to drug taking and having free sex with classmates. Malini committed suicide by jumping from her twelfth floor window. Vikram writhed with remorse and pain and knew it was too late to do anything. "Somewhere, he seemed to have given up on his daughter. It was not easy and he felt his heart ripped out of him. The new world was proving too much for him" (31). Through the narrative, the writer has very subtly opened before us the pangs of dislocation felt by individuals within the nation and outside.

Complex ideas of time and displacement are linked and evoked with great sensitivity, linking the past, present and the future. Set in post-independent India, the novel takes cognizance both of Pakistan and Bangladesh with characters travelling to Bangladesh, United States and Europe. Europeans and Americans also travel to India. Thus the dislocations work in both directions and both exile and attraction work simultaneously. While some characters are exiled or ousted or choose self-exile to ignominy, others seek affiliation with alien cultures and are reluctant to return. Space is an important detriment of the kind of relationships which are produced and power structures indicating exclusion and inclusion are spatial in nature. But what is at the core is the quest for independence and social justice. The village youth, whether Rahul or Hamid, fight for justice. The policymakers are people from the cities but the most affected by practical upheavals are the villagers who are at the centre of displacement. The villagers, irrespective of caste, creed and status survive harmoniously side by side but after independence, politicians hungry for power raise conflictual issues to exploit the strength of the villagers for their own interest.

Village is the centre where love and family are nurtured along with nature. The healing effect of nature on men close to it, is noticed. Sambhu Narain would renew himself in the wind and the rain, "they sang the same songs his heart sang and whispered the same incantations that poured from his lips" (3). Rahul when in a perturbed state of mind when in States, would link his thoughts with the nature around him, drawing peace and yet feeling the eeriness. Memories of the homeland haunted him and mixed with his feelings, perturbed him and out of sudden dark, obscure corners of his mind he would see:

> Barbaric forests where naked men poured wailing music out of hollowed branches and naked women flailed their arms at the sky. He would peer cautiously into this edge of time and exult in the blind power surging through him, until he felt himself moving with the wind, one with the power of the wind. But sometimes the wind was still, and he would see the hot sun striking down petals that had flared too quickly, too passionately. (119)

But above all this is the personal search for the centre that matters in an individual's life. Ashis Gupta himself has talked about the question of independence in context of his own life. In an interview given to Veena Singh he says, "I honestly do not know if I am any more 'independent' today than I would have been had I never left India in 1971....., my fugitive Indian personality haunts me incessantly" (42). Ashis Gupta has metaphorically expressed the entire process of displacement and relocation through nature imagery at the end of the novel, "The wind poked around, turning the odd leaf all the way on its side, lifting others off the ground. Some of the leaves swirled and danced in the air before they fell; others scattered on the water and floated away or piled up in an oozy mass at the riverbank" (318).

References

Deleuze, Gilles. *Bergsonism*. Trans. Hugh Tomlinson and Barbara Marbberjam. London: Zone Books, 1990.

Gupta, Ashis. *Dying Traditions* (1992). Delhi: Spantech Publishers Pvt. Ltd, 1992.

Jain, Jasbir (ed.). *Dislocations and Multiculturalisms*. Jaipur: Rawat Publications, 2004.

Singh, Veena. "The Fragile Self-Image of an Immigrant Writer: Interview with Ashis Gupta", *Writers of the Indian Diaspora*. Ed. Jasbir Jain. Jaipur and Delhi: Rawat Publications, 1998.

22

Recreating the Village

Davidar's *The House of Blue Mangoes*

PREETI BHATT

In an article in *The Hindu,* David Davidar, a contemporary Indian writer, discusses his debut novel *The House of Blue Mangoes* (2002) and the motive behind his decision to locate his narrative in a village. He states, "If you look at a lot of our writers, they tend to have very urban concerns. I didn't want to write a book that was set in Bombay or Delhi and talked about servants and the lack of electricity . . . it struck me as odd: of this cosmopolitan audience, most are no more than three generations removed from a village" (Roy). Davidar's novel traces the rural and ethnic origins of all Indians by focusing on a fictitious village, Chevathar, situated near Kanyakumari in Andhra Pradesh in South India. It portrays the vicissitudes in the lives of three generations of the members of a fictional non-Brahmin Christian clan named Dorai settled in Chevathar in the period between 1899 and 1947.

Davidar's novel with its setting in an imaginary village recalls R.K. Narayan's Malgudi and Thomas Hardy's Wessex. However *The House of Blue Mangoes*, unlike the works of Narayan or Hardy, is not a novel about characters or situations, but is a novel about time. It is a voluminous work, focusing on the influence of time on Chevathar as three generations of the

Dorais attempt to preserve and protect it from destructive forces. With the change in the attitudes of the Dorais with the passage of time, Chevathar too is shown to undergo a change with a major part of it developed into a modern colony of houses which accommodates the kinsfolk of the Dorais and is named Doraipuram, but which retains the essential characteristics of a village with close interdependence and sense of community among its residents.

The present paper examines the literary devices and narrative strategies in *The House of Blue Mangoes* and argues that Davidar employs specific narrative techniques to build the ambience and the atmosphere of a village in the narrative. These strategies serve to reinforce the rural setting of the novel as also to explore the concept of space as a metaphor. By drawing on the resources of language, myth and religious traditions David Davidar recreates the eternal village in his novel – the village that was the greatest contributing force in the economic, productive and labour-generating infrastructure of India a century ago. In the contemporary times, the villages with their inherent emphasis on the sense of bonding, close interdependence and kinship among people, have been pushed to the margins due to urbanization and technological development in the country. In this context the cultural values and social relationships nurtured in the villages in the early twentieth century as depicted in Davidar's novel acquire great significance.

By locating the village within a historical framework, the writer also simultaneously revives the strong cultural ties of the people of different communities in India a hundred years ago. Stuart Hall in "Cultural Identity and Diaspora" states "our cultural identities reflect the common historical experiences and shared, cultural codes which provide us, as 'one people', with stable, unchanging and continuous frames of reference and meaning beneath the shifting divisions and vicissitudes of our actual history" (111). In *The House of Blue Mangoes* Davidar represents the multifarious ways in which the village coped with historical changes and pressures and yet preserved and propagated Indian culture, beliefs and values. Leela Gandhi in *Postcolonial Theory: A Critical Introduction* (1998) asserts, "The novel and the newspaper are ... the two principal print forms capable of containing and representing, in one place, the impossible diversity that is the nation. Thus, the novel becomes a sort of proxy for the nation" (151). The village of Chevathar, as delineated by Davidar, comes alive with the conflicts and concerns, which beset the entire nation during the last fifty years of its colonial history. The idyllic agrarian settlement becomes a microcosm of the nation as it grapples with the destructive forces, and nurtures the ameliorating ones, and in the process, undergoes a transition into a land which promises greater prosperity and happiness to its natives.

In the epilogue to the novel, the writer narrates an episode relating to Auvaiyar, a well-known Tamil poetess and saint who lived sometime between the twelfth and fourteenth centuries. The story emphasizes the significance of perspective in one's understanding of reality. Davidar comments, "Ways of seeing. Every reality is perceived differently, depending on who is doing the looking, so let's take the road ourselves to see what we can see" (413). Through this reference Davidar foregrounds the need for the post-colonial reader to re-examine history from one's own perspective, and not from received ones. Chung-Hsiung Lai in "On Narrative: Story, Truth and History" while comparing history with narrative, also stresses the importance of perspective in narration. Lai states, "Rather than posing as definitive, narrative selects its material, proposing that we see the world from a certain perspective and that we arrange what can be seen in a specific way. In this sense, narrative mediates between the "is" and the "ought" inasmuch as it possesses the capacity not only to characterize an existing situation but also to predispose us in favor of a specific line of action" (35). Davidar's representation of the history of the last fifty years of the British rule over India with the focus on its influence on the village forces the reader to re-examine Indian history at the grassroot level from the point of view of those who do not form the mainstream.

The map of early twentieth century appended to *The House of Blue Mangoes* illustrates the geographical location of the villages, towns and districts, both real and imaginary, as conceived by the writer. It underlines the "real" presence of the village of Chevathar, and consequently, the reality of the entire narrative. Brian McHale in *Postmodernist Fiction* (1987) draws attention to the use of maps in postmodernist novels wherein maps are redrawn to accommodate non-existent places, which figure in that work of fiction. These maps, McHale asserts, reflect on a smaller scale the structure of the text of which they are a part. In these novels, "real space does not determine the map but the other way round, the map determines the real space" (McHale 53). The shape of the fictional work thus depends on the map which includes both the real and the anomalous. Historical authenticity, however, is imparted by Davidar by the retention of the original names of the cities as they were called in the period in which the novel is set – Tinnevelly for Tirunelveli, Madura for Madurai, Madras for Chennai, and so on. The map of southern India in Davidar's novel is an independent narrative device, which supplements the descriptive narrative.

The title of the novel holds symbolic significance for it implies a focus on the locale of action and not on the characters or on the situation. In the middle of the novel Daniel Dorai assigns the name "Neelam Illum" or the House of Blue Mangoes to the magnificent house which he builds for himself in Doraipuram at the place where his father Solomon's house stood in Chevathar (213). To restore the ancient beauty of the landscape, groves of blue mango trees are especially planted around the mansion (207-8), hence it is named the House of Blue Mangoes. The title of the novel instantly captures the attention of the reader, who is, generally speaking, aware of mangoes of different shades of yellow, orange, red or green, but not of blue. Blue mangoes, though not exactly blue in colour, however are a reality, and are popular in south India especially in Tamil Nadu. They are called "Neelam" in Tamil, a name that Davidar alludes to throughout his novel[1].

The blue mangoes find mention in the opening page of the novel when it is stated by an omniscient narrator in the fourth paragraph, "The locals will tell you that the Chevathar Neelam, which has made the Dorai name famous throughout the district, is so sweet that after you've eaten one you cannot taste sugar for at least three days" (3-4). The headman of the village of Chevathar and also the principal character of the novel – Solomon Dorai's love and fascination with the blue mangoes is depicted early in the novel. While references to the blue mangoes abound in the novel, the epilogue focuses yet again on their charm and power. Solomon's grandson Kannan is shown to be experiencing anxiety for the future of his ancestral village. He is in a mango orchard, and he goes close to a tree, reaches up to a ripe Neelam, caresses and picks it from the tree, and inhales its strong fragrance, "The bouquet explodes upon his senses: a huge delectable sweetness, overlaid with notes of freshness, lightness, sun and blue, counterpointed by a deep rolling melody of an almost corrupt muskiness" (416). This instinctive action, which every generation of the Dorais has been repeating time after time, lifts the gloom from his heart (415-16).

Davidar underlines the metaphorical significance of the blue mango in the middle of the novel when Daniel is shown to embark on a journey covering the whole of India to ascertain that the Chevathar blue mango is the sweetest variety in the country. Predictably, after the journey is over, Daniel concludes that "the Chevathar Neelam is the greatest mango in the world" (220), and begins the Blue Mango Festival in Doraipuram. The blue mango metaphorically stands for all that is represented as good in the novel – the Dorai clan, Chevathar, and also at a larger scale – India.

In the title *The House of Blue Mangoes* as well as in the text, the house in which Solomon Dorai has lived, called "the Big House" (3) and which is renovated by Daniel Dorai and renamed as "Neelam Illum", is very significant. The house in Jungian philosophy is an archetype, which carries powerful emotional and psychological associations with it. Gaston Bachelard in *The Poetics of Space* (1958) states "the house is one of the greatest powers of integration of the thoughts, memories and dreams of mankind" (6). The house shelters the human psyche offering it the protective warmth of a cradle as soon as it is born. Through dreams the human soul connects with the past, reliving memories of protection, of homes inhabited earlier, as heartwarming space. Bachelard writes, "An entire past comes to dwell in a new house. The old saying: 'We bring our lares with us' has many variations. And the daydream deepens to the point where an immemorial domain opens up for the dreamer of a home beyond man's earliest memory" (5). Human consciousness is deeply attached to the house where it has found protection, and memory helps to associate all past images of homes lived in, and gives comfort to the soul.

In the novel, the house inhabited earlier by Solomon and later by Daniel is an important symbol indicating the protagonists' attempt to preserve past values, emotional and familial ties and cultural bonds. When Daniel shifts to Nagercoil with his mother after Solomon's death, memories of Chevathar come flooding back to him: "These acts of remembering provoked an immense nostalgia in him for the place of his birth. All said and done, he mused, he was of the soil of Chevathar" (157). Daniel visits his ancestral home, anxious to reclaim his lost world, after his brother Aaron, a revolutionary in the Indian struggle for independence, dies in prison. He is disconcerted when he sees the dilapidated state of the Big House and vows to recover the house and the village for the sake of his dead brother. He rebuilds the house, giving it the shape of a huge mansion surrounded by beautiful gardens and groves of blue mango trees. Later when Kannan returns to Doraipuram from Pulimed he too experiences a deep sense of attachment for the place, thinking, "I'm glad I'm here, it is the place of my heart" (412). The ancestral home of the Dorais houses their souls, offering them eternal warmth and a nourishing environment.

The setting of the events in *The House of Blue Mangoes* is pivotal to the plot of the novel, as is apparent in the titles of the three sections into which the narrative is divided – "Chevathar", "Doraipuram" and "Pulimed"[2]. The novel has a circular structure, opening with Chevathar, moving on to the places around it with the movements of the protagonists, and coming back a full circle with Kannan's homecoming. Chevathar thus becomes the centre of action of the novel, and the narrative is held in place through the setting. The village of Chevathar is the protagonist of the novel, and it exerts its powerful influence on all the principal characters of the three generations of the Dorais. It forms the interconnected ground that becomes the hub of the going and coming of characters. In spite of shifting to other places earlier, Daniel and Kannan are unable to free themselves of its pull, and their concerns and aspirations revert to the progress and development of their native village in their later years.

Gaston Bachelard discusses the importance of journeys during which the unconscious is dislodged temporarily from the protective space of the home. Movement is essential for the growth of the inner self for it gives "an exterior destiny to the interior being" (11). Bachelard moves on to discuss life as a metaphor for a journey on the road of time. In *The House of Blue Mangoes* elaborate journeys undertaken in quest for something, or for a particular purpose, in fact occur like a refrain. Almost all the major characters are depicted as embarking on a long voyage with a specific motive. Solomon Dorai, early in the novel, anxious due to the lack of rainfall in the months of April and May, tours all the villages that are in his care (55-61), in order to assess the situation. In the midst of a picturesque description of Solomon's journey on a bullock-cart, reference is made to another journey which Solomon undertook "nearly twenty-five years ago now, when Joshua and he had decided to follow the river all the way to its source" (57). The turbulence and flooding of the river Chevathar had forced him and his cousin to abandon the journey in the middle. With Aaron, the travelling is for a patriotic cause, to raise "the nationalist consciousness of the people" (151). Aaron's journey, undertaken in 1909, ten years after his father's journey upon his agricultural land, offers a contrast for he travels by train and experiences a sense of awe for the modern machinery, "the great black locomotives hissing and snorting out of dimly lit stations, expelling steam from every joint, their fiery hearts driving them through the endless dark" (151). In the concluding section of the novel Kannan's painstaking quest for the man-eating tiger in the jungles of Pulimed is more a desperate attempt to save the honour of the Indians, the browns, including himself, from being falsely indicted of having attacked and killed a white clergyman.

The use of Tamil words in regular print spelt out in English in the narrative is a remarkable feature of the book. These words at times are explained in a short phrase and sometimes are not explained at all. The reader is expected to deduce the meaning of such words from the context in which they are used. Words like "thalaivar" (5), "paati" (171), "kumkumam" (4), "appa" (100) "anna" (145), "aiyah" (147), "chithappa" (19), "and thylam" (167) are few of the instances of the use of the regional dialect in the novel. Several words of the Hindi dialect are also used by the writer in the narrative. Words like "thali" (137), "tahsildar" (209), "poojari" (37), "Dipty" (23) are used frequently in the novel. The use of the regional dialect in the narrative gives it a local flavour and adds to the ethos and ambience of an Indian village.

An important narrative device which foregrounds the rural setting of the novel is the allusion to Hindu myths to explain the significance of contemporary events. *The Oxford Concise Dictionary of Literary Terms* defines the term "myth" as a "rudimentary narrative sequence, normally traditional and anonymous, through which a given culture ratifies its social customs or accounts for the origins of human and natural phenomena, usually in supernatural on boldly imaginative terms" (Baldick 143). Myths serve to reinforce cultural beliefs and enable people to relate to complex phenomena which are beyond human comprehension by interpreting them in a simplified manner.

Several Hindu myths are referred to in the novel in the context of the situations and incidents. The myth of the Gods churning the ocean looking for "amrita, the elixir of eternal life" is mentioned early in the narrative. The first product which came out from the ocean was the deadly poison Halhala. Father Ashworth reinterprets the myth in the present context of the casteism rampant in the country and states, "As discontent, envy and unhappiness swirl through the castes, communities and creeds in this land, it's inevitable that poison, hate and envy will be generated" (29). At another point in the novel the myth of Hiranyakashipu and his son Prahlada is interpreted in the novel with reference to Gandhi. To put an end to the tyranny of Hiranyakashipu who becomes the unchallenged ruler of the three worlds, God acquires the strange form of a man's body with a lion's head and devises a way to kill the king who had earlier defied natural death. Gandhi's non-violent methods of resistance to the British authorities are interpreted in the context of this myth, "Faced with an astonishingly complex problem, the Lord came up with a solution that was intricate, unusual and supremely effective. And that's what Mr Gandhi is doing, and it's driving Government crazy" (212).

The House of Blue Mangoes follows the linearity of time in the sequencing of incidents, which helps to root the narrative firmly in reality. Interspersed in the novel are references to the past historical events in India as a result of which the temporal scale of the novel is widened. The narrator states, "In the second half of the nineteenth century, the Madras Presidency was visited by famine seven times: in 1853-4, 1865-6, 1876-8, 1888-9, 1891-2, 1896-7 and 1899-1900" (82). Similarly, while the novel focuses on the village of Chevathar, references to political events in India and the world broaden the spatial dimension of the novel: "The skirts of the Great War brushed past India. Over one hundred thousand Indian soldiers were killed or wounded at Mons and Verdun, Ypres and Gallipoli, but the subcontinent itself was threatened only briefly" (181). Davidar uses this effective narrative strategy to relate the events depicted in Chevathar and the temporal setting of the novel to distant periods and places. Instead of delimiting the narrative to a small settlement, the writer expands the scale of time and distance to encompass historical events and their locales.

The narrative is punctuated with descriptions of the landscape, of natural phenomena like the sunrise and the sunset, with an almost photographic reproduction of the activities of birds, animals, insects and sea-creatures, as observed by the different characters: "As the sun subsided into the sea, a marvellous play of light and colour opened up. Shimmering bolts of orange, red, gold and a delicate lilac spread out in every direction" (35). The detailed description of the beauty of the landscape relaxes the pace of the narrative and imitates the slow tempo of life in rural areas. Agricultural activities of farmers and workmen are described with precision. A toddy tapper skillfully performing his task, as observed by Solomon, is described in detail, "The man, short, wiry and almost as black as the trunk of the tree, slipped a short loop of rope around his feet, then took a little jump and gripped the rough, serrated bark with the instep and soles of his feet and his powerful arms on which the muscles rippled like silk . . . . At the top he reached for the fleshy spathe of flowers and made a delicate incision with a small curved knife he carried" (58). These elaborate descriptions transpose the reader to the scene as it is gradually created through words that are colourful, lively and picturesque.

Descriptions of local festivals recur in the novel. These serve to emphasize the sense of community and kinship among village folk and their faith in religion and religious ceremonies. Village festivals are often celebrated to mark the change of the seasonal cycle or to relate to agricultural activities. However, to emphasize the political and social unrest in the country before independence, the festivals described in Davidar's novel carry images of violence, sadness and pain. During the festivities of the Panguni Uthiram, a village girl is raped which catalyses a caste war in Chevathar. The narrator, depicting the scene of the fair, states, "Gypsies in bright clothes wandered among the soberly dressed villagers, little stalls offered tempting trinkets and foodstuffs, and the world seemed to go on much as before, largely unaware of the terrifying future that was in store" (19). The description of the procession of devotees in the Chitra Pournami festival presents shocking images of the bodies of devotees being pierced with spears: "Then, holding the point of the spear to the devotee's cheek, he pierced it swiftly and precisely. He thrust the leaf-shaped tip of the spear through, then pierced the other cheek, and pulled the spear all the way over, so that its length was balanced nicely"(66). The harsh images presented in the novel relating to festivals however echo the sense of anxiety and tension pervading India during the struggle for independence.

Local customs and traditions find repeated mention in the narrative. "In Chevathar, the birth of a son was greeted with the kuruvai – a long drawn-out call ululating from the throats of aunts and sisters" (31). Wedding ceremonies depicting South Indian traditions are described intricately. Similarly traditional dishes are named frequently – "neimeen kolambu" (180), "appalam" (135), "puttu" (10), "fish biryani" (10), "paruppu payasam" (137), "atharasam" (318), and so on. References to Indian spices and other condiments abound in the novel – "cinnamon, cardamom, clove, nutmeg, aniseed, cumin seed, cake seed, and mace" (11) are referred to repeatedly. These help to conjure up a picture of South India with its abundance of spices. The village narrative thus becomes animated with images which lend colour, sound, fragrance and even taste to the descriptions.

The diverse strategies Davidar employs to capture the multiplicity of the village narrative, themselves form a conjunction of forces. Through the ingenuous use of narrative elements which underline the rural setting of the novel Davidar gives the visible a perceptible form, and foregrounds the theme of the novel, a theme which focuses on the attempt of individuals settled in remote parts of India to come to terms, at a personal level, with the social and political transitions occurring all around them in the first half of the twentieth century. Davidar manoeuvers narrative strategies effectively to represent the village as a centre of radical action, and contributing to the growth and development of the individual and the nation in pre-Independence India.

Notes

1. Blue mangoes derive their name from the blue sheen present on the dark green skin of the fruit of this particular variety.
2. A brief description of the plot of the novel will allow the reader to examine its circular structure. The first section titled "Chevathar" focuses on the violent form, which the caste conflict between the two groups, the Andavars and the Vedhars acquires in the village of Chevathar. This section ends with the death of Solomon Dorai, the village Headman who leads the Andavars, and the death of Muthu Vedhar, the leader of the Vedhars, and that of Father Ashworth, a Christian missionary settled in Chevathar, who is portrayed sympathetically by Davidar as a peacemaker. The second section "Doraipuram" describes the lives of Solomon's sons Daniel and Aaron, as they move in and out of Chevathar. Aaron's anti-British activities lead to his imprisonment and his tragic death in the Ranivoor prison. Daniel becomes a successful practitioner of Siddha medicine, and "Doraipuram" is the name he assigns to a family settlement he establishes in Chevathar, "which sprawled for miles by the Chevathar and provided a striking contrast to the existing village, more than half of which it had swallowed" (214). The third section "Pulimed" moves to the fictitious district of Pulimed with its tea-estates where Daniel's son Kannan works as a planter with the British officials, and lives with his Anglo-Indian wife Helen. As

Kannan's fascination with British ideals and way of life meets a bitter end, he returns to Doraipuram towards the end of the novel, resolving to work for the survival of his late father's dream and for the prosperity of Doraipuram in the future.

References

Baldick, Chris. *The Oxford Concise Dictionary of Literary Terms*. Oxford: OUP, 1990.

Bachelard, Gaston. 1958. *The Poetics of Space*. Trans. Etienne Gilson. Boston: Beacon Press, 1969.

Davidar, David. *The House of Blue Mangoes*. Delhi: Penguin, 2002.

Gandhi, Leela. *Postcolonial Theory: A Critical Introduction*. Oxford: OUP, 1998.

Hall, Stuart. "Cultural Identity and Diaspora." *Contemporary Postcolonial Theory: A Reader*. Ed. Padmini Mongia. New Delhi: OUP, 1997.

Lai, Chung-Hsiung. "On Narrative: Story, Truth and History." *Journal of Contemporary Thought* 21 (Summer 2005): 25-42.

McHale, Brian. *Postmodernist Fiction*. London: Routledge, 1987.

Roy, Nilanjana. "Malgudi, Ayemenem, and now Chevathar." *The Hindu Magazine* Jan. 13, 2002. Internet 30 Oct. 2005. Available http://www.hinduonnet.com/the hindu/mag/2002/01/13/stories/2002011300510100.htm

Contributors

Anisur Rahman is Professor of English at Jamia Millia Islamia, New Delhi.

Renuka Pamecha teaches Political Science at Kanoria Postgraduate Mahila Vidyalaya, Jaipur.

Kumool Abbi is in the Department of Sociology, Punjab University, Chandigarh.

Santosh Gupta, a senior professor, is currently working on a research project on Prison Writings, and is based in Jaipur.

Avadhesh K. Singh is Professor of English at Saurashtra University, Rajkot.

Ameena Ansari teaches English at Jamia Millia Islamia, New Delhi.

Bandana Chakravarty is presently based at Government College, Kala Dera.

Usha Bande former IIAS fellow is located at Shimla.

Veena Jain teaches English at Government College, Alwar.

Madhuri Chatterjee is located in Jaipur and teaches English at Subodh College, Jaipur.

Vrinda Mathur is on the faculty of English at Satya Sai College for Girls, Jaipur.

Neelam Raisinghani teaches English at Dungar College, Bikaner.

Sarojini is located at Jaipur.

Rama Rani Lall teaches English at Jaipur.

Jessy Mani teaches in Government College, Alwar.

Avinash Jodha is a lecturer in English at Bikaner.

Urmil Talwar is currently posted at Government College for Girls, Shahpura.

Sonu Shiva teaches at Dungar College, Bikaner.

Preranna Bishnoi has completed her research on diasporic writers and is freelancing at present.

Supriya Agarwal teaches English at Khandelwal P.G. College for Girls, Jaipur.

Preeti Bhatt is a lecturer in English at Sant Jaya Acharya College, Jaipur.

Jasbir Jain is an independent writer and critic, based at Jaipur.

Index